VIOLENCE IN THE
DOMESTIC SPHERE

VIOLENCE IN THE DOMESTIC SPHERE

INGRID WESTENDORP
RIA WOLLESWINKEL
(editors)

Antwerpen – Oxford

Distribution for the UK:
Hart Publishing
Salter's Boat Yard
Folly Bridge
Abingdon Road
Oxford OX1 4LB
UK
Tel: + 44 1865 24 55 33
Fax: + 44 1865 79 48 82

Distribution for North America:
Gaunt Inc.
Gaunt Building
3011 Gulf Drive
Holmes Beach
Florida 34217-2199
USA
Tel: + 1 941 778 5211
Fax: + 1 941 778 5252

Distribution for Switzerland and Germany:
Schulthess Verlag
Zwingliplatz 2
CH-8022 Zürich
Switzerland
Tel: + 41 1 251 93 36
Fax: + 41 1 261 63 94

Distribution for other countries:
Intersentia Publishers
Groenstraat 31
BE-2640 Mortsel
Belgium
Tel: + 32 3 680 15 50
Fax: + 32 3 658 71 21

Violence in the domestic sphere
Ingrid Westendorp and Ria Wolleswinkel (eds.)

© 2005 Intersentia
Antwerp – Oxford
http://www.intersentia.com

ISBN 90-5095-526-6
D/2005/7849/89
NUR 824

ACKNOWLEDGEMENTS

The editors wish to express their appreciation to all contributors to this volume, many of whom also actively participated in annual meeting of the School of Human Rights Research in Maastricht on 29 October 2004. A great deal of time and effort was put in preparing the presentations and in adapting the contributions for publication.

A word of thanks should also be addressed to our student-assistant Ida Nylund who has painstakingly checked all the footnotes and to Chantal Kuijpers who not only took care of the organisational and logistical aspects of this annual meeting, but who also prepared the manuscript for publication.

TABLE OF CONTENTS

INTRODUCTION

In October 2004, the Annual Meeting of the School of Human Rights Research was devoted to the theme of 'Domestic Violence'. The organizers at the Maastricht Centre for Human Rights selected this topic as it is suitable for an interdisciplinary approach, and the meeting coincided with the launching of Amnesty International's campaign on Violence against Women.

The title 'Violence in the domestic sphere' was chosen to indicate, as most of the authors do, that this type of violence may transgress various boundaries. Violence by intimates does not necessarily happen at the domicile, while harm at home is not exclusively inflicted by intimates. Some people's (temporary) homes are outside the family sphere, such as care centres, shelters, asylums, hospitals or prisons. It has become clear that dependency will create vulnerability and subsequently, a great diversity of victims and perpetrators exists. To complicate matters even more, some people may be both victim and perpetrator, either at the same time or at different stages of their lives. Violence in the domestic sphere appears to be a theme full of dilemmas in need of academic research and pragmatic solutions.

In this book, State responsibility for violations of citizens' rights is assumed, based on human rights standards and case law, also of human rights bodies. It has been proven that the traditional public-private dichotomy is problematic concerning violence in the domestic sphere, since the perpetrators are private persons. That is why the principle of due diligence is accepted when States fail to prevent, investigate, or punish acts of domestic violence, or when they fall short as regards providing legal remedies and reparation.

Violence in the domestic sphere predominantly affects women in all stages of their lives and in all societies, regardless even of their social status. Socio-cultural diversities, however, are reflected in various manifestations of violence.
The paternalistic control of women's sexuality appears to be rather common, making specific, moral demands on women. Some risk factors are indicated such as post-war aggression, poverty, and intergenerational violence. The realization of some human rights standards, like adequate housing, or the participation of women in public life, labour and education seems to be a deterrent to violence,

although new risks may rise especially in societies and institutions in transgression.

Although families differ all over the world, generally speaking, not all family members are equally empowered and family relations are gendered in many ways. Children are often powerless and because of that, the most vulnerable within the family. In addition, their vulnerability is gendered, too.

On reading this book, the different backgrounds and approaches of the authors becomes clear. Experts in international law and human rights issues tend to set standards at a high (universal) level and seek for best practices to inspire human rights bodies or to illustrate how standards might work. They notice the difficulties of implementation. But implementation at the domestic level is left to national experts and communities. For example, experts in criminal law start looking at how human rights standards can be implemented in the existing national law system. They also use best practices from abroad, often from geographically or culturally related countries, for comparison and sometimes for harmonization, but more often to underline the differences between law systems.

Social scientists deal with practices, they offer empirical studies (apart from case law although often related), they describe phenomena and give a broad view on differences, difficulties and dilemmas.

Non-governmental organizations (NGOs) are most of the time rooted in the community by giving a voice to vulnerable citizens and promoting their interests.

In this book, we have placed the chapters in an order that reveals this variety of approaches, which makes the topics relevant to scholars and students.

The starting chapter is that of Ingrid Vledder. As a representative of Amnesty International she gives a compilation of the Amnesty Report on Violence against Women. She also pays attention to the limitations of criminal justice solutions and the existence of flaws in the legal framework. Not all forms of violence in the domestic sphere are covered by law in all countries. Exceptions are made, depending on the particular country. Some of her examples are also explored in other chapters, like marital rape by Boerefijn, honour crimes by Römkens and female genital mutilation by Kool.

In the second chapter, Ineke Boerefijn gives an exhaustive, reader-friendly and useful oversight of all valuable documents on violence against women and more specifically on violence in the domestic sphere. She gives a great deal of historical and practical information and she has included the very first views adopted by CEDAW under the Optional Protocol to the Women's Convention. They concerned a case of domestic violence in Hungary.

While Vledder already paid attention to rape as a form of torture during war and post war conflicts, Theo van Boven and Sabine Puig in their chapter take the lead in proposing to identify domestic violence as a form of torture. In their argumentation they relate for example to a rather recent General Comment of the Human Rights Committee, the observations of the Committee Against Torture, and the interrelation between the concept of *due diligence* and *positive obligations* as used by the European Court on Human Rights.

Renée Römkens makes the connection between human rights standards and their implementation in Afghanistan. She criticizes the practical effectiveness under the current political and legal situation as well as the impact on how Afghan women are portrayed in for example Western media. The complexity of the traditions of a particular country has to be taken into account to get *cultural legitimacy* of international human rights law. Otherwise, it will be impossible to provide any substantial protection of women's rights. 'The existence of a gap between human rights standards and local women's rights should not necessarily be seen as a failure but as an inevitable yet challenging paradox', she writes.

Renée Kool struggles with the criminal law approach of female genital mutilation (FGM) in Western Europe. 'At international level the widest agreement appears to exist on the need to abolish female genital mutilation.'(quote Boerefijn) In the Netherlands, the question rises whether a specific provision against FGM has to be made in criminal law, because under general provisions against physical abuse no cases have been prosecuted till now. The same is true for other European countries, regardless of the existence of specific provisions, with the exception of France, where some cases have been brought before a court. Kool compares Dutch (general abuse) and Belgian (specific FGM) law and proposes to add a specific paragraph to increase the terms of imprisonment in cases of FGM in Dutch criminal law.

In her chapter, Ingrid Westendorp explains how violence in the domestic sphere falls within the scope of women's right to adequate housing. One of the elements determining adequacy is security. The privacy of the home has to be protected from interference, but if the threat comes from the inside, from intimates, the authorities will have to interfere. Westendorp gives a wide range of measures that can be taken by public authorities. As far as housing rights of a victim are concerned, she points at two different approaches; providing shelter for battered women (and their children) or evicting the perpetrator from the family home.

In addition to Westendorp, Katinka Lünnemann describes and compares the legal arrangements for eviction of the perpetrator in Austria and Germany and she links them to a recent proposal in The Netherlands. She pays special attention to crisis intervention and to the need for assistance to victims by advisory agencies that offer social and legal support. Also, perpetrators need support in case they want to change their violent behaviour. Lünnemann states that special attention should be paid to young children who are victims or witnesses of violence in the domestic sphere.

Jan Willems focuses on children as victims of abuse and introduces as the core risk factor in Western society the so-called *transism*, which he understands to be 'the patriarchal or parentiarchal ideology of "privacy" and "parental autonomy" that is, of not preparing adolescents for parenthood and not preventatively supporting parents.' Willems argues that preparation for parenthood and support and supervision of parents are to be seen as fundamental rights of the child. The law should define what is expected from parents and what parents can expect from society and the State, all in terms of a continuum of care.

At the end of this book Frans Koenraadt and Marieke Liem, at the continuum of violence in the domestic sphere, focus at the worst case scenario; homicides. From real case studies in The Netherlands they distinguish various forms of fatal killings within families and they elaborate gender related issues. They also take into account different ages of victims and perpetrators and how predictable structural violence might be for killing in the end. Especially suicide-related killings in the family seem to be the exception or, as stated by Koenraadt and Liem: 'Ongoing violence appears to be characteristic of all non-suicide filicides.'

In a way, this book is open-ended. Many questions and areas are not covered yet and many new questions may have risen. Violence in the domestic sphere needs more research, both in empirical studies to show various manifestations, but also in legal and theoretical studies. A great deal of creative solutions is needed to set standards in a changing world, in changing societies and in changing families. The legal discourse has to be opened for socio-cultural differences to be effective for the victims that are involved. Victims need to be heard themselves or they have to be represented in a proper way in case they have no voice or no means to participate in political or legal debates. Violent relations between intimates are complex, and inextricably linked to (abuse of) power positions. The only way to handle or to change violent and threatening patterns is by opening debates and setting standards. Not just to stereotype and isolate 'suspects', but to fulfil human rights for all people by creating effective (legal, social and economic) frameworks and solutions.

Ingrid Westendorp
Ria Wolleswinkel

IT'S IN OUR HANDS. STOP VIOLENCE AGAINST WOMEN

Ingrid Vledder[1]

'I was sleeping when the attack on Disa started. I was taken away by the attackers, they were all in uniforms. They took dozens of other girls and made us walk for three hours. During the day we were beaten and they were telling us "You, the black women, we will exterminate you, you have no god." At night we were raped several times. The Arabs[2] guarded us with arms and we were not given food for three days'.[3]

1. INTRODUCTION

Violence against women is the greatest human rights scandal of our time. From birth to death, in times of peace as well as war, women face discrimination and violence at the hands of the State, the community and the family. Violence against women is not confined to any particular political or economic system, but is prevalent in every society in the world and cuts across boundaries of wealth, race and culture.

1.1. A human rights scandal

The statistics of violence against women reveal a worldwide human rights catastrophe.

- At least one of every three women has been beaten, coerced into sex, or otherwise abused in her lifetime, according to a study based on 50 surveys from around the world. Usually, the abuser is a member of her own family or someone known to her.[4]

---

1   This article is for the greater part an abstract made by Ingrid Vledder of AMNESTY INTERNATIONAL'S REPORT, *It's in our Hands. Stop Violence against Women* (Amnesty International Report), 2004, available at: <http://web.amnesty.org/library/index/engact770012004>.

2   The term Arabs is used here to indicate people predominantly from nomadic groups, who speak Arabic as their first language.

3   A female refugee from Disa (Masalit village, West Darfur), interviewed by Amnesty International delegates in Goz Amer camp for Sudanese refugees in Chad, May 2004.

4   L. HEISE, M. ELLSBERG, M. GOTTEMOELLER, *Ending Violence against Women*. Population Reports, Series L., No. 11. Baltimore, John Hopkins University School of Public Health, December 1999, 1.

- The World Health Organization (WHO) has reported that up to 70 percent of female murder victims are killed by their male partners.[5]
- The Council of Europe has stated that domestic violence is the major cause of death and disability for women aged 16 to 44 and accounts for more death and ill-health than cancer or traffic accidents.[6]

Violence against women is under-reported because women are ashamed or fear skepticism, disbelief or further violence. In addition, definitions of the forms of violence vary widely in different countries, making comparisons difficult. Many States lack good reporting systems to determine the prevalence of violence against women. The failure to investigate and expose the true extent of violence allows governments, families and communities to ignore their responsibilities.[7]

1.2. Locations: violence against women

These include, but are not limited to:

- Violence in the family. This includes battering by intimate partners, sexual abuse of female children in the household, marital rape and female genital mutilation and other traditional practices harmful to women.
- Violence against women in the community. This includes rape, sexual abuse, sexual harassment and assault at work, in educational institutions and elsewhere. Trafficking, forced prostitution and forced labour fall into this category, which also covers rape and other abuses by armed groups.
- Gender-based violence perpetrated or condoned by the State, or by 'State actors' - police, prison guards, soldiers, border guards, immigration officials and so on. This includes, for example, rape by government forces during armed conflict, forced sterilization, torture in custody and violence by officials against refugee women.[8]

In any of these categories, violence may be physical, psychological, and sexual. It may be manifested through deprivation or neglect as opposed to overt acts of violence or harassment. These are not mutually exclusive categories. Physical violence by an intimate partner is often accompanied

---

[5] WORLD HEALTH ORGANIZATION (WHO), World Report on Violence and Health, Geneva, 2002, 118.

[6] PARLIAMENTARY ASSEMBLY OF THE COUNCIL OF EUROPE, Domestic Violence against Women, Recommendation 1582, adopted 27 September 2002.

[7] Amnesty International Report, supra n. 1, 4-5.

[8] Ibid., 3.

by sexual violence, deprivation, isolation and neglect, as well as by psychological abuse.[9]

1.3. A definition

Amnesty International bases its work on the definition in the United Nations Declaration on the Elimination of Violence against Women (UN Declaration) 'any act of gender-based violence that results in, or is likely to result in, physical, sexual or psychological harm or suffering to women, including threats of such acts, coercion or arbitrary deprivation of liberty, whether occurring in public or in private life'.[10]

According to the Committee on the Elimination of Discrimination against Women (CEDAW) gender-based violence is violence 'directed against a woman because she is a woman or that affects women disproportionately.'[11] In other words, not all acts which harm a woman are gender-based and not all victims of gender-based violence are female. Some men are victims of gender-based violence, for example, gay men who are harassed, beaten and killed because they do not conform to socially approved views of masculinity.[12]

Progressive interpretations of the definition found in the UN Declaration affirm that acts of omission - such as neglect or deprivation - can constitute violence against women. More recent international legal instruments broaden the definition, in particular to include structural violence i.e. harm resulting from the impact of the organization of the economy on women's lives.[13]

2. CONFLICT AND VIOLENCE AGAINST WOMEN

For women, both peace and war are times of discrimination and violence.[14] Heightened levels of violence are seen in societies which are

---

9   *Ibid.*

10   Art.1 of the Declaration on the Elimination of Violence against Women, General Assembly Resolution 48/104 of 20 December 1993,.

11   CEDAW, General Recommendation no. 9, on Statistical Data, 1992, UN Doc. A/47/38, para.6.

12   Amnesty International Report, supra n. 1, 4.

13   See The African Union's Protocol on the Rights of Women in Africa (July 2003); The Council of Europe, Committee of Ministers, Recommendation Rec. (2002) 5, on the protection of women against violence (30 April 2002).

14   AMNESTY INTERNATIONAL'S REPORT, *Lives blown apart. Crimes against women in times of conflict,* December 2004, available at: <http://web.amnesty.org/library/index/ ENGACT770752004>.

becoming increasingly militarized, in wars, in countries where conflict is endemic and intergenerational, and in post-conflict situations. In Vietnam, for example, patterns of domestic abuse from the experience of war are prevalent more than 30 years later. The form, circumstances and extent of violence varies, but there is a continuum between violence in conflict and violence in peacetime.[15]

2.1. Militarization

Militarization has been defined as a process whereby military values, ideology and patterns of behaviour achieve a dominating influence on the political, social, economic and external affairs of a society. Violence is not a by-product of militarization but one of its central features, and increased violence in society tends to lead to increased levels of gender-based violence against women.[16]

Militarization is a growing reality in societies all over the world, seen in the use of force to resolve international and internal disputes, foreign occupation, internal conflicts and the proliferation of arms. The global arms trade is both a manifestation of this trend and a contributory factor to increased conflict and aggression. This trade has rapidly expanded over the past few decades. Global military expenditures in the early 1990s were more than 60 per cent higher in real terms than in the 1970s and twice as high as in the 1960s.[17]

2.2. Violence in war

Instability and armed conflict lead to an increase in all forms of violence including genocide, rape and sexual violence. During conflicts, violence against women is often used as a weapon of war in order to dehumanize the women themselves, or to persecute the community to which they belong. Women are likely to form the greatest proportion of the adult civilian population killed in war and targeted for abuse. Women and children are also usually the majority of refugees and internally displaced people forced to flee their homes because of armed conflict.[18]

The wars in Bosnia-Herzegovina and Rwanda in the 1990s drew public attention to the horrific levels of violence against women committed in

---

[15] Amnesty International Report, supra n. 1, 49.

[16] *Ibid.*

[17] RUTH LEGER SIVARD, *World Military and social Expenditures 1991* (USA: World Priorities Inc.).

[18] Amnesty International Report, supra n. 1, 50.

conflict. Murder, systematic and widespread rape and other forms of sexual violence were used not only to destroy the morale of the enemy, but also literally to decimate them. In Rwanda, for example, gang-rape, sexual mutilation and sexual humiliation (for example, making Tutsi women parade naked in public) were prevalent in the genocide.[19]

Women may be targeted for violence because of their roles as community activists and leaders, or those of male relatives. During the Indonesian occupation of East Timor from 1975-1999, women suspected of sympathizing with the pro-independence armed opposition or being related to its members were subjected to sexual violence.[20] During a hearing of the Commission on Reception, Truth and Reconciliation in Timor-Leste, former Governor Mario Carrascalao testified about the common practice by the Indonesian military of holding dance parties where young Timorese women were forced to entertain the soldiers.[21] He also stated that wives of armed opposition combatants were forced into sexual slavery by the Indonesian military.[22]

In Nepal, two young girl cousins were abducted by army personnel in April 2002 and were alleged to have been repeatedly raped. The soldiers were pursuing the father of one of the girls who had escaped to India.[23]

During the period following the 1991 military coup in Haiti, a number of women were raped because they or their husbands were political organizers.[24] In the conflict between the Sri Lankan armed (Comment: as I am born Sri Lankan, I insert the general term used for author's review) forces and the Liberation Tigers of Tamil Eelam (known as the 'Tamil Tigers'), women in custody have been blindfolded, beaten, and raped by army, police and navy officials. For example, in March 2001, Sinnathamby Sivamany and Ehamparam Wijikala, two young Tamil women, were arrested by members of the navy in the coastal city of Mannar and taken to the office of a special police unit. Ehamparam Wijikala was brutally raped by two officers inside the police station. Sinnathamby Sivamany was blindfolded, undressed and raped in a van

---

19   *Ibid.*
20   *Ibid.*
21   COMMISSION ON RECEPTION, TRUTH AND RECONCILIATION IN TIMOR-LESTE, *National Public Hearing on Women and Conflict*, CAVR National Headquarters, former Comarca balide, Dili, 28-29 April 2003.
22   Amnesty International Report, supra n. 1, 51.
23   *Ibid.*
24   Report of the Special Rapporteur on Violence Against Women, Addendum: report on Mission to Haiti, UN Doc. E.CN.4/2000/Add.3, para. 58.

outside the station. Later, both women were forced to parade naked and then suspended for about 90 minutes by their hands and legs from a pole placed between two tables. They were also pinched and beaten with a thick wire.[25]

Of course, men and boys are also victims of violence in war. In recent conflicts, civilian men and boys have been singled out in towns and villages and then killed, raped, forcibly conscripted or made to commit acts of violence against women. However, in cases where men, rather than women are disproportionately targeted, whether as combatants or civilian victims, women constitute the majority of displaced populations and face new problems as a result.[26]

2.3. Violence in conflict, violence in the home

Women living through conflict not only have to endure assaults or the threat of assault by the other side, but they also face increased levels of violence from within their families. Conversely, at the same time, they are relied upon to rebuild their communities from the ground up.[27]

Since the *intifada*, Palestinian women have been exposed to increased levels of violence - not only through the destruction of their homes and communities by Israeli forces, but also through increased domestic violence. A poll conducted by the Palestinian Center for Public Opinion in 2002 showed that '86 percent of respondents said violence against women had significantly or somewhat increased (Comment: Author to review phrase 'significantly or somewhat increased')as a result of changing political, economic and social conditions of Palestinian women', up 22 percentage points from the previous year.[28]

2.4. After the war, the violence continues

Violence doesn't necessarily reduce once the conflict has abated. In the USA, domestic violence and murder by soldiers returning from combat is emerging as a serious issue.[29] One study, conducted by the US Army,

---

[25] Amnesty International Report, supra n. 1, 51.

[26] *Ibid.*

[27] *Ibid.*, 52.

[28] Domestic Violence against Palestinian Women, *Middle East Times*, 20 September 2002, based on reporting from the Agence France-Presse.

[29] Amnesty International Report, supra n. 1, 52.

found the incidence of 'severe aggression' against spouses was reportedly three times as high in army families as in civilian ones.[30]
The WHO notes that 'in many countries that have suffered violent conflict, the rates of interpersonal violence remain high even after the cessation of hostilities -- among other reasons because of the way violence has become more socially acceptable and the availability of weapons'.[31]

Iraqi women have suffered severe hardship for decades: loss of male relatives in the 1980-1988 Iran-Iraq war; mass expulsions to Iran of entire families declared by the authorities to be of 'Iranian descent'; Government repression including the chemical weapons attack on Halabja in 1988; the 1991 Gulf War and the subsequent suppression of the Shi'a uprising; 13 years of UN sanctions from 1991 to 2003 and the US-led military action in 2003.[32]

Under the Government of Saddam Hussein, women 'disappeared' and were arbitrarily arrested, tortured, and executed by the authorities on political grounds. In 2000, hundreds of women were said to have been beheaded in public by the paramilitary group *Feda'iye Saddam*, accused of prostitution.[33]

After the US-led invasion and occupation of Iraq in 2003, during which an unknown number of civilians were killed, the sudden political and security vacuum led to widespread looting and gun crime, and growing reports that women were afraid to leave their homes because of rapes and abductions. However, their homes are not necessarily safe either. The following case was documented by an Amnesty International researcher in Baghdad.[34]

Nineteen-year-old Fatima (not her real name) was shot in the legs by her husband in front of his family and their neighbours on 21 May 2003. Fatima was married to her husband at the age of 12 and was treated as a servant and regularly beaten in her husband's family home. On the day she was shot she had tried to run away to her own family, but they sent her back. According to Fatima, when her husband came,

---

[30]   Cited in JON ELLISON AND CATHERINE LUTZ, Hidden Casualties, *Southern Exposure*, 15 May 2003.
[31]   A study in Northern Ireland showed that the increased availability of guns meant that more dangerous forms of violence were used against women in the home.
[32]   Amnesty International Report, supra n. 1, 52.
[33]   *Ibid.*
[34]   *Ibid.*, 53.

'He was very angry and he took his Kalashnikov... I could not believe that he would shoot, his sister was standing beside him...But then he didn't stop, he shot my legs, I could not feel them, they were numb, the sun was setting, I was looking at the sky, I said to the men 'I don't want to die'. They took me to the hospital'.[35]

Despite the number of eye-witnesses and the seriousness of the crime, her husband was not arrested.

Research by the Non-Governmental Organization (NGO) Medica Zenica in Bosnia-Herzegovina showed that 24 per cent of the women interviewed had experienced domestic violence over a long period of time, dating from before the war.[36] The majority also reported that the incidence and intensity of violence increased after the end of the war in 1996. Although it is difficult to ascertain the real level of increase, many groups report 'shockingly high percentages of violence against women and children.' Social stigma and a lack of services are exacerbated by a criminal code that distinguishes between an 'assault' and 'light bodily injury committed by a spouse or cohabitant'. In the case of the latter, the victim must bring a prosecution against the perpetrator. The State typically doesn't intervene'.[37]

A recently identified trend in post-conflict societies is a rise in violence against women associated with the presence of international peace-keeping forces. For example, women have been trafficked into Kosovo for forced prostitution since the deployment of an international peacekeeping force (KFOR) and the establishment of a UN civilian administration (UNMIK) in 1999. They come from countries including Moldova, Ukraine and Bulgaria, and the majority is reportedly trafficked through Serbia. Trafficking was identified as a problem soon after UNMIK's arrival, but the number of premises where women believed to have been trafficked are forced to work as prostitutes has continued to rise, reaching more than 200 by July 2003.[38]

In a report on trafficking of women and girls to post-conflict Bosnia-Herzegovina, Human Rights Watch (HRW) gave convincing evidence of the direct responsibility of local police in trafficking - as bar owners and

---

[35]   *Ibid.*, 53-54.

[36]   Medica Zenica 1999, in: CHEYWA SPINDEL, ELISA LEVY, MELISSA CONNOR, *With An End in Sight: Strategies from the UNIFEM Trust Fund to Eliminate Violence Against Women,* UNIFEM, 2000.

[37]   JULIA POUCHER HARBIN, 'Families at War', Institute for War and Peace Reporting, 5 September 2001.

[38]   Amnesty International Report, supra n. 1, 54.

as employees of establishments holding trafficked women and girls. Local police also reportedly received bribes and free services, and tipped off owners about planned police raids, among other forms of complicity and participation. The report also shows the involvement of the UN police monitoring force and the NATO-led peacekeeping troops in trafficking as clients, purchasers of women and in retaliation against whistle-blowers.[39]

Other peace-keeping troops have committed acts of violence against women in the communities they are charged with protecting. For example, a sergeant from the Third Parachute Battalion of Belgium stationed in Somalia in 1993 allegedly procured a teenage Somali girl as a birthday present for a paratrooper. She was reportedly forced to perform a strip show at the birthday party and to have sexual relations with two Belgian paratroopers. In 1998 a military court sentenced the sergeant to 12 months' imprisonment, six of them suspended, a fine, and exclusion from the army. Italian troops were also found to have committed sexual violence while stationed in Somalia on the peacekeeping mission in 1993-4. An Italian Government commission found credible evidence of a number of instances of gang-rape, sexual assault and theft with violence. There were also reports of sexual violence committed by Italian peacekeeping troops in Mozambique in 1994.[40]

Too often, violence against women is relegated to the sidelines of peace and conflict resolution processes. Moreover, peace processes have routinely failed to include women and to deal with gender issues, which can result in gender-based persecution and violence being rendered invisible in peace agreements and not taken into account in their interpretation and implementation. For example, an Amnesty International delegation which visited Sierra Leone in 2000 reported that the process of disarmament, demobilization and reintegration of former combatants was failing to address the experiences of the many girls and women who had been abducted by rebel soldiers and forced to become their sexual partners. It appeared that when they reported for disarmament and demobilization, they were often not interviewed separately from their 'husbands' and not offered a genuine opportunity to leave, if they wished to do so. These women and girls, many either pregnant or with young children, required support to either return to

---

[39] HUMAN RIGHTS WATCH (HRW), *Hopes Betrayed: Trafficking of Women and Girls to Post-Conflict Bosnia and Herzegovina for Forced Prostitution*, November 2002.
[40] Amnesty International Report, supra n. 1, 55.

their families where possible or to re-establish their lives together with their children.[41]

2.5. Abuses by armed groups

There are many different - and passionate - views on whether and when it is legitimate to use violence to achieve change or to confront State power. Amnesty International takes no position on this issue - we do insist, however, that groups which resort to force respect minimum standards of international humanitarian law, justice and humanity. Armed groups, no less than governments, must never target civilians, take hostages, or practice torture or cruel treatment, and they must ensure respect for basic human rights and freedoms in territory they control.[42]

Although international legal rules extend to armed groups, in practice these rules have had little impact. Over the past several years armed groups operating in all regions of the world have been responsible for some of the worst human rights abuses, including brutal and systematic acts of violence against women.[43]

Armed groups tend to operate either in opposition to State power, or in situations where State power is weak or absent. In either case, in practice, the State in the territory affected cannot be expected to address - in a fair and effective way - the human rights abuses these groups commit. While this poses particular challenges, it does not mean that armed groups are beyond accountability. They need and depend on support, resources and finance from other States, private organizations and sympathetic communities abroad and all of these can wield considerable control over armed groups. The international tribunals for the former Yugoslavia and Rwanda have successfully prosecuted leading members of armed groups and the establishment of the International Criminal Court opens new avenues for pursuing international criminal prosecutions. Human rights advocates all over the world are seeking ways to pressure and engage armed groups to respect human rights, and these efforts must be strengthened. As part of these efforts, greater attention must be given to ensuring armed groups respect

---

[41] *Ibid.*, 55-56.

[42] *Ibid.*, 56.

[43] *Ibid.*

women's basic rights, and disciplining forces under their command, responsible for violence against women.[44]

In many parts of Afghanistan, security and legitimate Government have not been established since the fall of the Taliban regime in November 2001. In this power vacuum, armed groups have abducted, raped and abused women and girls with impunity. Incidents reported to Amnesty International include the rape of four girls by members of an armed group. The youngest, aged 12, was unconscious due to her injuries when brought to hospital by her parents.[45]

Armed groups frequently use rape and other forms of sexual violence as part of a strategy to instil terror. In Sierra Leone, during a decade of conflict, armed opposition forces undertook a deliberate campaign of mutilation. Civilians had limbs amputated or the letters RUF (initials of the armed opposition Revolutionary United Front) carved into their flesh. Abduction of girls and women, rape and sexual slavery were systematic and widespread. Most victims had sexually transmitted diseases and many became pregnant. Abortion is illegal in Sierra Leone, leaving such women with few options. A 14-year-old sex worker told the UN Development Fund for Women (UNIFEM) that she would have terminated her pregnancy but did not have enough money to pay for it. The cost of an 'underground' abortion was $100, 'more than the average annual income of most Sierra Leoneans and more money than the girl had seen throughout her whole life'.[46]

During the rebel incursion into Freetown in January 1999, rebel combatants went from home to home, collecting girls. Those who were not selected to be the 'wife' of a rebel commander were repeatedly raped by other rebel combatants. On 8 January 1999 in the Cline Town area in the east of Freetown, a rebel commander ordered that all girls who were virgins report for a physical examination by a woman colleague. Those confirmed to be virgins were ordered to report each night to the rebel commander and other combatants, who raped and sexually abused them.[47]

---

[44] *Ibid.,* 56-57.

[45] *Ibid.*

[46] ELISABETH REHN AND ELLEN JOHNSON SIRLIEF, 'Women War Peace: The Independent Experts' Assessment', progress of the World's Women 2002, UNIFEM, Vol. 1, p. 40.

[47] Amnesty International Report, supra n. 1, 58.

In some cases, armed groups want to make certain that their victims know who is responsible for their torment. In others, confusion serves as a convenient mechanism for committing acts of violence and escaping responsibility.

Members of armed groups as well as governments have a legal responsibility under the basic principles and rules of international humanitarian law, to respect the rights of civilians not to suffer violence of any kind, including torture and inhuman or degrading treatment.[48]

3. ROOTS OF VIOLENCE

The underlying cause of violence against women lies in discrimination which denies women equality with men in all areas of life. Violence is both rooted in discrimination and serves to reinforce discrimination, preventing women from exercising their rights and freedoms on a basis of equality with men.[49]

The UN Declaration states that violence against women is a 'manifestation of historically unequal power relations between men and women, which have led to domination over and discrimination against women by men' and that 'violence against women is one of the crucial social mechanisms by which women are forced into a subordinate position compared with men'.[50]

Despite its pervasiveness, gender-based violence is not 'natural' or 'inevitable.' Violence against women is an expression of historically and culturally specific values and standards. Social and political institutions may foster women's subservience and violence against them. Certain cultural practices and traditions - particularly those related to notions of purity and chastity - may be invoked to explain or excuse such violence.[51]

Although violence against women is universal, many women are targeted for specific forms of violence because of particular aspects of their identity. Race, ethnicity, culture, language, sexual identity, poverty

---

[48]   *Ibid.*
[49]   *Ibid.*, 5.
[50]   *Ibid.*, 5-6.
[51]   *Ibid.*, 6.

and health (particularly HIV status) are some of the many risk factors for violence against women.[52]

Control of women's sexuality is a powerful means by which men exert their dominance over women. Women who transgress norms of femininity often face severe punishments and have little hope of redress. Men's ability to control women's sexual expression and their reproductive lives is reinforced by the actions or inaction of the State. Violence against women is rooted in discrimination because it denies women equality with men in terms of control over their own bodies and their physical, psychological and mental well-being.[53]

Violence in conflicts devastates the lives of both men and women, but systematic rape as seen in many recent conflicts, is primarily directed at girls and women. Rape, mutilation and murder of women and girls are common practices of warfare, committed both by government forces and armed groups.[54]

Gender-specific forms of violence are also endemic in militarized or war-torn societies. In societies heavily influenced by gun culture, the ownership and use of arms reinforces existing gender inequalities, strengthening the dominant position of men and maintaining women's subordination. Violent disputes in the home often become more lethal to women and girls when men have guns. In the USA, 51 per cent of female murder victims are shot. In South Africa, more women are shot at home in acts of domestic violence than by strangers on the streets or by intruders.[55]

4. HUMAN RIGHTS

4.1. Guiding principles

As the world's largest non-governmental human rights organization, Amnesty International uses the human rights framework in combating violence against women. Four premises form the foundation for claiming women's right to equality and to be free from discrimination:
Human rights are universal - they belong to all people equally.[56]

---

[52] *Ibid.*

[53] *Ibid.*, 7.

[54] *Ibid.*

[55] Examples cited in 'Gender and Small Arms', WENDY CUKIER, Small Arms/Firearms Education and Research Network (SAFER-Net).

[56] Amnesty International Report, supra n. 1, 12.

The universality of human rights has been increasingly challenged by governments and other groups on the grounds that local culture and tradition should take precedence. Cultural relativist arguments are more frequently invoked over issues of gender and sexuality than in any other area within the international human rights movement. These arguments are used to claim that gender-based violence is justified by culture and tradition, despite the fact that cultures are neither static nor unitary. Rather, cultures change and adapt to contemporary circumstances.

The UN Special Rapporteur on Violence Against Women has vigorously tried to counter cultural relativism in matters of sexuality. In her contribution to the 2001 World Conference against Racism in Durban, South Africa, she drew attention to lesbian women of colour, whose experience of discrimination is often compounded by racism, sexism and homophobia.

In responding to challenges to universality, human rights activists need to confront the tension between respecting diversity and difference and affirming the universality and indivisibility of rights. Certain principles are absolute: violence against women is never acceptable, whatever the justification offered.

- They are indivisible - one right is not more important than another right. All rights are of equal value and urgency and they cannot be separated;
- Human rights cannot be taken away or abrogated. The exercise of some rights can be limited, but only temporarily and under very exceptional circumstances;
- Human rights are interdependent, so that the promotion and protection of any one right requires the promotion and protection of all other rights.[57]

4.2. International human rights law and violence against women

The Universal Declaration of Human Rights (Universal Declaration) states that everyone should enjoy human rights without discrimination. The UN Charter affirms the equal rights of women and men. However, 'gender blindness' has meant that in practice, gross violations of women's human rights have often been ignored and structural discrimination against women has gone unchallenged.[58]

---

[57] Amnesty International Report, supra n. 1, 12.
[58] *Ibid.*, 67.

Historically, many interpretations of human rights law have drawn stark distinctions between the 'public sphere' - political, legal, and social institutions - and the 'private' sphere of the home and family, and have only offered protection from abuse in the 'public' realm. Doctrines of privacy and protection of the family, found both in international and national laws, have been used to reinforce this artificial divide. Progress in establishing that all forms of violence against women, wherever they take place, can constitute a violation of human rights, for which the State can be held accountable, is a major achievement of women's human rights activists.[59]

Using international human rights law as a framework for addressing violence against women presents a methodology for determining government obligations to promote and protect the human rights of women. It also points to the mechanisms available for holding governments to account if they fail to meet those obligations.[60]

The UN Convention on the Elimination of All Forms of Discrimination against Women (Women's Convention) expressly requires States parties (those Governments that have agreed to bind themselves to the Convention) to 'take all appropriate measures to eliminate discrimination against women by any person, organization or enterprise' (Article 2 [e]).[61]

4.3. Violence as a form of discrimination

The Universal Declaration, which recognizes the human rights which are fundamental to the dignity and development of every human being, states that everyone should enjoy human rights without discrimination on grounds of sex. The right not to be discriminated against is so fundamental that it is one of the rights that cannot be set aside (derogated from) under any circumstances.[62]

4.4. Human rights standards

The detailed mandate to secure equality between women and men and to prohibit discrimination against women is set out in the Women's Convention. (Comment: is 'Women's Convention' an abbrev. Reference

---

[59] *Ibid.*
[60] *Ibid.*
[61] *Ibid.*, 68.
[62] *Ibid.*

not clear)This mandate finds its source in core human rights documents.[63]

While these human rights standards lay the foundation for the women's right to be free from violence, this was crystallized in 1992 when CEDAW adopted General Recommendation no. 19 on Violence Against Women.'[64] General Recommendation no. 19 defines violence against women as a form of discrimination.

General Recommendation no. 19 specifies the nature of governments' obligation to take comprehensive action to combat violence against women. It notes that it applies specifically to violence perpetrated by public authorities, but emphasizes that governments are responsible for eliminating discrimination against women by any person, organization or enterprise, and that governments are required to prevent violations of rights by any actor, punish these acts and provide compensation.[65]

In 1993, the UN declared violence against women to be a human rights violation, requiring urgent and immediate attention and proclaimed that women's rights are human rights. Soon after, in December 1993, the UN Declaration was adopted, setting out the mandate for addressing violence against women as a human rights issue.[66]

One of the most significant outcomes of lobbying by women in NGOs and in government delegations is the far-reaching Beijing Declaration and Platform for Action, agreed at the Fourth World Conference on Women in 1995. The Beijing Platform for Action (and its five-year review in 2000) has been augmented by agreements from a series of other UN world conferences held in the 1990s and into the 21st century.[67]

The Rome Statute of the International Criminal Court (Rome Statute), finalized in 1998, has been a significant development in addressing crimes of violence against women. Several forms of violence against women, including rape, were included in the Rome Statute as war crimes

---

63 *Ibid.*

64 *Ibid.*, 69.

65 *Ibid.*

66 *Ibid.*

67 Importing milestones in the 1990s were the World Conference on Human Rights (Vienna, 1993); the International Conference on Population and Development (Cairo, 1994); the World Summit on Social Development (Copenhagen, 1995); the Fourth World Conference on Women (Beijing, 1995); Beijing plus five (New York, 2000); UN Special Session on HIV/AIDS (New York, 2003).

and crimes against humanity. In addition, gender-based persecution was included as a crime against humanity. The draft Elements of Crimes outlines gender-sensitive definitions of crimes. For example, the definition of rape refers to 'invasion of the body' 'committed by force, threat of force or coercion, such as that caused by fear of violence, duress, detention, psychological oppression, or abuse of power... or the person was incapable of giving genuine consent (including age-related incapacity)'.[68] Draft Elements of Crimes and the Rome Statute contains progressive provisions. Amnesty International urges States to use these provisions in domestic criminal law.

The work of the UN Special Rapporteur on Violence Against Women has deepened the international community's understanding of the causes and manifestations of violence against women throughout the world. In addition, the mandates of other UN Special Rapporteurs have increasingly included an explicit commitment to address the gender dimensions of the area being covered. This applies both to those reviewing human rights abuses in particular countries and those examining particular issues, such as the right to the highest attainable standard of health, the right to education and the right to housing.[69]

4.5. States' obligations

States are required under international human rights law to 'respect, protect, and fulfill' human rights.[70] States are under an obligation to take effective steps to end violence against women. Under this obligation, States must not only ensure that their agents do not commit acts of violence against women, they must also take effective steps to prevent and punish such acts by private actors. If a State fails to act diligently to prevent violence against women - from whichever source - or fails to investigate and punish such violence after it occurs, the State can itself be held responsible for the violation. This is known as the standard of *due diligence*. This does not absolve the actual perpetrators and their accomplices from being prosecuted and punished for the initial acts of violence.[71]

States must take a comprehensive approach to eliminating *all* forms of violence against women and adopting measures designed to eradicate all

---

[68]   Amnesty International Report, supra n. 1, footnote 101.
[69]   *Ibid,* 72.
[70]   *Ibid.*
[71]   *Ibid.,* 73.

forms of violence and discrimination. States have an ongoing obligation to monitor the situation and respond accordingly, changing - or supplementing - tactics when progress subsides.[72]

The recent adoption of an Optional Protocol to the Women's Convention has strengthened the apparatus with which violence against women can be opposed. The Optional Protocol offers women a direct means for seeking redress at the international level for violations of their rights under the Women's Convention. It is a mechanism that allows victims of violations or those acting on their behalf (including NGOs) to make a complaint directly to CEDAW when all domestic avenues of redress have been exhausted or are ineffective (unless such a process will be unreasonably prolonged or unlikely to bring effective relief). It also allows CEDAW to undertake investigations of systematic abuses. As of September 2003, 75 States had signed the optional protocol, and 55 had ratified or acceded to it.[73]

Many of the States that have ratified the Women's Convention have entered reservations to it. Reservations which are 'incompatible with the object and purpose of the treaty' are prohibited.[74] The effect of reservations is to weaken States' commitment to uphold the rights in the treaty, particularly by reducing their obligation to change their domestic laws. There are many reservations to the Women's Convention on the issue of the general commitment to implementing equality between men and women and specifically in relation to family and nationality law. These, impact on women victims of violence, as difficulties in obtaining divorce, custody of their children or a passport, will affect their ability to leave abusive situations.[75] Let me give you an example. Saudi-Arabia entered the following reservation: 'In case of contradiction between any term of the Convention and the norms of Islamic law, the Kingdom is not under obligation to observe the contradictory terms of the Convention.' By entering such reservations, States are effectively denying women's equality, which is the main purpose of the Convention. Amnesty International urges States to ratify the Convention without reservations.

---

[72] *Ibid.*

[73] *Ibid.*

[74] Art. 19 of the Vienna Convention on the Law of Treaties.

[75] Amnesty International Report, supra n. 1, 73-74.

4.6. Due diligence

A leading case defining the doctrine of *due diligence* is *Velásquez Rodríguez*, Judgment of 29 July 1988, Inter-American Court of Human Rights, describes the degree of effort which a State must undertake to implement rights in practice. It is particularly valuable in assessing the accountability of governments for the acts of private individuals and groups. States are required to make sure that the rights recognized under human rights law are made a reality in practice. In addition, if a right is violated, the State must restore the right violated as far as is possible and provide appropriate compensation. The standard of due diligence is applied in order to assess whether they have carried out these obligations.[76]

According to the UN Declaration, States should 'exercise due diligence to prevent, investigate and, in accordance with national legislation, punish acts of violence against women, whether those acts are perpetrated by the State or by private persons'.[77]
A range of measures is open to a State to ensure that the rights of women and men are respected; the specific course of action is to be determined within the context of each country, in view of its particular political, economic, religious, cultural and social institutions. However, social and cultural practices may not be used to justify or excuse inaction or inadequate measures on the part of the State.[78]

4.7. Rape as torture

International human rights courts and international criminal tribunals have affirmed that the pain and suffering caused by rape are consistent with the definition of torture. In many circumstances under international law, rape has been acknowledged as a form of torture owing to the severe mental and physical pain and suffering that is inflicted on the victim. Not every case of rape, however, engages the responsibility of the State under international law. The State is accountable under international human rights law for rape by its agents. It is also accountable for rape by private individuals when it has failed to act with due diligence to prevent, punish or redress it.[79]

---

[76] *Ibid.*, 74.
[77] *Ibid.*
[78] *Ibid.*, 74-75.
[79] *Ibid.*, 76.

Amnesty International's recent worldwide campaigns against torture have included a focus on women and on torture and ill-treatment based on sexual identity. Amnesty International makes the case for acts of violence against women in the home or community constituting torture, for which the State is accountable, when they are of the nature and severity of torture and the State has failed to fulfill its obligation to provide effective protection. Amnesty International notes that the prevalence of sexism and homophobia in societies puts lesbians at grave risk of abuse in the home and in the community.[80]

4.8. Impunity

Impunity, literally the absence of punishment, is the failure to bring to justice, perpetrators of human rights violations. Most acts of violence against women are never investigated, and perpetrators commit their crimes safe in the knowledge that they will never face arrest, prosecution or punishment. Impunity for violence against women contributes to a climate, where such acts are seen as normal and acceptable rather then criminal, where women do not seek justice because they know they will not gain it, where the original pain and suffering are prolonged and aggravated by the denial that a serious violation of human rights has been committed. While investigation and prosecution are the responsibility of the State, individuals and communities have vital roles to play in overcoming impunity.[81]

When we discuss violence in the home, the issue of responsibility and accountability is complex because usually the family, the community and the State are all implicated. Women who seek to expose abuse are told that it is a private matter, and as a result, domestic violence is committed with impunity in countries all over the world. In Amnesty International's experience, such impunity is a major factor in prolonging the pattern of violence.[82]

When women pursue legal action, they are often faced with a hostile and abusive criminal justice system. Deeply held attitudes that denigrate women, deny them equal rights and portray them as property are built into many penal and family codes, criminal investigation procedures and rules of evidence and customary legal systems. For example, in many penal codes, rape is considered to be a 'crime of honour', placing the

---

[80] *Ibid.*, 76-77.
[81] *Ibid.*, 84.
[82] *Ibid.*, 83-84.

woman's morality and her sexual behaviour before the court for analysis, and thereby treating her as the suspect. If a woman has had an active sexual life, she may in effect be held to have given her 'consent'.[83]

5. THE LIMITATIONS OF CRIMINAL JUSTICE SOLUTIONS

This campaign led Amnesty International as a primarily legal organization to confront the limitations of criminal justice solutions. Even when the law prohibits violence against women, social institutions, cultural norms and political structures in every country sustain and maintain it, making the law a dead letter. Impunity remains the norm because of inadequate implementation, monitoring, documentation and evaluation of the law. Acts of violence against women, therefore, go unchecked and unpunished.[84]

Discriminatory attitudes within the criminal justice system can undermine law reforms and lead to perverse outcomes, where women's rights, rather than being enhanced are further restricted - women are under-policed but over-criminalized. In the USA, rape crisis centres have documented how victims are sometimes penalized because of poorly drafted or poorly implemented legislation. Women from marginalized communities may be particularly reluctant to press charges or act as witnesses, having little or no confidence in the outcome of interaction with the police and criminal justice system.[85]

Some progress has been made in holding to account, perpetrators of violence against women at the international level. However, this is often not reflected in national prosecutions. For example, despite the ground-breaking decisions of the International Criminal Tribunal for the former Yugoslavia (ICTY) in prosecuting sexual violence, there have been no domestic prosecutions solely for rape in Bosnia-Herzegovina.[86]

5.1. Flawed laws

There are flaws in the legal framework of some countries which contribute to impunity. For example, even though constitutional provisions may affirm women's right to a life free from violence, the definition may not cover all forms of violence against all women. Among

---

83 *Ibid.,* 84.
84 *Ibid.,* 85.
85 *Ibid.,* 86.
86 *Ibid.*

the forms most frequently absent from legislative prohibition is sexual harassment in the workplace or in school. Laws may cover some forms of violence but not others - for example, the law may punish domestic violence, but may omit marital rape from the definition. This is the case in countries with otherwise progressive domestic violence legislation, such as Thailand.[87]

Laws against violence against women - especially domestic violence - frequently emphasize family reunification or maintenance over the protection of victims. In some countries, laws allow so-called 'honour crimes' or allow a defense of honour to mitigate criminal penalties, putting the right of the family to defend its honour ahead of the rights of individuals in the family.[88]

Some countries, such as Brazil and Lebanon, have laws that suspend rape sentences if the perpetrator marries the victim.[89] Sometimes, the detailed provisions of a law undermine its stated purpose. In Egypt, for example, there is a law prohibiting female genital mutilation, but it refers only to operations performed outside hospitals by people without a medical qualification.[90]

5.2. Discriminatory laws

In some countries, even if legislation does not condone violence directly, it is discriminatory - the laws treat women differently from men, and confer fewer or lesser rights on women. Examples of such gender bias in statutory law include women being unable to sign official documents without their husband's permission or needing their husband's consent in order to get a passport, use contraception, or acquire property. Women in many countries have fewer rights than men to inheritance or property ownership. In many countries, including Gabon, a wife must get her husband's permission to travel abroad. In other countries, women are unable to pass their citizenship on to their children. Many women are thus trapped in abusive situations, or face the invidious choice of staying or leaving without their children.[91]

---

[87] NIKKI JECKS, 'Ending Violence Against Women: Regional Scan for East and Southern Asia', UNIFEM, 2002, 7.

[88] Amnesty International Report, supra n. 1, 87.

[89] *Ibid.*, 88.

[90] Report of the Special Rapporteur on Violence Against Women, UN Doc. E/CN.4/1996/53, para. 726.

[91] Amnesty International Report, supra n. 1, 88.

Sometimes, there is gender bias in the application of the law. Under Afghan law, adultery is a criminal offence carrying a prison sentence of up to 10 years or, where certain evidentiary requirements are met, the punishment of stoning (to Amnesty International's knowledge, this punishment has not been applied during the transitional period). In many parts of Afghanistan, there is a strong emphasis on prosecuting girls and women for offences such as adultery, 'running away from home' and sex before marriage, which are known as zina crimes. A few men have been accused or convicted of zina crimes, but the criminal justice system places disproportionate emphasis on the prosecution of women for zina crimes.[92]

5.3. Failure to implement the law

Even where the legal framework outlawing violence against women is in place, it may fail at the implementation stage. For example, the appropriate enabling legislation may not be passed, or inadequate provisions might be made for enforcement. Jurisdiction may not be unambiguously established, and if and when it is, judges may prefer to use civil, rather than criminal codes, resulting in much more lenient treatment of acts of violence.[93]

5.4. Community complicity

At the local level, when the suffering of women victims of violence is ignored or disparaged, impunity is reinforced. When women depart from what the community holds to be 'appropriate' behaviour, whether by asserting their sexuality or in other ways, they are often met with violent retribution - by their families, members of the community, or the State. Common forms include abductions, rapes, killings and incarceration. In many societies, marriage patterns and customs already infringe upon the fundamental rights of women and men to equally choose their spouse, to consent to sexual activity in marriage or to end a marriage. So women may transgress community norms merely by seeking to assert their fundamental rights. This structural violence puts women's rights to life and bodily integrity at risk. The State remains accountable for ensuring women's basic rights, even when they choose to depart from community norms. In the struggle against impunity, the

---

[92] *Ibid.*
[93] *Ibid.*, 89.

silent complicity of not only the State, but also individuals and communities, has to be confronted and overcome.[94]

6. CAMPAIGNING FOR CHANGE - MAKING A DIFFERENCE

Violence against women is universal but it is not inevitable. A recent WHO Report points out that communities that condemn violence, take action to end it and provide support for survivors, have lower levels of violence than communities that do not take such action. In a comparative study of 16 countries, researchers found that levels of partner violence are lowest in those societies with community sanctions (whether in the form of legal action, social approbation or moral pressure) and sanctuaries (shelters or family support systems).[95]

All over the world, women's rights activists have led efforts to expose violence against women, to give victims a voice, to provide innovative forms of support, to force governments and the international community to recognize their own failure to protect women and to hold all those responsible to account. They have shown that organizing to combat violence against women can make a real difference. Amnesty International launched its campaign to mobilize its more than 1.5 million members and supporters worldwide to add their voices to this struggle to stop violence against women.[96]

6.1. Making rights matter

One of the main reasons for engaging a human rights framework to oppose violence against women is the credibility it lends to the claim that contesting violence against women is a public responsibility, requiring legal and social redress. It also makes the more powerful appeal that violence against women, no matter what the cultural context, is not a legitimate practice and that the individual woman's body is inviolable. Often, making this point has required courageous work on the part of women's organizations.[97]

---

[94]   *Ibid.,* 93.

[95]   BELMA BACIRBASIC AND DZENNA SCECIC, *Invisible Causalities of War: Bosnia's raped women are being shunned by a society that refuses to see them as victims,* WHO 2002, 176.

[96]   Amnesty International Report, supra n. 1, 101.

[97]   *Ibid.*

6.2. Naming violations

The suffering caused by acts of violence against women can be life-long, and so can the struggle for redress. An estimated 200,000 women from across Asia were forced into military brothels during the Second World War by the Japanese Imperial Army. These so-called 'comfort women' began demanding acknowledgement of the violations they had suffered only in the late 1980s and 1990s. By this time, some no longer had any family who might be 'shamed' and women's activists had begun to link the issue with the problem of sexual oppression of women as a whole.[98] Eventually, in 2001, the non-governmental Women's International War Crimes Tribunal concluded that Japan's late Emperor Hirohito, and his Government, were responsible for forcing women into sexual slavery during the Second World War. It described the system as 'State-sanctioned rape and enslavement'.[99]

6.3. Raising awareness

Anti-violence activists - from grass-roots, community-based initiatives, to large national and regional networks to international organizations and UN agencies - have engaged in a wide variety of efforts to break the silence about violence against women, educate women about their rights, teach men that violence against women is a human rights abuse and a crime and mobilize communities to take responsibility for ending violence against women.[100]

6.4. Engaging human rights mechanisms

NGOs and legal advocates have used international human rights law not only to raise awareness and build pressure on governments but also more directly. In some cases, the injunction to abide by international human right standards has taken hold in courts and criminal proceedings. The Turkish Constitutional Court has extensively referred to the Women's Convention in decisions whose effect, among other things, has been to decriminalize adultery. Only two weeks after its ratification by Afghanistan, Amnesty International observed the Chief Judge of the District Court of Kabul considering the Women's Convention in a case in which a husband who had left for several years returned to find that his wife had married again. The husband was

---

[98] GEORGE HICKS, *The Comfort Women: Japan's Brutal Regime of Enforced Prostitution in the Second World War* (W.W. Norton. W.W. Norton & Company, Incorporated, 1995).

[99] Amnesty International Report, supra n. 1, 103.

[100] *Ibid.*, 104.

asking the court to force her to return to him and to have her prosecuted for adultery.[101] At the same time, she was petitioning for a divorce, due to desertion, at the advice of the National Human Rights Commission. In a lower court, the judge had refused to deal with the case, noting the country's recent ratification of the Women's Convention, and arguing that the judgment he would have normally delivered would conflict with women's rights to equality. The Chief Judge, noting the conflict of rights, decided to refer the case to the Chief Justice of the Supreme Court.[102] Regional human rights systems have also been an important site for combating discriminatory laws and demanding an end to impunity.[103]

6.5. Civil sanctions

Women's rights activists in some countries are promoting various forms of civil sanctions as well as criminal penalties as a means of countering and redressing violence against women. Such civil sanctions can include protection orders, fines, and removal from the home.[104] For example, in Italy, judges can order payments to victims who lack resources, including through withholding the sum from the aggressor's pay. Aggressors may be required to attend public or private centres for therapy.[105]

6.6. Demanding local action

Advocates for ending violence against women have also sought to harness the capacity of local, regional and municipal government. Human rights organizations have traditionally focused on holding States accountable at the national level for their failure to protect rights and ensure access to justice and adequate protection for women escaping violence. In many countries, however, local and municipal governments control education, rights in marriage and access to key services for women. They are also often responsible for protection through the police, courts, shelters and hospitals. In light of this, anti-violence activists are 'bringing human rights home,' engaging in advocacy at the local level to make governments more accountable and to challenge unbridled impunity.[106]

---

[101] The First CEDAW Impact Study.

[102] Amnesty International Report, supra n. 1, 105.

[103] *Ibid.*

[104] *Ibid.*, 106.

[105] Queen Sophia Centre, Valencia, Spain, Database on violence against women.

[106] Amnesty International Report, supra n. 1, 107-108.

Women have taken enormous strides to counter violence and achieve justice and equality. They have organized support services - sometimes with, though often without the support of their governments. They have initiated local, national and international campaigns to raise awareness about the rampant nature of violence against women and to shame their governments into taking action. Further, they have lobbied for the repeal of discriminatory laws and the adoption of legislation to address violence against women and they have developed national, regional and international networks that have changed the face of global organizing. One by one, they have confronted their abusers, left violent situations, and claimed their right to live free from violence. In the face of the pervasive shame and stigma attached to women speaking out about violence committed against them, they have asserted – 'silent no more'.[107]

---

[107] *Ibid.*

DOMESTIC VIOLENCE AGAINST WOMEN IN INTERNATIONAL HUMAN RIGHTS LAW

Ineke Boerefijn

1. INTRODUCTION

It is currently undisputed that violence against women constitutes a violation of their human rights, even if most of that violence occurs in the family and is mainly perpetrated by private individuals, not by representatives of the State.[1] Violence against women is a form of discrimination which severely restricts the rights and fundamental freedoms of women to live on equal terms with men. The human rights at risk of violation are the right to life, the right not to be subjected to torture or to cruel, inhuman or degrading treatment or punishment, the right to liberty and security of person, the right to equal protection under the law, the right to equality in the family and the right to the highest attainable standard of physical and mental health.

The responsibility of the State lies in the fact that violence against women is not a matter of crimes committed on an incidental basis by individual men. It is a structural phenomenon that is symptomatic of the structural inequality of men and women in society. It has taken a long time for this view to gain general acceptance, partly due to the fact that very few women were involved in the regular circuit of human rights fora. Matters involving largely or exclusively women's issues have tended to be dealt with in separate international fora. As a result, human rights developments have not focused sufficiently on gender-specific human rights violations. It has even been claimed that human rights have been defined 'by the criterion of what men fear will happen to them.'[2] However, a great deal of ground has been covered since the early nineties, thanks mainly to well-organized lobbying by the women's

---

[1] *Further actions and initiatives to implement the Beijing Declaration and Platform for Action*, UN Doc. A/RES/S-23/3, Annex, para. 13. See also I. BOEREFIJN, M.M. VAN DER LIET-SENDERS, T. LOENEN, *Het voorkomen en bestrijden van geweld tegen vrouwen. Een verdiepend onderzoek naar het Nederlandse beleid in het licht van de verplichtingen die voortvloeien uit het Vrouwenverdrag (Preventing and combating violence against women. In-depth research into Dutch policy in the light of obligations under the Women's Convention)*, (The Hague: Ministry of Social Affairs and Employment, 2000). Section 2 of this report examines the developments in international fora and the theoretical basis for this position.

[2] This was said by Hilary Charlesworth, quoted in URSULA O'HARE, 'Realizing Human Rights for Women', in Human Rights Quarterly, Vol. 21, 1999, 364-402, p. 367.

movement before and during the World Conference on Human Rights held in Vienna in 1993 and the Fourth World Conference on Women, held in Beijing in 1994. The early nineties saw the creation of a number of important instruments, including General Recommendation no. 19 (1992)[3] adopted by the Committee on the Elimination of Discrimination against Women and the UN Declaration on the Elimination of Violence against Women (1993).[4] Further, the Sub-Commission for the Promotion and Protection of Human Rights appointed a Special Rapporteur on Harmful Traditional Practices, the Commission on Human Rights appointed a Special Rapporteur on Violence Against Women (1994), the Council of Europe adopted a declaration (1993) and the Organization of American States created a convention which came into force in March 1995.

Violence against women is currently a prominent issue on the agenda of many international fora, especially within the United Nations framework. A number of instruments are specifically aimed at combating this phenomenon, but many other human rights instruments have played an important role in further defining the concept of violence against women in general and specific forms of violence, such as domestic violence, and elaborating on States' obligations. When examining the state of the art with respect to the scope of domestic violence and States' obligations under international human rights law, various sources can be used. This contribution focuses on relevant United Nations instruments – legally binding instruments as well as soft law instruments – and the interpretation thereof by expert bodies, individual experts and political organs. Section 3 will look at the Convention on the Elimination of All Forms of Discrimination Against Women (Women's Convention), the Covenant on Civil and Political Rights, the Convention Against Torture and Other Cruel, Inhuman or Degrading Treatment or Punishment, the Convention on the Rights of the Child and the Convention on the Elimination of all forms of Racial Discrimination and the respective treaty monitoring bodies; the UN Declaration on the Elimination of Violence Against Women and the work of the Special Rapporteur on Violence Against Women, the Special Rapporteur on Extrajudicial, Summary or Arbitrary Executions, the Special Rapporteur on Migrant Workers, and the resolutions adopted by

---

3   CEDAW, General Recommendation no. 19, Violence Against Women, adopted on 30 January 1992, UN Doc. A/47/38, Ch. I.
4   *Declaration on the Elimination of Violence Against Women*, adopted on 20 December 1993, UN Doc. A/RES/48/104.

the Commission on Human Rights and the General Assembly.[5] Significant elements of the work of the organs have been selected to demonstrate that they complement and reinforce each other. First, section 2 will provide insight into the scope of domestic violence by looking at the definition and the various forms of domestic violence that fall within the scope of the definition. Section 4 will deal with obligations of States, as can be derived from the various instruments. Finally, the question will be raised whether a legally binding instrument is needed.

2. DEFINING DOMESTIC VIOLENCE AGAINST WOMEN

In 1993 the United Nations General Assembly adopted the UN Declaration on the Elimination of Violence against Women (hereafter referred to as the UN Declaration) without a vote.[6] This Declaration is the first international instrument entirely devoted to violence against women. Article 1 gives the following definition of the term 'violence against women':

Any act of gender-based violence that results in, or is likely to result in, physical, sexual or psychological harm or suffering to women, including threats of such acts, coercion or arbitrary deprivation of liberty, whether occurring in public or in private life.

This definition reaffirms the definition adopted by CEDAW in General Recommendation no. 19. Article 2 of the Declaration distinguishes three areas in which physical, sexual and psychological harm against women occurs:

(1) In the family, including battering, sexual abuse of female children in the household, dowry-related violence, marital rape, female genital mutilation and other traditional practices harmful to women, non-spousal violence and violence related to exploitation;

(2) In the general community, including rape, sexual abuse, sexual harassment and intimidation at work, in educational institutions and elsewhere, trafficking in women and forced prostitution;

(3) Violence perpetrated or condoned by the State, wherever it occurs.

---

[5]   This contribution does not deal with the important work done by organizations such as WHO, UNIFEM, UNICEF, UNFPA, regional organizations (in particular South America and Africa) and numerous non-governmental organizations.

[6]   *Declaration on the Elimination of Violence Against Women*, adopted on 20 December 1993, UN Doc. A/RES/48/104.

This contribution focuses mainly on the forms of violence listed under (1).

It is highly significant that Article 4 of the UN Declaration specifically states that States should condemn violence against women and should not invoke any custom, tradition or religious consideration to avoid their obligations with respect to its elimination. In 17 subparagraphs the Declaration imposes a series of obligations on States including the obligation to refrain from engaging in violence themselves and the obligation to exercise *due diligence* to prevent, investigate and in accordance with national legislation, punish acts of violence against women.

The World Conference on Human Rights, held in Vienna in 1993, called on the Commission on Human Rights to appoint a Special Rapporteur on Violence Against Women, which the Commission did in its session in March 1994.[7] The Special Rapporteur's mandate relates to gender-based violence in the family, within the general community and when perpetrated or condoned by the State. In 2003, the mandate was extended, the new resolution calls upon States to take action whether acts of violence against women are perpetrated by the State, by private persons or by armed groups or warring factions.[8]

When trying to find an answer to the question of the forms of domestic violence on which there is agreement, it becomes clear that there are still controversial issues. In their practice, both the independent experts and the political organs usually list various forms of domestic violence, thereby emphasizing that a specific form is to be considered to be a violation of human rights. This has, however, resulted in debates on various forms, especially over certain cultural or traditional practices, and the question whether or not they ought to be condemned as a form of domestic violence. Forms that have not explicitly been condemned by the Commission on Human Rights or the General Assembly are thus not generally recognized as falling within the definition of Article 1 of the UN Declaration, despite the fact that it was agreed in general terms that States should not invoke culture, tradition or religious considerations. This is not a debate on the violent or otherwise harmful nature of the various forms, but rather on their 'acceptability'.

---

[7]   Commission on Human Rights Resolution 1994/45. From 1994 - July 2003, Ms. Radhika Coomaraswamy (Sri Lanka) performed this function, since August 2003, Dr. Yakin Ertürk (Turkey) is Special Rapporteur.

[8]   Commission on Human Rights Resolution 2003/45, adopted on 23 April 2003.

The Special Rapporteur on Violence Against Women has devoted various reports to domestic violence, which give much insight in its manifestations.[9] In her reports, the Special Rapporteur on Violence Against Women has called for a broad understanding of the term 'family' to include the multiplicity of family forms and provide protection for those within the family, irrespective of family form. She defined violence in the family as 'violence perpetrated in the domestic sphere which targets women because of their role in that sphere or as violence which is intended to impact, directly and negatively, on women within the domestic sphere. Such violence may be carried out by both private and public actors and agents.' It is, therefore, the sphere in which the violence takes place rather than the perpetrator that makes a specific occurrence of violence, 'domestic.'[10] As forms of violence in the family, she has mentioned *inter alia*, woman-battering, marital rape, incest, forced prostitution, violence against domestic workers, sex-selective abortions, female infanticide, forced and early marriage, preference of sons over daughters and female genital mutilation.[11] At a later stage, she also included honour crimes (see next section). The Special Rapporteur on Violence Against Women further made it clear that women encounter violence in different stages of their lives. In her report she referred to various manifestations of violence that fall within the scope of economic and social rights. With respect to girls and the unborn, she pointed to issues such as 'enforced malnutrition', unequal access to health care, mental and physical assault; as well as trafficking in children for prostitution and bonded labour. Adult women may become victims of dowry violence, domestic murder, *sati* (widow burning), forced pregnancy, abortion and sterilization.[12] In her 2002 report, the Special Rapporteur also drew attention to beauty in Western countries. She observed that the culture of impractical ideals results in many practices that cause a great deal of abuse to the female body.[13]

---

[9] See in particular, Report of the Special Rapporteur on Violence Against Women, its causes and consequences, Ms. Radhika Coomaraswamy , UN Doc. E/CN.4/1996/53; *Violence against women in the family*, Report of the Special Rapporteur on Violence Against Women, its causes and consequences, Ms. Radhika Coomaraswamy, submitted in accordance with Commission on Human Rights Resolution 1995/85, UN Doc. E/CN.4/1999/68 and Cultural practices in the family that are violent towards women, Report of the Special Rapporteur on Violence Against Women, its causes and consequences, Ms. Radhika Coomaraswamy, submitted in accordance with Commission on Human Rights resolution 2001/49, UN Doc. E/CN.4/2002/83.

[10] UN Doc. E/CN.4/1999, 68, ibid, para. 16.

[11] *Ibid.*

[12] UN Doc. E/CN.4/1996/53, supra n. 9, paras. 54-55.

[13] UN Doc. E/CN.4/2002/83, supra n. 9, para. 96.

Most of the forms identified by the Special Rapporteur have been recognized as forms of (domestic) violence against women also by other organs, though not the forms that violate women's economic and social rights.

The General Assembly's special session on the follow-up to Beijing constituted an important landmark.[14] It noted forms of violence such as battering, sexual abuse of female children in the household, dowry-related violence, marital rape, female genital mutilation and other traditional practices harmful to women, non-spousal violence and violence related to exploitation.[15] It called on States to eradicate harmful customary or traditional practices, including female genital mutilation, early and forced marriage and so-called honour crimes, which are violations of the human rights of women and girls and obstacles to the full enjoyment by women of their human rights and fundamental freedoms.[16] Furthermore, the outcome document called on States to take all measures towards the elimination of violence against women and girls including forms of commercial sexual exploitation, as well as economic exploitation including trafficking in women and children, female infanticide, crimes committed in the name of honour, crimes committed in the name of passion, racially motivated crimes, abduction and sale of children, dowry-related violence and deaths, acid attacks and harmful traditional or customary practices, such as female genital mutilation, early and forced marriages.[17] The widest agreement appears to exist on the need to abolish female genital mutilation. The 2002 UN Special Session on Children set a goal to end female genital mutilation and cutting by the year 2010.[18]

In 1999, the Special Rapporteur on Violence Against Women was the first to include so-called honour crimes as a form of violence in the family in her reports, because of the numerous communications she received.[19] The question of honour crimes has also been addressed by the Special Rapporteur on extrajudicial, summary and arbitrary executions. The

---

14   For some critical comments on the document, see *Towards an effective implementation of international norms to end violence against women, Report of the Special Rapporteur on Violence Against Women*, its causes and consequences, Yakin Ertürk, UN Doc. E/CN.4/2004/66, paras. 26-28.
15   Further actions and initiatives to implement the Beijing Declaration and Platform for Action, UN Doc. A/RES/S-23/3, Annex para. 14.
16   *Ibid.*, para. 69(d).
17   *Ibid.*, para. 96(a).
18   UN Doc. A/RES/S-27/2, *A world fit for children*, Annex, para. 43.
19   UN Doc. E/CN.4/1999/68, supra n. 9, paras. 17-18.

latter Special Rapporteur investigates both overtly state-sanctioned honour crimes, and cases where the perpetrators go unpunished because the practice has either overt or tacit approval. Honour crimes can take a variety of forms. Sometimes young girls and women are driven to suicide after public condemnation of their behaviour or open threats. Acid burns have permanently mutilated or even killed many women. The Special Rapporteur has also received information that girls accused of immoral behaviour are sometimes whipped to death. The perpetrators, often members of the girls' or women's families, are usually proud of what they have done. Some countries continue to enforce legislation which provides for only very light punishments; in some of these countries, honour crimes are not even prosecuted. This systematic leniency is perpetuated by the courts, which either justify the crime on the grounds that the woman's disobedience was a 'provocation' or cite cultural norms as grounds for light sentences. Some governments try to 'protect' potential victims by imprisoning them or putting them in a custodial or correctional home, sometimes for years, while the potential perpetrators go free.[20] In a subsequent report, the Special Rapporteur expressed her concern about reports of women being condemned to death for adultery. She observed that this offence does not constitute a 'most serious crime' and that it is not an intentional crime with lethal or other extremely grave consequences.[21]

The fact that honour crimes is a particularly controversial issue also becomes clear when we look at the resolutions of the Commission on Human Rights and the General Assembly. In 2000 the General Assembly adopted a resolution solely on honour crimes. The preamble confirms that 'crimes against women committed in the name of honour are a human rights issue and that States have an obligation to exercise due diligence to prevent, investigate and punish the perpetrators of such crimes and to provide protection to the victims, and that the failure to do so constitutes a human rights violation.'[22] In 2002, it adopted a resolution that mentioned a large number of forms of violence including all forms of commercial sexual exploitation as well as economic exploitation including trafficking in women and children, female infanticide, crimes committed in the name of honour, crimes committed in the name of

---

[20] *Extrajudicial, summary or arbitrary executions*, Report of the Special Rapporteur, Ms. Asma Jahangir, submitted pursuant to Commission on Human Rights resolution 1999/35, UN Doc. E/CN.4/2000/3, paras. 78-84.

[21] *Interim report of the Special Rapporteur of the Commission on Human Rights on extrajudicial, summary or arbitrary executions*, UN Doc. A/59/319, para. 56.

[22] *Working towards the elimination of crimes against women committed in the name of honour*, adopted on 4 December 2000, UN Doc. A/RES/55/66.

passion, racially motivated crimes, the abduction and sale of children, dowry-related violence and deaths, acid attacks and harmful traditional or customary practices, such as female genital mutilation and early and forced marriages.[23] In 2003, however, honour crimes were not mentioned in the General Assembly's relevant resolutions. Instead, the General Assembly requested the Secretary-General to conduct an in-depth study on all forms and manifestations of violence against women.[24] A resolution dealing solely with domestic violence departed from previous practice by no longer listing the various forms of violence, but merely stated that domestic violence can take many different forms, including physical, psychological and sexual violence.[25] On the one hand, there is something to say for condemning domestic violence in general terms; in this case, however, it was clear that this approach was chosen because the General Assembly did not agree on the inclusion of honour crimes in the resolution. Nevertheless, in 2004, the General Assembly adopted a resolution in stronger terms, stressing the need 'to treat all forms of violence against women and girls, including crimes committed in the name of honour, as a criminal offence, punishable by law.'[26] It called on States to fulfil their obligations under the relevant human rights instruments and to implement the Beijing Declaration and Platform for Action and the outcome document of the special session of the General Assembly.[27] Hopefully, the General Assembly will continue to condemn this issue in the strongest terms. Other forms that have been mentioned by a number of expert bodies, but on which there is no agreement in the political organs, include forced abortion, forced sterilisation, forced pregnancy and polygamy.

3. PRACTICE OF ORGANS THAT DEAL WITH DOMESTIC VIOLENCE

As was stated before, many organs deal with violence against women, including domestic violence. It would go beyond the scope of this contribution to deal extensively with all forms of domestic violence

---

[23] Elimination of all forms of violence against women, including crimes identified in the outcome document of the twenty-third special session of the General Assembly, 'Women 2000: gender equality, development and peace for the twenty-first century', adopted on 18 December 2002, UN Doc. A/RES/57/181, para. 2.

[24] In-depth study on all forms of violence against women, 22 December 2003, UN Doc. A/RES/58/185.

[25] Elimination of domestic violence against women, 22 December 2003, UN Doc. A/RES/58/147.

[26] Working towards the elimination of crimes against women and girls committed in the name of honour, adopted on 20 December 2004, UN Doc. A/RES/59/165, preamble.

[27] UN Doc. A/RES/59/165, para. 3(a).

against women. As became clear in the previous section, there are numerous forms of violence on which there is, to a large extent, agreement that they fall within the scope of domestic violence. In the present section, attention will be paid to the practice of various organs that deal with violence against women, in order to provide a picture of the various instruments and relevant practice related thereto.

3.1. Committee on the Elimination of Discrimination Against Women

The Women's Convention does not contain any provisions which recognise women's right to physical integrity.[28] CEDAW, which is the body charged with supervising compliance with the Women's Convention, states that violence against women is a form of discrimination. An authoritative elaboration of this view can be found in CEDAW General Recommendation no. 19.[29] CEDAW stresses that gender-based violence is a form of discrimination that seriously inhibits women's ability to enjoy rights and freedoms on a basis of equality with men.

The General Recommendation comments on a number of specific Articles in the Convention which cover the following forms of violence:

- Articles 2(f), 5 and 10(c): family violence and abuse, forced marriage, dowry deaths, acid attacks and female circumcision.
- Article 6: traffic in women and exploitation of the prostitution of women. This also covers new forms of sexual exploitation, such as sex tourism, the recruitment of domestic labour from developing countries to work in developed countries, and organised marriages between women from developing countries and foreign nationals.
- Article 11: sexual harassment including physical contact and advances, sexually coloured remarks, showing pornography and sexual demands.
- Article 12: traditional practices including dietary restrictions for pregnant women, preference for male children and female circumcision or genital mutilation.
- Article 16 (and 5): compulsory sterilisation and abortion, family violence including battering, rape, other forms of sexual assault, mental and other forms of violence.

---

[28] See MARJOLEIN VAN DEN BRINK, '*Het recht op lichamelijke integriteit en het Vrouwenverdrag*', (The right to physical integrity and the Women's Convention), in: NJCM Bulletin 18, 1993, p. 660-673.

[29] General Recommendation no. 19, supra n. 3.

The General Recommendation pays due attention to the causes of violence, such as traditional attitudes by which women are regarded as subordinate to men or as having stereotyped roles that perpetuate widespread practices involving violence or coercion. Further, it provides an overview of the implications for all relevant provisions of the Women's Convention. In its practice under the reporting procedure, CEDAW has paid considerable attention to domestic violence, and has stated, among other things, that polygamy and forced marriages are incompatible with the Women's Convention.[30] Another relevant General Recommendation deals with the right to health.[31] The Recommendation states that violence against women is an important issue for women's health. It points out that harmful traditional practices such as female genital mutilation (FGM), polygamy and marital rape expose women and girls to HIV/AIDS and other sexually transmitted diseases.

The very first views adopted by CEDAW under the Optional Protocol to the Women's Convention concerned a domestic violence case in Hungary.[32] The author of the communication had been subjected to regular severe domestic violence and threats by her common law husband, father of her two children, one of whom is severely brain-damaged. No shelter in the country was equipped to take in a fully disabled child. Under Hungarian law, protection orders or restraining orders were not available. Criminal proceedings had been instituted against the author's common law husband, from whom she separated, but who continued to be violent against her. It took more than three years until he was convicted and fined 365 US$. In the meantime, he was not detained and the author had no possibility of obtaining temporary protection. After having determined that the communication was admissible, CEDAW turned to the merits of the case. It referred to General Recommendation no. 19 and examined whether Articles 2(a), (b) and (e); 5 and 16 of the Women's Convention had been violated.

With regard to Article 2(a), (b) and (e), CEDAW noted that there were no remedies to provide the author with effective protection against ill-

---

[30] See for example CEDAW, *Concluding observations on Israel*, UN Doc. A/52/38/Rev.1, Part II, para. 178.

[31] CEDAW, General Recommendation no. 24, Women and Health (Article 12), adopted on 2 February 1999, UN Doc. A/54/38/Rev.1, chapter I.

[32] CEDAW, Communication no. 2/2003, *Ms. A.T. v. Hungary*, views of 25 January 2005. At the time of writing, the views had not yet been published as an official UN document. They were available through the website of the Division for the Advancement of Women, available at: <http://www.un.org/womenwatch/daw/cedaw/>.

treatment by her former partner and that – despite efforts undertaken by the State party – the legal and institutional arrangements in the State party were not ready to ensure the internationally expected, coordinated, comprehensive and effective protection and support for the victims of domestic violence. Further, it became clear that domestic violence cases as such did not enjoy high priority in court proceedings. According to CEDAW, women's human rights to life and to physical and mental integrity could not be superseded by other rights, including the right to property and the right to privacy. CEDAW concluded that the obligations set out in Article 2(a), (b) and (e) extended to the prevention of and protection from violence against women and in the instant case, remained unfulfilled and constituted a violation of the author's human rights and fundamental freedoms, particularly her right to security of person.

With respect to Articles 5 and 16, CEDAW noted that traditional attitudes contributed to violence against women. When considering Hungary's report, CEDAW had expressed its concern about the persistence of entrenched traditional stereotypes regarding the role and responsibilities of women and men in the family. It stated that the facts of the communication revealed aspects of the relationships between the sexes and attitudes towards women that the Committee recognized vis-à-vis the country as a whole. It pointed again to the impossibility for the author to obtain effective remedies and to flee to a shelter. CEDAW concluded that, considered together, the facts indicated that the rights of the author under Articles 5 (a) and 16 of the Convention had been violated.

In formulating its recommendations, CEDAW referred to measures taken with respect to the author of the communication, as well as in general. It found that the State party should take immediate and effective measures to guarantee the physical and mental integrity of A.T. and her family; and ensure that A.T. is given a safe home in which to live with her children, receives appropriate child support and legal assistance and that she receives reparation proportionate to the physical and mental harm undergone and to the gravity of the violations of her rights. Measures recommended to improve the situation in general concerned, among others, protection, training on the Convention, implementation of CEDAW's concluding comments, the duty to investigate all allegations of domestic violence, access to justice and effective remedies and rehabilitation and programmes for offenders.

These views demonstrate the potential of the Women's Convention in the area of domestic violence, even though the right to physical integrity has not as such been guaranteed in the Convention. In its activities under the reporting procedure, CEDAW has developed its position in general terms and has now applied these to a concrete case. Some people may have feared that the restrictive terminology used in Article 2 of the Optional Protocol[33] would constitute an obstacle to finding violations of provisions such as Articles 2 and 5, but CEDAW has clearly acted in the spirit of the Convention and the Optional Protocol. The recommendations formulated by CEDAW are particularly noteworthy and relevant to all States parties to the Women's Convention.

3.2. Human Rights Committee

In its detailed and revolutionary recommendation on Article 3 of the International Covenant on Civil and Political Rights (ICCPR),[34] the Human Rights Committee comments on a number of aspects relevant to the subject of violence against women. It considers the causes of the continuing structural inequality between men and women. The Human Rights Committee examines the Articles of the ICCPR one by one. In respect of Article 6 the Human Rights Committee pays considerable attention to factors which are important to the right to life. It asks for statistics on births and on mortality as a result of pregnancy and childbirth, for information on unwanted pregnancies and measures to prevent women resorting to potentially fatal illegal abortions. It also calls on States to report on measures to protect women against practices which violate their right to life (such as female infanticide, widow burning and dowry-related murders) and on the consequences of poverty and deprivation which can put the lives of women at risk.

The Human Rights Committee's interpretation of Article 7, which deals with the prohibition of torture and other cruel, inhuman or degrading treatment or punishment, is particularly striking. Whilst the Committee Against Torture hardly pays attention to violence against women, the Human Rights Committee states that in order for it to monitor observance of Articles 7 and 24 (rights of children) it must be given

---

33 According to Article 2 of the Optional Protocol 'Communications may be submitted by or on behalf of individuals or groups of individuals, under the jurisdiction of a State Party, claiming to be victims of a violation of any of the rights set forth in the Convention (....)' (emphasis added, IB).

34 Article 3 ICCPR states: 'The States Parties to the present Covenant undertake to ensure the equal right of men and women to the enjoyment of all civil and political rights set forth in the present Covenant'.

information on national legislation and practices related to violence in the family and other forms of violence against women, including rape. It also wishes to receive reports on the availability of facilities for safe abortion following rape, on measures to prevent compulsory abortion and compulsory sterilisation and on the scale of FGM and measures designed to abolish it.

The Human Rights Committee states its position in respect of States which enforce clothing restrictions for women in public. It points out that subjecting women to corporal punishment for non-observance of these restrictions violates a number of human rights, including those under Article 7. It reserves some of its most forthright comments for the subject of polygamy and states that it should also be noted that equality of treatment with regard to the right to marry implies that polygamy is incompatible with this principle. Polygamy violates the dignity of women. It states that it is an inadmissible discrimination against women and that it should definitely be abolished, wherever it continues to exist. On honour crimes, it has stated that where these remain unpunished, they constitute a serious violation of the Covenant, particularly of Articles 6 (right to life), 14 (right to a fair trial) and 26 (right to equality and non-discrimination).

3.3. Committee on Economic, Social and Cultural Rights

The Committee on Economic, Social and Cultural Rights (ESC Committee) also considers the issue of violence against women, in particular, violence in the family. It largely bases its positions on Articles 10 and 12 (respectively the right to protection of the family and the right to the highest standard attainable of physical and mental health) of the Covenant on Economic, Social ad Cultural Rights. It tends to look at violence against women in connection with violence against children, either because violence against women has serious consequences for children in the families concerned or because children themselves are victims of domestic violence. The ESC Committee also observes violations of other rights under the Covenant, such as the right to housing. It notes that homeless women are particularly vulnerable to acts of violence and sexual abuse.[35] It notes that reductions in the funding of social welfare programmes and shortages of affordable and suitable housing constitute serious obstacles for women attempting to escape from violent domestic situations. This effectively forces women to choose

---

[35] General Comment no. 7, the right to adequate housing, 1997 (art. 11.1 of the Covenant): forced evictions, UN Doc. E/C.12/2000/4, para. 11.

between staying in or returning to a violent situation or exposing themselves and their children to the risk of homelessness, lack of food and clothing.[36]

3.4. Committee on the Rights of the Child

The Convention on the Rights of the Child contains a number of provisions related to violence, including domestic violence. Article 19 obliges States parties to protect the child 'from all forms of physical or mental violence, injury or abuse, neglect or negligent treatment, maltreatment or exploitation, including sexual abuse, while in the care of parent(s), legal guardian(s) or any other person who has the care of the child'. Article 24 of the Convention on the Rights of the Child recognises the right to the enjoyment of the highest attainable standard of health. Paragraph 3 states that 'States Parties shall take all effective and appropriate measures with a view to abolishing traditional practices prejudicial to the health of children'. In the examination of country reports, the Committee on the Rights of the Child (CRC Committee) devotes much attention to the practice of female genital mutilation.

3.5. Committee Against Torture

The Committee against Torture (CAT Committee) has paid scant attention to gender-specific violence. In certain cases it has welcomed the adoption of laws against violence against women as 'positive developments.' For example, in the case of Venezuela the CAT Committee notes that such laws were intended to provide greater protection to this vulnerable group, who are often the victims of discrimination, abuse or cruel, inhuman or degrading treatment.[37] The Division for the Advancement of Women (DAW, a division of the UN Secretariat) indicates that two points in the Beijing Platform for Action are relevant to CAT; violence against women and women in situations of armed conflict. DAW draws attention to the fact that while individual members may have highlighted gender-specific forms of torture such as the rape of women in detention by police officers, these issues have never been raised in a country report. DAW recommends that the CAT Committee includes these issues in its country reports since they are much more accessible than the reports of the Committee's sessions. DAW observes that to date, the CAT Committee has concentrated almost

---

[36] ESC COMMITTEE, *Concluding observations on Canada*, adopted on 4 December 1998, UN Doc. E/C.12/1/Add.31, para. 28.

[37] CAT COMMITTEE, *Concluding comments on Venezuela*, adopted in Spring 1999, UN Doc. A/54/44, adopted in Spring 1999, para. 133.

exclusively on violence perpetrated by officials of the State, meaning that violence against women in the family or in the community has been ignored. DAW requests that in future, the CAT Committee will look into the issue of the responsibility of States for preventing violence and for introducing measures on violence perpetrated by private citizens.[38]

In the examination of individual communications under Article 22 of the Convention Against Torture, the CAT Committee adopted one decision that is highly relevant for the issue of violence against women. An Iranian woman, the widow of a martyr, was supervised by the Committee of Martyrs. She had been forced into a *sighe* or *mutah* marriage (a short-term marriage) with an ayatollah. She fell in love with a Christian man whom she met secretly. The relationship was discovered, and subsequently she was beaten by her husband. After she had fled to Sweden, she was tried *in absentia* and sentenced to death by stoning for adultery. The CAT Committee took into account the numerous reports from the Special Representative of the Commission on Human Rights on Iran and from non-governmental sources which confirmed that married women had indeed been stoned to death for adultery. The CAT Committee decided that Sweden was under an obligation not to expel the woman to Iran, in accordance with Article 3 of the Convention.[39]

3.6. Committee on the Elimination of Racial Discrimination

In its General Recommendation on gender-related dimensions of racial discrimination,[40] the Committee on the Elimination of Racial Discrimination (CERD) paid attention to a number of forms of violence. It noted that certain forms of racial discrimination may be directed towards women specifically because of their gender. Among the forms of domestic violence, it referred to the coerced sterilization of indigenous women and abuse of women workers in the informal sector or domestic workers employed abroad by their employers. It also stated that racial discrimination may have consequences that affect primarily or only women, such as pregnancy resulting from racial bias-motivated rape and that in some societies women victims of such rapes may also be ostracized. In its concluding comments it deals with these issues. Upon concluding the examination of Slovakia's report, for example, it expressed its concern about reports of cases of forced sterilization of

---

38 DAW, Women 2000, *Integrating a gender perspective into UN human rights work,* p. 6-7.

39 CAT COMMITTEE, Communication no. 149/1999, *A.S. v. Sweden,* views of 24 November 2000. UN Doc. A/56/44, Annex VII.A.10, p. 173-186.

40 CERD COMMITTEE, *General Recommendation XXV on gender related dimensions of racial discrimination,* adopted on 24 March 2000, UN Doc. A/55/18, Annex V.A.

49

women without their full and informed consent. The CERD Committee strongly recommended that Slovakia take all necessary measures to put an end to this practice and to provide the victims with just and effective remedies, including compensation and apology.[41]

3.7. Special Rapporteurs of the Commission on Human Rights[42]

Much of the important work carried out by the Special Rapporteur on Violence Against Women has already been dealt with in previous sections of this contribution. This Rapporteur pays much attention to the causes and consequences of the various forms of violence against women, including violence in the family. When studying the various forms of domestic violence, it becomes clear that this Special Rapporteur has taken the lead in qualifying a particular practice or custom as a form of violence that falls within the scope of the definition of the UN Declaration and other human rights instruments. She has proved to be a true advocate for the cause of eliminating violence against women, by calling upon individual States and international organizations to recognize violence against women as a human rights violation, and to take all possible measures, despite the fact that many forms of violence are deeply rooted in society. In challenging such practices, women's cultural identity and cultural respect must be taken into consideration. She points to the fact that many traditional practices challenge the very concept of universal human rights. She notes that many of them are 'torture like' in their manifestation, and should therefore receive maximum international scrutiny and agitation. The Special Rapporteur refers in particular to practices such as female genital mutilation, honour killings, *sati*, the pledging of girls for economic and cultural appeasement, witch hunting and other cultural practices that brutalize the female body.[43]

Also other Special Rapporteurs pay attention to the issue of violence against women. As was stated above, the Special Rapporteur on Extrajudicial, Summary, or Arbitrary Executions has stated that the issue of honour killings that go unpunished, or where government officials were complicit or had failed to take action falls within her mandate.

---

41 CERD COMMITTEE, *Concluding comments on Slovakia*, adopted on 18 August 2004, UN Doc. CERD/C/65/CO/7.

42 In 2004, the Commission on Human Rights decided to establish a Special Rapporteur on Trafficking in Persons , especially in women and children. This Special Rapporteur is due to report to the Commission for the first time in 2005. See resolution 2004/110.

43 UN Doc. E/CN.4/2002/83, supra n. 9, para. 6.

Furthermore, she has expressed her grave concern about women who are condemned to death for adultery.[44]

The Special Rapporteur on Migrant Workers devoted a significant portion of her 2004 report to the human rights of migrant domestic workers, in which she focused principally on the situation of female domestic workers.[45] Various factors make migrant domestic workers an extremely vulnerable category. Many such workers are heavily dependent on their employer, particularly when legal residence in the country depends on the work contract. Furthermore, their vulnerability is frequently exacerbated by the fact that their immigrant status is not legal. Many migrant domestic workers work under the explicit or psychological threat of deportation or violence. Many women are deceived and are unaware of the type and terms of their employment. Owing to the very nature of the violation, and, in the absence of watchdog mechanisms, it is very difficult for migrant domestic workers to report the abuses they suffer. This may lead to a situation that a female domestic worker who has been raped by her employer or another member of the household is forced to remain in the house. Other forms of abuses that occur include physical and sexual abuse, deprivation of liberty, murder and disappearance.

In this section, the Sub-Commission's activities also need to be mentioned. In the 1980s the Sub-Commission appointed a 'Working Group on Traditional Practices Affecting the Health of Women and Children', consisting of experts from the Sub-Commission, UNICEF, UNESCO and the WHO, as well as representatives from NGOs. The group met three times in 1985-1986 before submitting a report to the Commission on Human Rights.[46] The Commission asked the Sub-Commission to investigate national and international measures taken in this area. The mandate is currently entitled 'The elimination of traditional practices affecting the health of women and the girl child.' The Special Rapporteur appointed on this mandate paid particular attention to the practice of female genital mutilation.

---

[44] UN Doc. A/59/319, supra n. 21, paras. 54-56.

[45] *Migrant workers, Report of the Special Rapporteur*, Ms. Gabriela Rodríguez Pizarro, submitted pursuant to Commission on Human Rights resolution 2003/46, UN Doc. E/CN.4/2004/76.

[46] Report of the Working Group on Traditional Practices Affecting the Health of Women and Children, UN Doc. E/CN.4/1986/42.

4. OBLIGATIONS OF STATES

As was made clear in the previous section, there are numerous forms of domestic violence against women. The problem is universal and must be addressed in a comprehensive manner. Section 3 described the practice of various organs that deal with the manifestations of violence against women, whereas the present section provides an overview of States' obligations under international instruments, as interpreted by the expert bodies.[47] Obligations of States can be divided into categories such as general measures, legislative measures, protective measures, remedies and preventive measures. The following sections will give examples of measures to be taken in each of these categories.

4.1. General measures

Various provisions in international instruments oblige States to take 'appropriate' measures, which is often understood as giving States a wide margin of appreciation in adopting measures. It must be understood in such a way, that a government has an obligation to determine what measure is 'appropriate' in a given situation. Governments should undertake research to gain proper insight into the nature, scale and consequences of the different forms of violence against women in their societies, taking into account the diverse composition. Structural research should serve as a basis for policy, preferably in a comprehensive national action plan to eliminate all forms of violence against women. Policy documents must set measurable objectives. If research shows that some or all of the objectives are not being achieved, the means must be adjusted. Policy that is considered to be 'good' must be vigorously pursued.

The gender-specific nature of the issue must be kept in mind at all times. For instance, gender mainstreaming must not lead to a situation in which the general issue of violence – such as random violence in the public sphere – is at centre stage while woman-battering, assault and rape of adult females are pushed into the background.

Changing a culture is a delicate undertaking. It should be emphasized that cultures are dynamic rather than static. The conviction that practices which are detrimental to the health and dignity of women should be

---

[47] This section is largely based on previous research, I. BOEREFIJN ET AL., supra n. 1, and INEKE BOEREFIJN, *Violence against women. An overview of current international law particularly with regard to traditional practices harmful to women* (unpublished background paper submitted to the Advisory Council on International Affairs, January 2001).

eliminated from a culture does not necessarily imply any lack of respect for that culture. Criticism of a culture must never be allowed to turn into a form of racism or demonisation of that culture. It is imperative to adopt an intersectional approach to the introduction and implementation of policy aimed at changing a culture. This means inviting representatives from all the communities concerned - including schools, community groups and local government bodies – to participate in the policy making process. Attempts to find ceremonies and rites as alternatives to harmful practices should be part of this process.

The government must clearly acknowledge that violence against women is a human rights issue and an issue for the entire community, not just a private problem. It should give high priority to tackling the issue – at least as high as that given to the issue of public acts of violence – and allocate structural resources for this purpose.

Proper coordination and policy cohesion are essential. There should be high-level government commitment to the issue and a national plan of action to tackle violence against women should be introduced. A good starting point would be the five principles developed by UNICEF: prevention, protection, early intervention, rebuilding the lives of victims and accountability.[48]

It is essential to recognise the important contribution made by NGOs and to involve them in policy development and implementation. They should be given the resources to perform this work on a structural basis rather than in individual projects.

4.2. Legislative measures

A variety of legislative measures is necessary to effectively combat violence against women. Criminal law measures as well as civil law measures must be taken. States parties should ensure that laws against family violence and abuse, rape, sexual assault and other gender-based violence give adequate protection to all women, and respect their integrity and dignity. Domestic violence, including marital rape, incest and honour killings should be a criminal offence. In respect of honour killings, it is also necessary to amend the criminal law to the effect that defence of the honour cannot be used as an attenuating circumstance resulting in a lesser penalty. Legislation must be effective and should

---

[48] UNICEF, 'Domestic violence against women and girls', *Innocenti Digest*, No. 6, May 2000.

provide for strong sanctions. The burden of proof in cases of sexual violence should not be higher than the burden of proof requested with regard to other offences against the person. States should exercise due diligence to prevent, investigate and punish violence against women. The Special Rapporteur on Violence Against Women has drawn up a list of questions she uses to judge the extent to which a state has complied with its obligation to use due diligence.[49] Where a woman commits a crime against the person who subjected her to long-term abuse, she should have the possibility to invoke an exclusionary ground. The law should provide for access to remedies, including complaints procedures, rehabilitation and compensation of victims. Complaints procedures should be easily accessible and provide effective protection to women. Counselling and treatment of offenders should be regulated by law.

4.3. Protective measures

Victims of violence should be given access to high quality support services, legal and other assistance. These facilities should be approachable and widely available. The police, prosecutors, the courts and the medical profession should receive gender-sensitive training to detect and be able to deal adequately with violence against women. They should be capable of recognising situations in which women are the victims of violence and of dealing appropriately with these situations. The government should allocate sufficient funding to gender-sensitivity training to achieve this end. Further, there should be adequate shelter facilities and support services; women should have access to legal, social, psychological and medical counselling. Hospitals should develop health care protocols and hospital procedures on how to deal with violence against women. If one of the partners leaves the house, it should be the offender, rather than the victim. Victims should be protected from secondary victimisation. Rehabilitation programmes should address both the victim and the offender.

Specific legislative measures with extraterritorial effect should be introduced to address female genital mutilation of women and girls. It goes without saying that public information and education campaigns are required alongside criminal law provisions.

---

[49] UN Doc. E/CN.4/1999/68, supra n. 9, para. 25.

4.4. Complaints procedures and remedies

Provision should be made for low-threshold complaints procedures. The use of complaints procedures should be encouraged; in this respect, NGOs can play an important role. Investigation and prosecution should be possible also when another person than the direct victim submits a complaint. Procedures should provide for compensation, the rehabilitation of victims and protection against secondary victimisation.

4.5. Preventive measures

Universal ratification of the major UN Conventions on Human Rights (including the Women's Convention) has not yet been achieved. Governments should be encouraged to ratify all major human rights treaties, to withdraw all reservations to these conventions, and to accept individual complaints procedures.

Of course, ratification alone is not sufficient. Women and girls should be made more aware of their rights and the legal remedies available to them. Governments can play a significant role in this process. The text of the relevant conventions and other instruments (*e.g.* the UN Declaration on the Elimination of Violence Against Women) should be translated into national languages and be made available to the public in an accessible form. Translations should also be made available of the outcomes of the work of the treaty bodies, such as the general recommendations and the concluding observations.

The major policy focus should be on economic independence for women, a fundamental reallocation of care tasks, and empowerment for women in the more general sense. Women's empowerment (which includes their right to decide how many children they have and the interval between them) can contribute to a structural solution. High priority should also be given to the elimination of male and female stereotyping through general public information campaigns and in schools (see also Articles 5 and 10 of the Women's Convention). In this area, the media has an important role to play. Such measures should also be aimed at men and boys.

5. IN CONCLUSION – TOWARDS A LEGALLY BINDING TREATY?

The process of changing traditional attitudes is fraught with difficult and sensitive issues. However, this does not alter the need for States, civil-society organizations and the international community to make much more concerted efforts to fulfil their obligations than they have done in the past.

At first sight it seems as though the process of setting standards has been largely completed. A number of serious forms of violence against women have been universally condemned. However, the international community has not explicitly condemned all forms of violence against women. Condemnation of several forms of violence which can be classified as harmful traditional practices has come only from independent experts such as Special Rapporteurs and treaty bodies rather than from the political institutions. Governments should continue to put in considerable efforts to persuade the General Assembly to condemn honour crimes in a resolution. After all, these forms of violence constitute a serious violation of women's right to life. It is to be hoped that a State takes the lead on other serious forms of violence which have not yet been condemned by the UN General Assembly. These include widow burning, early and forced marriages, wife inheritance and polygamy.

Much attention is paid to physical abuse. However, violence against women is not just a matter of physical and sexual violence. Psychological violence can have equally serious consequences. For instance, the threat of violence, the threat of abandonment, imprisonment, destruction of objects, isolation, verbal abuse and permanent humiliation. Especially in the case of domestic violence against women, it must be borne in mind that abuse of women often involves a complex mix of factors that are not limited to physical and sexual abuse.

Economic and social rights are factors that improve the social status of women. Violations of these economic and social human rights can be considered forms of violence in some cases. Examples include enforced malnutrition, inferior nutrition for girls/women or unequal access to health care and education. So far, international organs do not give these issues the attention they deserve.

At the regional level, a number of positive developments in the field of standard-setting have taken place. The Inter-American Convention on the Prevention, Punishment and Eradication of Violence Against Women is the only legally binding instrument devoted in its entirety to violence against women. Article 3 guarantees women the right to be free from violence in both the public and the private sphere. Complaints about violations of the Convention can be submitted to the Inter-American

Commission on Human Rights and – subject to the acceptance of the Court's jurisdiction – to the Inter-American Court of Human Rights. The African Union adopted an Additional Protocol to the African Charter on Human and Peoples' Rights on the rights of women in Africa.[50] The Protocol contains very strong language on, among other subjects, women's right to physical integrity and the elimination of harmful practices. The (future) African Court is charged with the interpretation of the Protocol.

In light of the recent controversies encountered in the General Assembly on agreed language on hot issues such as honour killings, the present time may not be opportune to attempt to draft a legally binding Convention at the global level. It should therefore be thoroughly investigated whether a legally binding instrument at European and international level would have an added value. Furthermore, it became clear that much could be achieved if States were willing to comply with their obligations under already existing international instruments, and accept the interpretations by the various independent expert organs. Many States are not willing to accept that eradication of all forms of violence against women requires changes of cultures and traditions, as was recently made clear by CEDAW in its first substantive decision under the Optional Protocol to the Women's Convention. It is at present the implementation of already-existing standards that represents the major obstacle to eliminating violence against women rather than the lack of adequate norms.

As demonstrated above, the human rights treaty bodies each played a significant part in addressing the problem of violence against women. It would be useful if the treaty bodies would adopt a joint general comment in which they codify their interpretations and views for future steps to be taken. Such a general comment would give insight into the sum of the obligations existing under the various human rights instruments and allow for a comprehensive approach which is necessary to effectively combat domestic violence.

---

[50] Adopted on 11 July 2003, not yet entered into force.

DOMESTIC VIOLENCE AGAINST WOMEN AND TORTURE

Theo van Boven and Sabina Puig

1. INTRODUCTION

In this paper, the basic question will be raised and discussed whether domestic violence against women should be considered and described as a form of torture under international human rights law. This question will be examined from the perspective of the most specific anti-torture instrument, the United Nations Convention against Torture and Other Cruel, Inhuman or Degrading Treatment (UNCAT) but also in the light of views and opinions by authoritative bodies and mechanisms interpreting and monitoring other international and regional human rights instruments. It will be argued that the public-private dichotomy which used to inhibit the labelling of domestic violence as a human rights abuse is losing its adverse effect, and that with the acceptance of the principle of due diligence, States have positive obligations to prevent, to punish and to provide remedies for abuses in the domestic sphere. These positive obligations are to be enforced under international human rights standards in order to protect the physical and mental integrity of the human person and as a means to combat domestic violence against women. This paper will finally argue that the qualification of domestic violence against women as a form of torture constitutes a powerful strategic device in public and legal campaigns to combat and to end the plague of domestic violence against women.

2. THE CONVENTION AGAINST TORTURE AND OTHER FORMS OF CRUEL, INHUMAN OR DEGRADING TREATMENT OR PUNISHMENT (UNCAT)

It was correctly pointed out by the Special Rapporteur on Violence Against Women, its Causes and Consequences, that domestic violence against women and torture as defined in Article 1 of UNCAT have a series of similarities: '(…) it is argued that, like torture, domestic violence commonly involves some form of physical and/or psychological suffering, including death in some cases. Secondly, domestic violence, like torture, is purposeful behaviour which is perpetrated intentionally (…). Thirdly, domestic violence is generally committed for specific purposes including punishment, intimidation and the diminution of the woman's personality. Lastly, like torture, domestic violence occurs with at least the tacit involvement of the State if the State does not exercise *due diligence* and equal protection in preventing domestic abuse. This argument contends that, as such, domestic violence may be understood to constitute a form of torture'.[1]

While the first two elements constitutive of the torture definition – *i.e.* intentional infliction of severe pain or suffering – may indeed apply without doubt to domestic violence against women, those relating to the purpose and the State involvement are more controversial, in particular the latter.

As far as the purposive element of the definition of torture is concerned, it may be argued that the purposes included in Article 1 of UNCAT – obtaining information or a confession, punishment, intimidation or coercion, or discrimination – reflect only State purposes. Thus, Sir Nigel Rodley stated, 'It is not by accident that the purposive element of torture reflects precisely State purposes or, at any rate, the purposes of an organized political entity exercising effective power'.[2]

However, other authors have divergent views and consider that the purposes reflected in UNCAT apply to domestic violence as well. Rhonda Copelon has conducted an analysis on the purposes intrinsic to domestic violence and has concluded that they correspond to the UNCAT definition of torture.[3] Firstly, 'whether precipitated by rage, jealousy, or a real or feared loss of control, domestic violence has its own interrogation, its own questions, accusations, insults and explicit or implicit orders'.[4] Further, 'intimate violence is a systematic form of punishment which bypasses all the procedural guarantees of due process and serves an absolutist system of power'.[5] Thirdly, 'domestic violence is also designed to intimidate both the individual woman who is the target, and all women as a class. On the individual level, the goal of domestic violence is to 'domesticate' her, to terrify her into obedience, to prevent or deter her assertion of difference or autonomy [...] Battering undermines women's self-esteem and sense of alternatives; it limits them

---

1   Commission on Human Rights, 52nd Session, UN Doc. E/CN.4/1996/53, para. 44.

2   N. RODLEY, 'The Definition(s) of Torture in International Law', in: *Current Legal Problems*, Vol. 55, 2002, 467.

3   R. COPELON, 'Domestic Violence as Torture', in: *Columbia Human Rights Law Review*, Vol. 25, 1994, 291.

4   *Ibid.*, 333.

5   *Ibid.*, 337.

to coping within a narrow frame'.[6] And finally, 'violence against women is undoubtedly a form of discrimination against women insofar as it targets women disproportionately and is based on and perpetuates the subordination of women'.[7]

With regard to the State involvement element, the traditional framework of international human rights law establishes a distinction between public and private acts, and in this sense, the UNCAT has been interpreted as being limited to the public context. For instance, during an Expert Seminar on the Definition of Torture organized in November 2001 by the Association for the Prevention of Torture (APT), one expert emphasized that according to the *travaux préparatoires* of the UNCAT, the Convention was not supposed to extend to private spheres.[8] In the Handbook on the Convention against Torture and Other Cruel, Inhuman or Degrading Treatment, setting out the origin and the drafting history of UNCAT it is written that 'only torture for which the authorities could be held responsible should fall within the article's definition. If torture is committed without any involvement of the authorities, but as a criminal act by private persons, it can be expected that the normal machinery of justice will operate and that prosecution and punishment will follow under the normal conditions of the domestic legal system'.[9]

Commenting on the status of the perpetrator as defined in Article 1 of the Convention, Nigel Rodley wrote, 'The fundamental idea is that, as is conceptually appropriate in the context of giving legal form to human rights principles, the State violates the right through its agents, human rights being the normative articulation of the fundamental rules mediating the relationship of the organs of organized society – typically the State – and the individual members of the society. This fits neatly with the basic approach of international law, which identifies legal obligations as a matter of State responsibility and violations of those obligations as breaches of state responsibility'.[10] Accordingly, this approach, combined with the view that UNCAT does not reflect personal purposes would have the effect of excluding private acts for purely personal ends from the scope of torture as defined in UNCAT.

---

[6]   *Ibid.*, 338.

[7]   *Ibid.*, 339.

[8]   ASSOCIATION FOR THE PREVENTION OF TORTURE (APT), *The Definition of Torture*, Proceedings of an Expert Seminar, 2001.

[9]   J.H. BURGERS, H. DANELIUS, *The United Nations Convention against Torture; A Handbook on the Convention against Torture and Other Cruel, Inhuman or Degrading Treatment or Punishment* (Dordrecht/Boston/London,1988) 119-120.

[10] RODLEY, supra n. 2.

3. PUBLIC-PRIVATE DICHOTOMY AND STATE RESPONSIBILITY

However, the public-private dichotomy in international law is progressively fading. It is now more commonly accepted that in certain circumstances, States may be held responsible for acts perpetrated by private individuals, which would thus constitute human rights violations.

The assumption that Article 1 of UNCAT applies to violence committed by private individuals in the conjugal and familial sphere is open to debate.[11] Nevertheless, the wording of this Article 'at the instigation of or with the consent or acquiescence of a public official or other person acting in an official capacity', read in conjunction with international and regional jurisprudence, gives some room for holding States responsible for human rights violations committed by non-state actors. Indeed, there is an increasing tendency to extend State responsibility into the private sphere, including responsibility for domestic violence against women.

In its General Comment no. 20, the Human Rights Committee (HRC) clarified that 'it is the duty of the State party to afford everyone protection through legislative and other measures as may be necessary against the acts prohibited by Article 7, whether inflicted by people acting in their official capacity, outside their official capacity or in a private capacity'.[12]

More recently, the Committee reaffirmed such a view in its General Comment no. 31:

The positive obligations on States Parties to ensure Covenant rights will only be fully discharged if individuals are protected by the State, not just against violations of Covenant rights by its agents, but also against acts committed by private persons or entities that would impair the enjoyment of Covenant rights in so far as they are amenable to application between private persons or entities. There may be circumstances in which a failure to ensure Covenant rights as required by Article 2 would give rise to violations by States Parties of those rights, as a result of States Parties permitting or failing to take appropriate measures or to exercise due diligence to prevent, punish,

---

[11] C. VILLÁN DURÁN, 'La práctica de la tortura y los malos tratos en el mundo. Tendencias actuales', in: ARARTEKO, *La prevención y erradicación de la tortura y malos tratos en los sistemas democráticos.* VITORIA, ARARTEKO, colección *Jornada sobre derechos humanos*, n° 7, 2004, 185, 33-115.

[12] General Comment no. 20, replaces General Comment 7 concerning prohibition of torture and cruel treatment or punishment (Art. 7), 10/03/92, UN Doc. CCPR/C/21/Rev.1/Add.9, para. 2.

investigate or redress the harm caused by such acts by private persons or entities. States are reminded of the interrelationship between the positive obligations imposed under Article 2 and the need to provide effective remedies in the event of breach under Article 2, paragraph 3 (...) it is also implicit in Article 7 that States Parties have to take positive measures to ensure that private persons or entities do not inflict torture or cruel, inhuman or degrading treatment or punishment on others within their power.[13]

One of the questions triggered by the wording 'within their power' used by the Committee is, to what extent are female individuals, by the mere fact of being women, in the power of their male partners and relatives? While this appears to be true in virtually all families, one should not jump too fast to generalized conclusions, without looking into all actual circumstances of persons involved.

The first Special Rapporteur on Torture, Peter Kooijmans, took a position similar to the HRC on this issue:

(...) private acts of brutality (...) should not imply State responsibility, since these would usually be ordinary criminal offences under national law. Nevertheless, the authorities' passive attitude regarding customs broadly accepted in a number of countries (i.e. sexual mutilation and other tribal traditional practices) might be considered as "consent or acquiescence" particularly when these practices are not prosecuted as criminal offences under domestic law, probably because the State itself is abandoning its function of protecting its citizens from any kind of torture.[14]

Although the Special Rapporteur referred to very specific acts of brutality, such a statement could be interpreted as opening the door to a more far-reaching interpretation of State responsibility in cases of domestic violence.

The European Court on Human Rights also considered that:

The obligation on the High Contracting Parties under Article 1 of the Convention to secure to everyone within their jurisdiction the rights and freedoms defined in the Convention, taken together with Article 3, requires States to take measures designed to ensure that individuals within their jurisdiction are not subjected to torture or inhuman or degrading treatment or punishment, including such ill-treatment administered by private individuals.[15]

Another recent development indicating that international law is expanding its scope to private spheres is reflected in the Advisory

---

13   General Comment no. 31, the nature of the general legal obligation imposed on States Parties to the Covenant, 2004, UN Doc. CCPR/C/21/Rev.1/Add.13, para. 8.

14   UN Doc. E/CN.4/1986/15, para. 38.

15   *A. v. The United Kingdom* (Appl. no. 25599/94), ECtHR 23 September 1998.

Opinion on International Norms: Gender-Related Persecution and Relevance to 'Membership of a Particular Social Group' and 'Political Opinion', submitted on 9 January 2004 by the United Nations High Commissioner for Refugees (UNHCR) to the United States of America Attorney General. In this Advisory Opinion, the UNHCR held that Ms. Rodi Alvarado Peña, a Guatemalan woman who fled her country to escape from continued severe domestic violence and who had sought protection to Guatemalan authorities to no avail, should be recognized as a refugee.[16]

Once it has been admitted that States do have responsibilities with respect to private violence, it is essential to define their obligations in this connection.

4. DUTIES TO RESPECT, PROTECT, AND FULFIL

The Committee on Economic, Social and Cultural Rights elaborated on the typology of obligations States have with respect to human rights; the duties to respect, protect, and fulfil.[17] This terminology has been used in many other international standards and jurisprudential cases.[18]

With respect to State responsibility for violence against women, it is clear that state agents have the obligation to *respect* the physical and mental integrity of all individuals within the State jurisdiction.

Furthermore, States have the obligation to *protect* women from violence against non-state actors, including the most intimate spheres. Protection also means preventing harm against individual women known to be at specific risk. In this sense and to use the same wording as the European Court on Human Rights, there is a failure to protect the victim from harm committed by a non-state actor when the authorities do not do all that could be reasonably expected of them to avoid a real and immediate risk of which they have or ought to have knowledge.[19] In another case, the European Court held that '(a) failure to take reasonably available measures which could have had a real harm is sufficient to engage the

---

[16] Advisory Opinion available at: <http://w3.uchastings.edu/cgrs/documents/legal/unhcr_ra-amicus.pdf>.

[17] See in particular General Comment no. 14, on the right to the highest attainable standard of health, 2000, UN Doc. E/C.12/2000/4.

[18] The typology of obligations was originally created by Henry Shue in 1980.

[19] See *Osman v. The United Kingdom* (Appl. no. 0023452/94), ECtHR 28 October 1998 (note that in this case, the right examined by the Court is the right to life).

responsibility of the state'.[20] Furthermore, protection entails preventing harm against all potential victims through the establishment of law-enforcement machinery for the prevention, suppression and punishment of this type of violence.

Thirdly, States have the obligation to *fulfil* human rights by taking necessary global measures to ensure that protective measures are effective. In its report 'Making rights a reality: the duty of states to address violence against women', Amnesty International lists a number of measures that States should take to fulfil and promote women's rights so that they are respected by all. Among these measures, AI includes changes in criminal and civil laws, forbidding illegal defences, ensuring access to justice for women, appropriate punishments, civil remedies, training of professionals dealing with violence against women and of judicial and law-enforcement personnel. AI also makes some suggestions to make women's rights to freedom from violence a reality; proposals of national plans, studies and statistics, development of guidelines, local, regional and urban planning, public awareness, legal literacy, public education, education, cooperation with women's organizations and reports to international bodies.

5. DUE DILIGENCE

In case law and literature the concept of due diligence is progressively accepted as a viable construction to hold States responsible for violations of human rights by private persons if States have failed to adequately protect the victims against such acts. The first case explicitly holding a State accountable on the basis of lack of due diligence may be found at the regional level. In the *Velásquez Rodríguez* case the Inter-American Court of Human Rights held that:

> [a]n illegal act which violates human rights and which is initially not directly imputable to a State (for example, because it is an act of a private person or because the person responsible has not been identified) can lead to international responsibility of the State, not because of the act itself, but because of the lack of due diligence to prevent the violation or to respond to it as required by the Convention (...) What is decisive is whether a violation of the rights recognized by the Convention has occurred with the support or the acquiescence of the Government, or whether the State has allowed the act to take place without taking measures to prevent it or to punish those responsible (...). The State has a legal duty to take reasonable steps to prevent human rights violations and to use the means at its disposal to carry out a serious investigation of violations

---

[20] *E. and others v. The United Kingdom* (Appl. no. 33218/96), ECtHR 26 November 2002, § 99.

committed within its jurisdiction, to identify those responsible, impose the appropriate punishment and ensure the victim adequate compensation.[21]

In its General Recommendation no. 19, CEDAW stated that '[u]nder general international law and specific human rights covenants, States may also be responsible for private acts if they fail to act with due diligence to prevent violations of rights or to investigate and punish acts of violence, and for providing compensation'.[22] CEDAW listed a series of recommendations that States should follow to overcome all forms of violence against women 'whether by public or private act'. Further, States have also the duty to afford reparation to victims of human rights violations. In the context of domestic violations, victims should have access to just and effective remedies, rehabilitation measures, and appropriate compensation (including for monetary, physical, psychological, moral and social damage); available, accessible, acceptable and appropriate services to assist their recovery and witnesses and access to reproductive health services. Protection and support services for survivors should also be guaranteed.[23]

Specifically in relation with violence against women, the UN Declaration on Violence against Women states that States should 'exercise *due diligence* to prevent, investigate and, in accordance with national legislation, punish acts of violence against women, whether those acts are perpetrated by the State or by private persons'.[24]

The Special Rapporteur on Violence Against Women stated that:

[w]here the State does not exercise due diligence and equal protection to prevent and punish domestic abuse, it, like official torture or independent paramilitary violence, occurs with at least the tacit involvement of the State. Where the State permits this violence or is passive or half-hearted, it abandons the battered woman to the dominion of the batterer and tacitly supports that dominion. On these bases, it is contended that severe domestic violence can be understood as a form of torture while less severe forms may be sanctioned as ill-treatment under the ICCPR.[25]

In order to illustrate the complexity in assessing the State's responsibility and its failure to comply with its obligation, it is worthwhile to further

---

[21] *Velásquez Rodríguez* case, IACtHR 29 July 1988, Series C No. 4, in *Human Rights Law Journal*, Vol. 9, 1988, 212, para. 172-174.

[22] CEDAW, General Recommendation no. 19, on Violence Against Women, UN Doc. A/47/38, 1992, para. 9.

[23] *Ibid.*, 24.

[24] UN Doc. A/RES/48/104, 23 February 1994, Article 4(c).

[25] UN Doc. E/CN.4/1996/53, 5 February 1996, para. 48.

quote the Special Rapporteur on Violence Against Women, who explained:

Unlike for direct State action, the standard for establishing State complicity in violations committed by private actors is more relative. Complicity must be demonstrated by establishing that the State condones a pattern of abuse through pervasive non-action. Where States do not actively engage in acts of domestic violence or routinely disregard evidence of murder, rape or assault of women by their intimate partners, States generally fail to take the minimum steps necessary to protect their female citizens' rights to physical integrity and, in extreme cases, to life. This sends a message that such attacks are justified and will not be punished. To avoid such complicity, States must demonstrate due diligence by taking active measures to protect, prosecute and punish private actors who commit abuses'.[26]

6. IN CONCLUSION

There is no doubt that in present *opinio iuris*, domestic violence against women entails State responsibility whenever State authorities fail to exercise due diligence in their duties to take effective measures of prevention and to offer protection, remedies and reparation to victims and potential victims of domestic violence. Human rights courts, treaty bodies and special rapporteurs have advanced strong arguments to substantiate the responsibility of States in this respect. The civil responsibility of the States in the matter of domestic violence against women is matched by the criminal responsibility of the perpetrators.

While, therefore, there may be no doubt that domestic violence against women carries with it all the legal and moral consequences of human rights law in terms of duties to respect, protect and fulfill, the answer to the initial question raised in this paper, viz. whether domestic violence falls within the scope of torture, appears less straightforward. Would it matter to identify domestic violence against women as a form of torture? The answer to this question is clearly affirmative. As the European Court of Human Rights expressly stated, the qualification of torture carries a special stigma.[27] The identification of domestic violence as a form of torture is a powerful device in all strategies and policies to combat acts and practices of domestic violence. As Amnesty International's manual for action in combating torture has pointed out:

(...) Those campaigning to end domestic violence against women have pointed to the strategic benefits of applying international standards on torture in their work. (...) It underscores the gravity of violence in the family and helps to invalidate any attempts to

---

[26] Supra n. 1, 33.
[27] *Selmouni v. France* (Appl. no. 25803/94), ECtHR Judgment 28 July 1999, para. 26.

justify such abuses in the name of culture, religion or tradition, since under international standards torture can never be justified in any circumstances.[28]

Legally and politically, this position is supported by views of authoritative judicial and quasi-judicial bodies that interpret and apply the right to everyone, not to be subjected to torture or to cruel, inhuman or degrading treatment or punishment as enshrined in major world-wide and regional human rights instruments. Paradoxically, the answer is less clear-cut from the perspective of the more specific anti-torture instrument, the Convention against Torture and Other Forms of Cruel, Inhuman and Degrading Treatment or Punishment (UNCAT). While this Convention contains many provisions that must be considered pertinent for strategies and policies to combat domestic violence, it has other features such as the explicit separation and distinction of the notion of torture from other cruel, inhuman or degrading treatment or punishment, the non-refoulement principle and the notion of universal jurisdiction, which make the Convention a less amenable instrument in the struggle against domestic violence. It is important to note that the Committee against Torture appears to take significant steps in recent times towards bringing domestic violence under the scope of UNCAT. Thus, it recommended in concluding observations relating to a State party to 'establish programs to prevent and combat violence against women, including domestic violence'.[29] And most recently, the Committee in concluding observations relating to another State party identified under subjects of concern 'the reported prevalence of violence against women and girls, including domestic violence, and the reluctance on the part of the authorities to, *inter alia*, adopt legislative measures to counter this phenomenon', and it recommended the State party to 'adopt legislation and other measures to combat violence against women, within the framework of plans to take measures to prevent such violence, including domestic violence, and to investigate all allegations of ill-treatment and abuse.[30] Indeed there would be an inconsistency if general human rights law on torture would allow in matters of domestic violence a more advanced and liberal interpretation than the specific anti-torture Convention. The authors of this paper do not satisfy themselves by pointing out a conceivably anomalous interpretation of different legal texts. They support the view that human rights instruments are by their nature – as the European Court of Human

---

28 AMNESTY INTERNATIONAL, *Combating Torture: A Manual for Action* (London, 2003) 164.
29 Conclusions and recommendations on the initial report of Zambia, UN Doc. A/57/44, para. 66 (h).
30 Conclusions and recommendations on the fourth periodic report of Greece, UN Doc. CAT/C/CR/33/2, paras. 5 (k) and 6 (l).

Rights repeatedly stated – living instruments which must be interpreted in the light of present-day conditions. All these instruments are interrelated and mutually supportive. This applies in particular to the eradication of such a persistent, widespread and de-humanizing practice as violence in the domestic and family sphere.

IN THE SHADOW OF NO LAW. NAVIGATING CULTURAL LEGITIMACY AND LEGAL PROTECTION OF WOMEN AGAINST VIOLENCE IN AFGHANISTAN

Renée Römkens[1]

1. INTRODUCTION

Violence against women has become 'mainstreamed' and is no longer of mainly feminist or activist concern. It has become an established respectable subject on the international human rights agenda at the beginning of the 21st century as is reflected in growing attention for this issue from international human rights organizations like Human Rights Watch (HRW) and Amnesty International. The United Nations (UN) has become more vigilant as we can see in their long list of reports since the early 1990's appointment of its Special Rapporteur on Violence Against Women.[2] The International War Crime Tribunal of former Yugoslavia (ICTY) qualified rape as a war crime and the new International Criminal Court (ICC) is appointing victim-experts with special expertise in gender

---

1   Thanks to Katherine Franke, for the inspiring collaboration during a first research field trip to Kabul, Afghanistan in July 2004. Thanks also to Carolyn McCool, interim-head of UNIFEM Afghanistan and to Rachel Wareham, staff member of Medica Mondiale (Kabul) for generously sharing information on current developments in legal regulation and policy development in Afghanistan regarding violence against women. The title of my paper has been inspired by two earlier texts that relate in very different but pertinent ways to the subject of my article: ROBERT MNOOKIN and LEWIS KORNHAUSER , 'Bargaining in the Shadow of the Law. The Case of Divorce', In: *Yale Law Journal,* 88, (1978-1979), 950-997, and ART SPIEGELMAN (2004), *In the shadow of no towers.* New York: Pantheon Books.

2   The list of UN Resolutions and treaties explicitly addressing violence against women testifies to a growing political commitment of the international community at least on a political level. See particularly the Convention on the Elimination of All Forms of Discrimination Against Women (Women's Convention) and Committee on the Elimination of All Forms of Discrimination (CEDAW), General Recommendation no. 19, on Violence Against Women, 1992, UN Doc. A/47/38, 1992. See I. BOEREFIJN, M. VAN DER LIET-SENDERS, T. LOENEN, *Het voorkomen en bestrijden van geweld tegen vrouwen. Een verdiepend onderzoek naar het Nederlandse beleid in het licht van de verplichtingen die voortvloeien uit het Vrouwenverdrag* (Den Haag: Ministerie van Sociale Zaken en Werkgelegenheid, 2000). See also UN Security Council Resolution 1325 on women, peace and security, UN Doc. S/Res.1325 (2000). This resolution promotes a wide range of measures to promote and protect women's and girls' human rights. For an overview of UN-related initiatives and resolutions on women in Afghanistan, see: <http://www.un.org/womenwatch/afghanistan/links.html>.

violence. Violence against women as a gender-based violation of fundamental (human) rights is here to stay on the stage of international human rights-based legal practice and discourse. From a feminist legal perspective, that is a major achievement that deserves continuing careful reflection. Once a social problem becomes translated into a legal concern it can evoke unintended consequences given how powerful a legal context is in shaping the ensuing discourse and social practices. In this article I will focus on how the topic of violence against women figures in current legal development in Afghanistan. In focussing on Afghanistan I hope to raise wider socio-legal questions that are at stake when using an international human rights framework to address violence against women in a context of transitional justice and in a legal and social culture that is profoundly shaped by Islamic religious and cultural traditions.

Due to the mainstreaming of the issue of violence against women it has become a selling point for international political agendas of very different kinds. The Bush administration, for example, used in 2001 the urgent need to 'liberate' women in Afghanistan from their violent oppressors (*i.e.* the Taliban) as a major reason for the American-lead military invasion of Afghanistan. In the ensuing political rhetoric, the cruelties of the Taliban against women were addressed in great detail.[3] The fact that the United States had a long history of supporting the warring mujahaddin-militias who were known to rape Afghan women, had never been a reason to stop US support and was conveniently silenced.[4] Violence against women has become a useful topic in times of

---

[3]   Most notably mandatory veiling with the *burqa* was a flashpoint in that narrative. It is often upheld as the ultimate symbol of oppression and violence against Afghan women. Despite growing critique from the scholars of Islam and gender on the post-colonial attitude underlying this selective attention for the veil, many scholars on Islam and gender have addressed this long standing Western fixation on the veil, leading to the discursive construction of the veil as the icon of Islamic backwardness (at least) and oppression (at its worst) or, alternatively, as a symbol of resistance or cultural authenticity of Islamic women. See LILA ABU-LUGHOD, 'Introduction', in: *Remaking women: feminism and modernity in the Middle East* (Princeton, N.J.: Princeton University Press, 1998) 14.

[4]   In a radio speech of First Lady Laura Bush 'to the American people', 17 November 2001. On the issue of American support for mujahaddin who were committing atrocities against women, see CHARLES HIRSCHKIND AND MAHMOOD SABA, 'Feminism, the Taliban, and Politics of Counter-Insurgency', in: *Anthropological Quarterly*, 75(2), 2002, 339-354. See also, Afghanistan Justice Project, *Candidates and the past. The legacy of war crimes and the political transition in Afghanistan* (2004), available at: <http://www.Afghanistanproject.org> (retrieved January 15, 2005).

a growing tendency (and political need) to vilify Islamic fundamentalism
and make it virtually synonymous with violence and terrorism.[5]
At the same time we see many international non-governmental women's
organizations, women's grass roots organizations as well as UN
organizations such as UNIFEM rallying already for many years against
the oppression of Afghan women, expressing what seems to be a less
opportunistic political concern about violent abuse of Afghan women
like forced marriages, exchange of girls to resolve tribal conflicts,
domestic violence, illegal incarcerations of women who flee their home,
etcetera.

Despite varying political motives for concern about violence against
women, there is consensus in one crucial respect: that international
human rights law as well as the Convention on Elimination of All Forms
of Discrimination Against Women (Women's Convention) and related
resolutions[6] are the paradigmatic international legal (and political)
frameworks to address this problem. There is an overall endorsement of
the moral and legal rightness of the call to respect 'the rule of law'. In
this article I would like to critically reflect on the implications of the use
of a human rights and/or discrimination framework and its
compatibility with the current legal developments in Afghanistan. From
a political and legal point of view there are inevitably tensions between
Western based individualized international human rights law that
endorses gender equality norms on the one hand and local Afghan laws,
particularly customary law and Islamic law (*Shari'a*) that are more
community oriented and do not allow for gender equality *pur sang*. How
can Afghan women's needs be addressed in the context of complex
cultural tradition, without imposing a neo-colonial salvation project that
would inevitably resurrect the image of the Afghan woman as the
essential victim?[7]

---

5   The subordination of women in Muslim countries still holds political currency in 2005
     when it comes to selling the US military interventions (meaning in this case Iraq and
     Afghanistan) to 'bring freedom and liberty' as a 'solemn duty'. As George W. Bush
     pleaded in his inaugural speech for his second term as President of the United States:
     'America will not pretend (...) that women welcome humiliation and servitude, or that
     any human being aspires to live at the mercy of bullies' Inaugural Speech George W.
     Bush, 20 January 2005, available at: <http://www.whitehouse.gov/news/
     releases/2005/01/print/20050120-1.html>.

6   Women's Convention and General Recommendation no. 19, supra n. 2.

7   See CHANDRA TALPADE MOHANTY, 'Under Western Eyes Revisited: Feminist Solidarity
     through Anticapitalist Struggles', in: *Signs: Journal of Women in Culture and Society*, Vol.
     28, no. 2, 2002, 499 -535. See also LETI VOLPP, 'Feminism versus multiculturalism', in:
     Columbia Law Review, 101, 5, 2001, 1181-1218.

As necessary as human rights law is to help put the issue of violence against women on the international agenda, an old question keeps coming back. How can it be of support to achieve effective legal (or social, political) changes for women in developing countries, living in cultural and legal contexts that might not easily be compatible with international human rights standards? This inevitably raises the question of the *cultural* legitimacy of international human rights law in a context of transitional justice in Afghanistan. Many experts doubt whether international human rights law can play a meaningful role in the absence of an effectively operating judiciary. However, this begs the question whether and how the rhetoric of human rights, as the archetypical language of democratic transition, can affect concrete social or legal practices? We might argue that the ratification of the Women's Convention and the constitutional adherence to international human rights law might not present an enforceable body of law yet in Afghanistan but it nonetheless throws a shadow of law which might create a basis and context for women to become effective rights holders.[8] This article is a first and predominantly descriptive exploration of these issues. To clarify the complexities we face when trying to understand the role of law in bringing about legal and social changes for Afghan women who are facing violence, we need to contextualize these larger socio-legal issues in their concrete social and cultural context. I will therefore present a brief sketch of the situation with regard to women's rights and violence against women in Afghanistan (section 2), followed by an overview of current developments in the formal justice systems in Afghanistan (section 3) and its international influences (section 4). After a review of main developments in the informal justice system (section 4), recent attempts to strengthen women's civic participation are discussed (section 6). Concluding, I will tentatively address some of the dilemmas that are at stake if we want to improve protection for women and women's rights in the Islamic Republic of Afghanistan while using an international human rights framework.

2. HUMAN RIGHTS VIOLATIONS AND VIOLENCE AGAINST WOMEN IN AFGHANISTAN: A BRIEF EXPLORATION

Afghan culture is essentially tribal and patriarchal in nature and for many decades, conflict-ridden.[9] The wars that ravaged the country

---

[8] ROBERT MNOOKIN AND LEWIS KORNHAUSER, 'Bargaining in the Shadow of the Law. The Case of Divorce', in: *Yale Law Journal*, Vol. 88, 1978-1979, 950-997.

[9] See EDWARD GIRARDET AND JONATHAN WALKER (eds.), *Afghanistan: Essential field guide to humanitarian and conflict zones* (Geneva: Crosslines, 1998).

during the past two decades since the invasion of the Soviets in 1979
aggravated this cultural legacy of distrust and conflict. Till this very day,
despite the installation of a central government in Kabul and despite the
start of a democratization process guided by a process of disarmament of
local militias, this legacy of patriarchal fiefdoms is alive. Particularly in
rural Afghanistan, many incidents of violent intimidation and
lawlessness are still reported, directly related to rivalry and ongoing
power conflicts between local warlords and their militias. Without
exception, recent reports on human rights in Afghanistan deplore the
'rule of gun' that continues to haunt the reconstruction process and that
makes 'women suffer disproportionately' since it simply makes it
difficult if not impossible for women and girls to move around safely in
public.[10] Peace and security, specifically through the disarmament of
warlords, was mentioned by the majority of Afghan women and men
who were recently interviewed as one of the human rights in urgent
need of respect (followed by food, education and employment).[11]

Despite the earlier promises by the international community to the
women of Afghanistan, limited progress has been achieved to improve
their hardship and discrimination over the past years since the fall of the
Taliban.[12] Obviously the Taliban were not the only reason for women's

---

[10] HUMAN RIGHTS WATCH (HRW), *The Rule of the Gun, Human Rights Abuses and Political
Repression in the Run-Up to Afghanistan's Presidential Election* (September 2004), available
at <http://www.hrw.org/backgrounder/asia/afghanistan0904/>. HRW, *Between hope
and fear. Intimidation and attacks against women in public life in Afghanistan* (October 2004),
available at: <http://hrw.org/backgrounder/asia/afghanistan1004/>. HRW,
Humanity denied. Systematic violations of women's rights in Afghanistan (October 2001),
available at: <http://www.hrw.org/reports/2001/afghan3/afgwrd1001.pdf>.
HRW, *Climate of fear: sexual violence and abduction of women and girls in Baghdad* (July
2003), available at: <http://hrw.org/reports/2003/iraq0703/>.
AMNESTY INTERNATIONAL, *No one listens to us and no one treats us as human beings* (2003),
available at: <http://web.amnesty.org/library/index/engasa110232003>.
AMNESTY INTERNATIONAL, *Lives blown apart. Crimes against women in times of conflict*
(2004), available at: <http://web.amnesty.org/library/Index/ENGACT770752004?
open&of=ENG-373>.

[11] CENTER FOR ECONOMIC AND SOCIAL RIGHTS, *Human rights and reconstruction in
Afghanistan* (2002), available at: <http://cesr.org/low/node/view/499>. See also
HRW, 2002, 2003, 2004, *ibid.*

[12] The fact that women in particular suffer under these dire conditions is reflected in The
Gender Disparity Index, a composite index based on measurement of female life
expectancy, educational attainment and income. In the mid 1990s under the Taliban
Afghanistan ranked in the lowest position of any country in the world. See UNDP,
'Human Development Report 1995', quoted in: UNITED NATIONS ECONOMIC AND
SOCIAL COUNCIL, *Integration of the human rights of women and the gender perspective
violence against women. Report of the Special Rapporteur on violence against women.
Addendum. Mission to Pakistan and Afghanistan* (2000), UN Doc.
E/CN.4/2000/68/Add.4.

hardship nor the first.[13] Afghanistan's history shows that women and their rights under Islam have been the flashpoint of conflict, and successive attempts of reform and repression for more than a century.[14]

In the dominant picture in Western media and politics, the Taliban have been portrayed as the ultimate oppressors of Afghan women, suggesting that their removal was the major obstacle to women's 'freedom and liberty'.[15] That erased a more complex picture of obstinate patriarchal traditions that Afghan women, like many Muslim women, face in times of social change, most notably when their countries move away from former (colonial) regimes into projects of so-called 'liberation or 'modernisation'.[16]

However, some progress has been made in basic human rights and women's development areas such as education.[17] In Afghanistan, more girls can go to school than under the Taliban and women are slowly returning to their jobs. Still, only a third of primary school students are girls and only 9% go on to secondary school.[18] From the age of ten onward, girls are often withdrawn from school and kept in *purdah* (segregated from the other sex), confined to their houses as a means of ensuring their 'purity'.[19] All this is happening in the face of ongoing

---

[13] HRW, September 2004, supra n. 10, 5-6.

[14] There was an emerging participation of women in education, professional and political life during the 1950s to the 1990s. That was, however, limited to urban middle-class and elite women and not even without contestation. The forced politics of women's emancipation under the Soviet-occupational regime has been designated as 'a major cause for the ensuing popular resistance' against the Soviets. INGER W. BOESEN, *From subjects to citizens. Local participation in the National Solidarity Programme* (Afghan Research and Evaluation Unit (AREU), August 2004) 8-10, available at: <http://www.areu.org.af/publications>.

[15] HIRSCHKIND AND MAHMOOD, supra n. 4.

[16] QUDSIA MIRZA, 'Islamic feminism, possibilities and limitations', in: J. STRAWSON (ed.) *Law after ground zero* (Sydney: Glasshouse Press, 2002) 108-122. See also ABU-LUGHOD, supra n. 3; YVONNE HADDAD YAZBECK, JOHN ESPOSITO (eds), *Islam, Gender and Social Change* (New York/Oxford: Oxford University Press, 1998) 30-44.

[17] Behind 'eradication of extreme poverty' and 'achieving universal primary education', 'the promotion of gender equality and empowerment of women' is listed as number three in the top ten of the United Nations Millennium Development Goals. Empowerment of women is specified as 'Eliminating gender disparities in primary and secondary education by 2005'. *United Nations Millennium Declaration*, 18 September 2000, UN Doc. A/RES/55/2.

[18] Human Rights Research and Advocacy Consortium, *Report Card: Progress on Compulsory Education, Grades 1-9* (Afghanistan: Oxfam, 2004).

[19] UN COMMISSION ON HUMAN RIGHTS, *Other human rights issues. Women and human rights. Report of the Secretary-General on the situation of women and girls in the territories occupied by Afghan armed group* (2002), UN Doc. E/CN.4/Sub.2/2002/27, 6.

threats and violent attacks on women and girls.[20] The harsh reality is that the majority of girls, particularly in rural areas, still cannot attend school.[21]

Employment of women, already an area in Afghan society where women were under-represented, is increasing only slowly. Women are reluctant to travel out of fear for harassment and sexual violence. Female journalists, who speak out against violence against women or trafficking, report death threats, intimidation, obstruction or dismissal from their jobs.[22] Even female ministers, women in political leadership positions or male politicians, who speak out in support of women's rights are intimidated and threatened, and sometimes even forced to appear in Islamic Supreme Court to face accusations of blasphemy.[23] The absence of security in Afghanistan due to ongoing influence of local warlords is unanimously considered as key to understanding the overall endemic human rights abuse and as the most significant threat to national reconstruction and the protection of human rights.[24]

Domestic violence and sexual violence like rape and gang-rape are common problems throughout Afghanistan. The war and post-conflict situation in Afghanistan exponentially intensifies the inequities that women are living with. It has been noted that domestic violence in particular increases during and after conflict due to the availability of weapons, violence that male members of the family have experienced, lack of jobs, shelter and basic services. In those stressful conditions women become easy targets for men's frustrations and disappointments.[25] In the absence of enough shelters,[26] some women flee to police stations and are taken into 'protective custody'.[27]

---

20 UN GENERAL ASSEMBLY, *Report of the independent expert of the Commission on Human Rights on the situation of human rights in Afghanistan* (2004), UN Doc. A/59/370, 11.

21 TARAKHIL, SHAHABBUDIN, HAFIZULLAH GARDISH, 'Girls' schools become targets', in: *Afghan Recovery Report,* 24 June 2004 (London: Institute for War & Peace Reporting, 2004), available at: <http://www.iwpr.net;>. See also BOESEN, supra n. 14, 13.

22 HRW, October 2004, supra n. 10, 2.

23 HRW, *ibid.*; UN COMMISSION ON HUMAN RIGHTS, supra n. 19, 3-4.

24 CHRIS JOHNSON, WILLIAM MALEY, ALEXANDER THIER AND ALI WARDAK, *Afghanistan's political and constitutional development* (London: UK Department for International Development (DFID) - Overseas Development Institute, 2003); RUBIN R. BARNETT, 'Crafting a constitution for Afghanistan', in: *Journal of Democracy*, 15 (3), 2004, 5-20; UN General Assembly, supra n. 20, 11; UN ECONOMIC AND SOCIAL COUNCIL, *Report of the Secretary General to the Commission of the Status of Women on the status of women in Afghanistan,* 2004, UN Doc. E/CN.6/2004.5.

25 ELISABETH REHN AND ELLEN JOHSON SIRLEAF, *Women, War and Peace .The Independent Experts' Assessment on the Impact of Armed Conflict on Women and Women's Role in Peace-building* (New York: UNIFEM, 2002), available at: <http://www.parliament.gov.za/

The problem with rape is that few women dare to come forward out of fear of being accused of committing adultery (*zina*),[28] which is considered a very serious moral crime under Islamic law. Several incarcerated women in Kabul prison were accused of adultery after fleeing from an abusive husband.[29]

Women are facing illegal incarceration for behaviour such as running away from an abusive husband, or escaping a forced marriage.[30] In 2003, more than half of the women in Kabul prison were incarcerated for so called moral crimes and left without access to appropriate legal recourse to ensure fair trials.[31] All this makes it easier for family and community members to have women, in particular, arrested on the suspicion of having committed a 'moral crime'. Lawyers are discouraged to take up cases of 'bad' women and they face obstacles to get access to their client's files.[32] Due to lack of prison facilities for women, private confinement of women in the custody of tribal elders has recently been found to happen. The conditions of internment are described as 'slave-like'.[33] Women in prison are at least temporarily protected from relatives and potential lethal violence from the husband's family. In the face of the enormous social costs, the act of leaving their home is an equally desperate and courageous search for safety, but also a cry for justice and change. However, women pay dearly for it. They break the traditional custom in Afghanistan that does not allow a divorce initiated by a woman.[34]

---

pls/portal30/docs/FOLDER/PARLIAMENTARY_INFORMATION/PUBLICATIONS/UNIFEM/INDEX.HTM>.

[26] AMNESTY INTERNATIONAL, 2004, supra n. 10.

[27] Medica Mondiale/Afghanistan and Legal Aid Fund, *Report on Three Month Pilot Study 2003*, 10 (report on file with author).

[28] In some parts of Afghanistan *zina* refers to adultery, 'running away from home' and unlawful sexual activity, Amnesty International, 2003, supra n. 10, 4.

[29] Medica Mondiale/LAF, supra n. 27.

[30] UN GENERAL ASSEMBLY, supra n. 20, 6.

[31] Incarceration is often the outcome of the application of customary law and traditions, which in most of the cases is even incongruent with *Shari'a* (Islamic Law) and/or statutory laws. The situation is worsened by the fact that the criminal justice system is in disarray, many are susceptible to bribery due to being underpaid, and basic professional and technical expertise is lacking. UN GENERAL ASSEMBLY, *ibid.*

[32] Medica Mondiale/LAF, supra n. 27.

[33] The women are usually accused of so-called 'honour crimes' that are often unsubstantiated and the women are reportedly subjected to physical and sexual abuse. UN GENERAL ASSEMBLY, supra n. 20, 19.

[34] SHAHEEN SARDAR ALI, *Gender and human rights in Islam and International Law* (The Hague: Kluwer, 2000). Under *Shari'a* Law, divorce for women is possible in a few very narrowly circumscribed conditions, extreme violent behaviour of the husband would be one. The cultural tradition of shaming makes divorce for women in Afghanistan extremely difficult and virtually impossible.

Women who flee are at serious risk for further retaliation by the husband's family.[35]

Exchange of girls to resolve a conflict between families - *bad* or the paying of so-called 'blood money' - and more generally, forced child marriage and forced marriage of widows to a male relative from her deceased husband's family is a form of gender based violence that is deeply embedded in social and cultural traditions, common in rural tribal areas (where three quarters of Afghanistan's population live).[36] Approximately 57% of girls get married before the age of sixteen.[37] The exchange of girls to resolve conflict has been interpreted as a restorative justice approach[38] in which girls and women are apparently considered the socially acceptable price to pay for community peace and to avoid tribal warfare. The practice of exchange and forced marriage has led in several instances to suicides through self-immolation.[39]

Except for a few initiatives by International NGOs mostly in and around Kabul, there are no structural provisions to support or protect women and girls. The current slow pace in the prioritization of women's issues regarding violence in Afghanistan is not so much the result of a lack of political commitment on the side of the international community to push for women's interests, but is equally if not more, due to a reluctance or outright refusal of the local and national political and religious leaders in Afghanistan to engage the problem of violence against women.

As previous research on Islam and gender has indicated, in many cases it is precisely during times of change where Islamic culture meets Western practices and political influence that women become the site *par excellence* for a production of a rather traditional conservative discourse

---

[35] Shelters do not necessarily provide an alternative, if the women have no place to go after they leave the shelter. Leaving the shelter would seriously expose them to the risk of being killed. Medica Mondiale/LAF, supra n. 27, 10-11.

[36] UN GENERAL ASSEMBLY, supra n. 20, 6 and 18. See also, supra n. 18;
HAKIM BASHARAT (2004), 'Society abandons divorced women', in: *Afghan Recovery Report No. 124* (London: Institute for War & Peace Reporting, 5 July 2004), available at: <http://www.iwpr.net>.

[37] UN COMMISSION ON HUMAN RIGHTS, supra n. 19, 7. See also INTEGRATED REGIONAL INFORMATION NETWORK (IRIN), '*Afghanistan: Child marriage rate still high*', 13 July 2004, available at: <http://www.irinnews.org/report.aspReportID=42160&SelectRegion=Central_Asia&SelectCountry=AFGHANISTAN>.

[38] ALI WARDAK, 'Jirga: Power and traditional conflict resolution in Afghanistan', in: J.STRAWSON (ed.), *Law after ground zero* (Sydney: Glasshouse Press, 2002) 187-204.

[39] WOMAN AND CHILDREN AND LEGAL RESEARCH FOUNDATION (WCLRF), *Bad Painful Sedative: Research Report, First Part (Kabul and Surrounding Area)*, 2003 (Kabul; on file with author).

on cultural Islamic authenticity and national identity in which the Islamic woman is constructed in firm opposition to Western values and practices. Most notably women's sexuality is the ultimate object of social control since it is constructed as the basis of many social evils and therefore reason for their subjection to control.[40]

A few examples can illustrate this tendency that reflects a deepening of the antagonism between Islam and Western culture. In an interview with a mullah living close to Kabul and who is generally considered a liberal, he expressed his concern about girls going to school, 'There is no security. If someone violates her chastity, who will regain it?' He was also concerned about women going out by themselves without a male relative as guardian (*mahram*) to work in public spaces, 'they will get infected by HIV like the Europeans.'[41] At a conference in Bangkok (June 2004) several Afghan women pointed to a dilemma: Western presence can inadvertently contribute to a polarisation in which Western presence comes to symbolise contamination of a 'pure' Islamic culture that eventually corrupts Islamic women. In the words of an Afghan representative, 'The import of Western cultures and traditions, with the arrival of the citizens of many countries in Afghanistan, has created many moral problems in the society and this has led families to prevent their female members from attending educational or training courses'.[42]

A recent UN report on human rights in Afghanistan concludes that 'the human rights situation of women in Afghanistan remains of serious concern'.[43] Within several UN-bodies the topic is being addressed more consistently. The UN Development Fund for Women (UNIFEM) began to coordinate a working group on violence against women in 2004. This group was created in order to facilitate and coordinate with various Inter-Governmental Organizations (IGOs), NGOs and government bodies on gender-based violence. UNIFEM is also guiding and funding the Afghan Ministry of Women's Affairs, which is looking into the areas of legal research for women, legal education and advocacy. Representatives of Afghan civil society are also part of the UNIFEM Coordination group.[44]

---

[40] See ABU-LUGHOD, supra n. 3; MIRZA, supra n. 16.

[41] SUHAILA MUHSENI AND SHAHABUDDIN TARAKHIL, 'Cultures clash over women's rights', *Afghan Recovery Report*, 18 November 2004. (London: Institute for War & Peace Reporting), available at: <http://www.iwpr.net>.

[42] JAMILA AFGHANI, Director Noor Educational Centre Kabul, 2004.

[43] UN GENERAL ASSEMBLY, supra n. 20, 18.

[44] Personal communication with Carolyn McCool, Interim Head of UNIFEM Kabul, July 2004.

In Afghanistan the Afghan Independent National Human Rights
Commission (AIHRC) has been established with UN support in June
2002. It is charged with monitoring and investigating the human rights
situation in Afghanistan, also with respect to the situation of women and
girls in the country.[45] In interviews I conducted with staff in Kabul from
the AIHRC during July 2004, it was indicated that violence against
women, despite being designated as one of the areas of the commission's
work, had not received much attention so far in field missions. However,
an important step in terms of policy preparation has been made in
November 2004 when several Ministries, in collaboration with the
AIHRC, the Supreme Court and the General Prosecution Office, adopted
a joint resolution in which they announced the development of a
national plan to end violence against women to be launched by a
National Commission for the Elimination of violence against women.[46]
The focus in this resolution is on the need for implementation of 'the
laws of the country and the Islamic *Shari'a'* in order to punish
perpetrators and on the amendment of family law 'according to the
Constitution and the Islamic *Shari'a'*. Furthermore, marriage registration,
publicity campaigns on violence against women, most notably on *bad* are
announced. Forced marriage of children and widows are mentioned as
'indecent traditions' that the public needs to be 'informed about'. It is not
clear at this point whether or not a legal ban of those practices will
follow.

3. FORMAL LEGAL DEVELOPMENTS IN AFGHANISTAN

How relevant are current legal developments in Afghanistan in terms of
providing legal recourse to women? Can it provide tools for women who
want to gain access to justice?

On January 26, 2004 President Karzai promulgated the new Constitution
of Afghanistan.[47] It tries to reconcile Western based principles of
democracy and Islamic law (*Shari'a*). This has been the outcome of a
delicate political negotiation process in which international forces were
prominently present, and internal Afghan power struggles between
various military and political factions, fundamentalist Islamists and
more reform oriented politicians had to yield. As part of the Afghan

---

45 UN COMMISSION ON HUMAN RIGHTS, supra n. 19, 8.

46 Resolution on the 'Elimination of Violence Against Women'. Kabul, November 24, 2004
    (on file with author).

47 The   Constitution   of   Afghanistan,   26   January   2004,   available   at:
    <http://www.embassyofafghanistan.org/pdf's/Documents/AdoptedConstitutionEng
    lish.pdf>.

reconstruction process that started with help of the international community after the Bonn Agreement (December 2001), the Constitution has been drafted under the guidance of the international community, notably the United States[48] and the European Union. According to Rubin, international actors made clear to the Islamist leaders from the very start of the drafting 'what the international community's red lines were'.[49] While they accepted that the new Constitution would declare Afghanistan an Islamic state, they did not want any explicit reference to *Shari'a* in the text. The current text in Article 2 states that 'the religion of the state of the Islamic Republic of Afghanistan is the sacred religion of Islam' and Article 3 says that 'no law can be contrary to the beliefs and provisions of the sacred religion of Islam'. This provision to ban laws contrary to Islam is in some form, commonly incorporated in the Constitutions of predominantly Muslim countries. An important achievement in terms of the underwriting of democratic principles is Article 7 according to which Afghanistan 'will abide by the UN charter, international treaties, international conventions that it has signed', explicitly referring to 'the Universal Declaration of Human Rights'. Furthermore, gender equality has been provided in Article 22 without any of the usual qualifications found in *Shari'a*. 'Any kind of discrimination and privilege between the citizens of Afghanistan is prohibited. The citizens of Afghanistan - whether man or woman - have equal rights and duties before the law'.

Although according to some there is formally no supremacy of Islamic law,[50] the Constitution obviously implies basic tensions. Most notably the provision in Article 3, which grants the Supreme Court the power to review the constitutionality of legislation, presidential decrees, and international treaties, represents one of those obstacles. Rubin warns that this provision could have a profound political impact since the Supreme Court in Afghanistan is a body that has always been dominated by Islamic scholars (*ulama*) trained in Islamic jurisprudence rather than constitutional law, and many do not have any training in formal law at all.

---

[48] See also WERNER M. PROHL, *Promoting Democracy in Post-Conflict Societies* (2004), who points at American experts providing 'a guiding hand' in the drafting process. Paper presented as a contribution of the Konrad Adenauer Foundation at the Joint Meeting of the Scientific Committee of the International Centre for Human Sciences at Byblos, Lebanon, and the International Panel on Democracy and Development of UNESCO (March 7 -10, 2004, Byblos/Beirut, Lebanon). The article is available at: <http://www.kas.de/db_files/dokumente/7_dokument_dok_pdf_4504_2.pdf>.

[49] BARNETT R. RUBIN, 'Crafting a constitution for Afghanistan', in: *Journal of Democracy*, Vol.15 (3), 2004, 5-20.

[50] PROHL, supra n. 48.

*'It is almost inevitable that conflicts will arise between the constitution's acceptance of
international human rights standards and embrace of male-female legal equality, on the
one hand, and the requirement that no law may contradict the "beliefs and provisions" of
Islam, on the other. When that happens, one may safely predict that political rather than
purely interpretive considerations will shape the outcome'.*[51]

Furthermore, the Constitutional provisions concerning the Judiciary
perpetuate a system in which the Supreme Court is in full administrative
control of the judiciary.[52]

An example of this climate of unconstitutional yet quasi legalised
gender-conservatism in Afghanistan is a recent decree from the Supreme
Court, in which cable networks were banned because they broadcasted
'un-Islamic' material.[53] The recent accusations against a presidential
candidate for being 'blasphemic' because he campaigned for gender
equality rights signal the current legal conservatism in Afghanistan's
Supreme Court, particularly regarding gender issues.[54] How this is going
to be resolved remains unclear at this point in time.[55]

---

[51] RUBIN, 2004, supra n. 49.

[52] It has been admitted by Constitutional Commission members privately, according to
Rubin, that this system sustains an existing corrupt network of judges that consist of
Islamic scholars who are usually not trained in any other than Islamic law and do not
need to be either, according to the Constitution. He concludes: 'Given the expanded
powers of the Supreme Court and the interest of the *ulama* in keeping a monopoly of
the power to interpret Islam, the failure to create more constitutional space for judicial
reform could prove a serious barrier against needed change in the future'. See RUBIN,
ibid.

[53] I.e. Bollywood-movies with romantic scenes between men and women. *Daily Times
Pakistan,* 15 November 2004.

[54] According to broadcasts by the BBC and Bakhtar News Agency on 1 September 2004,
the Supreme Court of Afghanistan (Setare Mahkame) asked that the democratic
candidate Latif Pedram be barred from the list of presidential candidates and all
electoral activities. Pedram's position in favor of women's rights was qualified as
'blasphemous' by the Supreme Court, and they have consequently requested that a
judicial investigation of these charges be opened. Eventually this was suspended after
firm protests, also from high level government officials. Sima Samar, the current head
of the Afghan Independent Human Rights Commission faced similar accusations last
year, after speaking out on women's rights. Those accusations were eventually also
suspended.

[55] Obviously there is a tension between this religious provision in Article 3 of the
Constitution, with Article 22 on gender equality and with international human rights
treaties and most notably with the Women's Convention that has been ratified by the
Interim Afghan Authority.Article 58, Constitution of Afghanistan, designates the
AIHRC as the structure to guard against human rights abuses. But it has no substantive
power yet to influence any adherence to human rights in the absence of a functioning
independent judicial system in current Afghanistan. The AIHRC has been designated
in the Constitution as the platform to which citizens can turn to complain about human
rights violations, and the AIHRC does have the authority to 'refer cases of violation of

A major complicating factor is that in Afghanistan the judicial system is in complete disarray and *de facto* in the process of rebuilding, like most political and administrative systems in Afghanistan.[56] The Afghan Judicial Reform Commission has failed in its mission since it became a fourth player in the power struggles.[57] The current Interim Authority of Afghanistan is a transitional government and not very effective yet, mostly due to its lack of control over warlords and local stakeholders in rural areas. The first parliamentary elections are scheduled to take place in 2005. The legislative process after the parliamentary elections, however, is still rather unclear.

4. INTERNATIONAL INFLUENCE ON AFGHAN LEGAL DEVELOPMENTS

Over the past few years the United Nations Assistance Mission to Afghanistan (UNAMA) has been set up as the UN-based coordinating platform designated to guide the international community's support in rebuilding Afghanistan. In addition to UNAMA, several UN agencies are actively involved in human rights work. They include UNHCR, UNIFEM, UNICEF, UNDP, WHO and the World Bank. Several EU-countries are actively involved in the rebuilding process of the judicial system, most notably Germany (focusing on rebuilding and training of the police) and Italy (focusing on legal reform, drafting of laws and providing training).[58] Furthermore, many international and local Afghan NGOs have become active in developing projects to provide human rights training and improve the legal system. UNIFEM is actively supporting professional legal women in Afghanistan who are organizing themselves, like the Afghan Women Lawyers and Professional Association, the Afghan Women Judges Association and the Women Lawyers Council. Several female defense lawyers are currently trained by a German based NGO.[59] The general impression of actors in the judicial field is that currently many activities focusing on women's rights

---

human rights to the legal authorities, and assist in defending the rights of the complainant'.

[56] JOHNSON ET AL., supra n. 24; ALI WARDAK, *Jirga - A Traditional Mechanism of Conflict Resolution in Afghanistan* (2003), available at: <www.afghaninstitute-for-justice.org>.

[57] UNITED STATES AGENCY FOR INTERNATIONAL DEVELOPMENT (USAID), *Afghanistan Rule of Law Activities. Request for Task Order - Proposal 306-44 533*, 8 August 2004 (on file with author).

[58] *Ibid.*, 11-12.

[59] Medica Mondiale/LAF, supra n. 27.

are not well coordinated, an inevitable consequence of the local
administrative situation that is in transition and lacking transparency.[60]

In the fall of 2004, the United States Government via its US Agency for
International Development (USAID) has stepped in to play a major
steering role in the judicial reform process. It launched a $6 million
dollar programme on *'The rule of law in Afghanistan'* to be developed and
implemented over the next few years.[61] The launching document of the
programme addresses the challenge of how to integrate Islamic legal
principles with Western based democratic principles and rules of law. It
summarizes succinctly the main problems that we face in the current
legal arena in Afghanistan.

*'The programme is designed to target critical obstacles to the establishment of the rule of
law in Afghanistan: inadequate systems for handling and tracking cases in the formal
justice sector, a lack of educated and well-trained judges, lawyers and court
administrators, a disconnection between the formal and informal justice sectors, a lack of
public awareness regarding rights and procedures in the formal justice system and a lack
of clarity regarding the status of laws/law revision and lack of capacity to draft, codify
and disseminate legislation'.*[62]

It will take a number of years before results can be expected of any
programme focusing on judicial change. Its effectiveness will depend
ultimately on whether or not it will succeed in gaining legitimacy within
an Afghan political and legal context. In this programme three main
components are identified: (1) strengthening the court system and
education of legal personnel, (2) law reform and legislative drafting, and
(3) building linkages to the informal justice sector.

The programme aims to include what is called a 'gender component', in
this context meaning that the programme as a whole 'should benefit both
men and women. (...) Due to the shortage of women in the legal
profession (...) creative ideas on how to engage women are welcome.
Programme activities should seek to encourage more women to join the
legal profession; to support female law students and to provide
opportunities to women already in the profession.'[63] It is interesting to
note that the definition of the gender component refers only to a desired
increase of the number of women, and not to the required substantive

---

60 Personal interviews in July 2004 with representatives in Kabul of UNDP, UNIFEM,
   UNODC, AIHRC, Professor N. Abu Bakr-Gross (Kabul University), and Rachel
   Wareham (Medica Mondiale, Afghanistan).
61 USAID, supra n. 57.
62 *Ibid.*, 6.
63 *Ibid.*, 21.

and qualitative changes in the judicial system or legislation. It avoids the thorny issues that are at stake when claiming to change gender discrimination and particularly violence against women in a developing country where cultural traditions regarding gender relations are at odds with a dominant Western framework of gender equality.

In the face of a dysfunctional formal legal system in the current Afghan context, it will take a long time to get a functional system on track. Both the drafting of national statutory law in accordance with the new Constitution and the building of a functioning judicial infrastructure that ensures the independent implementation of the law, are major projects. Only the future will tell whether the Afghan Government will succeed in realising this. Until then, Afghan citizens, men and women will not yet be able to gain full access to justice and live a life where the rule of law is upheld. Furthermore, given the traditional cultural and religious context in which the law is currently operating, it is particularly not well-equipped to provide any meaningful protection or support to women who have been victimised. Violence against women is still seen as a private matter and there still is a debilitating stigma in Afghanistan attached to women seeking justice for sexual crimes in particular. Prosecutions for violence against women are rare and with limited resources for investigation, prosecutors mostly argue cases on the basis of allegations rather than on evidence. In addition, the majority of women remain unaware of their legal rights and do not have the support of the community to pursue their cases.

5. INFORMAL JUSTICE IN AFGHANISTAN: JIRGA OR SHURA AND WOMEN'S ACCESS TO JUSTICE

Given how weak the State's institutions currently are, the real power in local community is exerted by male heads of families and religious leaders. Because of the dysfunctional formal justice system at this point in time, existing informal justice systems continue to play an important role in Afghanistan. It basically has served most Afghan people for a long time in history already since few citizens have had access to formal systems to begin with, certainly in rural areas where the majority of Afghans live.[64] Customary law, heavily leaning on Islamic principles, has been traditionally the primal legal basis to resolve conflicts. The traditional tribal structure for conflict resolution as well as political

---

[64] USAID, supra n. 57, 12; ALI WARDAK, supra n. 38.

decision-making in Afghanistan is the *jirga* or *shura*.[65] At a local level, the
jirga or *shura* consists of a council of male elders, usually religious
scholars or landowners chosen for their charismatic characteristics
and/or their background of social influence. The original goal of the *jirga*
is one of conflict resolution.[66]

Over the centuries, *jirga* operated as an important mechanism of conflict
resolution and has contributed to the maintenance of social order in
Afghan society. Furthermore, culturally and socially speaking,
Afghanistan tribal areas are characterised by a tradition of profound
distrust in central government and their institutions which makes people
rather rely on local structures for conflict resolution. The authority of the
jirga rests upon authority coming from tradition and custom rather than
any sort of judicial power.[67]

Given how deeply rooted informal conflict resolutions mechanisms
executed via local *shura* or *jirga*, are, it is generally agreed that they need

---

[65] There exist some regional-ethnic differences between different kinds of *jirga* or *shura*.
The general *modus operandi* in that they represent a local decision making and conflict
resolving council of elders is similar though. See LYNN CARTER AND KERRY CONNOR, *A
preliminary investigation of contemporary Afghan councils* (Peshawar: Agency
Coordinating Body For Afghan Relief, 1998). WARDAK, *ibid.*; WARDAK, supra n. 56.

[66] CARTER AND CONNOR, *ibid.*; The council meets only in response to resolve a specific
conflict between unrelated individuals, families, groups of families or tribes. Conflicts
between family members within one family are considered private matters which are
to be resolved by the male head of the family. So conflicts related to violent abuse,
divorce, inheritance, arrangements of a marriage are considered private matters and
need to be settled behind closed doors in the private sphere of the family. An extended
family is the smallest social unit upon which Afghan society is built. Two or more
generations of blood-related relatives live together in a cluster of adjacent houses, and
women move in with the in-laws after their marriage. The eldest male member of the
family, usually the husband and father or, the grandfather, eldest brother or uncle, has
traditionally the authority to decide so-called private conflicts, even though they
obviously are often a party to the conflict.
The concept of *jirga* has been translated into national political culture in Afghanistan.
The lower house of parliament is named *wolasi jirga* and the upper house *mashrano
jirga*, and the periodically held grand Afghan assembly is the *Loya Jirga* (Wardak, supra
n. 56, 5). The new constitution of Afghanistan was accepted after consultation of a so-
called Emergency Constitutional Jirga, see RUBIN, supra n. 49.

[67] It is the social and moral authority of the members that provides legitimacy to their
decisions. Decision-making is not based on a democratic one-man-one-vote principle
but on an informal negotiation process geared towards consensus. The principle of a
quorum is not a pertinent one. Levels of personal influence and status of the members
present at the meeting ultimately define its outcome. Failure to accept a *jirga* decision
leads at a minimum to social ostracization (most extreme: leaving the area) or in rare
cases to punishment (e.g. burning of one's house). See CARTER ET AL, supra n. 65;
WARDAK, *ibid.*; WARDAK, supra n. 38.

to be integrated in any future legal system in Afghanistan.[68] Wardak argues that the *jirga* has the transformative capacity to express traditional values in a modern setting. He emphasizes, however, that the *jirga* must adapt, though, 'to the new social, economic and political environment (check where the quotation marks should appear) that a globalised 21st century presents as challenges'. It needs to learn from other cultures as much as they need to learn from it.[69]

The question is to which extent *jirga* can be transformative and more sensitive to the principles of human rights?[70] Can an institution which to this very day not only excludes women as members, but de facto closes its doors to women dealing with 'private' problems, and even worse, violates women's basic human rights by exchanging them to appease warring families, transform itself? In Afghan society the group as rights-bearer is historically considered more important than the individual.[71] Wardak does acknowledge that 'The individual - a woman in this case - often pays the price for the tribe's social survival in this patriarchal group-oriented society'. This does not mitigate his optimism for change though.[72]

6. FRAGILE WOMEN'S CITIZENSHIP AND LOCAL DEMOCRACY IN AFGHANISTAN

The very first efforts to make informal justice systems like *shura* or *jirga* more sensitive to women's participation reveal that it is very difficult to change traditional Afghan gender norms in relation to informal justice structures. Recent experiments in Afghanistan with the so-called National Solidarity Programme (NSP) illustrates how difficult it is to make local councils more inclusive toward women.[73] The programme aims at development of local democracy through the election of so-called local Community Development Committees (CDC), which are given

---

68 WARDAK, *ibid.*; USAID, supra n. 57, 12-14.
69 WARDAK, supra n. 38, 202.
70 WARDAK, supra n. 56, 17.
71 Recently, in one of the first explorative studies in which Afghans were interviewed about their understanding of human rights, the difference with Western conceptions of individualized rights became very clear. Respondents generally understood human rights from a family or community perspective – for example, emphasizing the needs of their children as part of the family. Respondents also associated human rights with economic and social rights, especially food security, education, work and health. This reflects the fact that the daily struggle for survival remains paramount for many Afghans.CESR, supra n. 11, 21.
72 WARDAK, supra n. 56, 11.
73 BOESEN, supra n. 14. All data on the National Solidarity Program presented here, are based on this report.

decision-making power on how to spend a development grant that is awarded to the community. The community then decides how exactly and on which particular development project the grant will be spent (like digging a well, building a school etcetera). The NSP heralds a historical change of the interrelations between the central government and local communities, particularly with regard to the role of women in local decision-making. The CDC is supposed to include and represent both men and women. In this respect, the idea of women's participation in public civic life such as community decision-making, challenges some of the most central Afghan norms: submission of women to male decision making. More generally, it is at odds with the custom of positioning the woman first and foremost as a member of the family - not as an individual - and more specifically as the bearer of the family honour. It is also at odds with the tradition of *purdah*, common in most rural areas in Afghanistan, and which is understood to uphold the women's honour and the family honour by segregating the sexes and by the virtually complete exclusion of women from public life to avoid public shame.

The NSP-programme is an attempt to introduce democracy 'from above'. First results are mixed. In only ten percent of the villages participating in the study, women were allowed membership of the local council.[74] Women's participation is described as 'the most difficult and sensitive problem in (this) approach to inclusive community development'.[75] Women were very interested and enthusiastic about the programme and they wanted to vote, but there is a generally fierce resistance from the male-dominated community.[76] Separate parallel structures were created to the local male committees as an alternative forum for the women to discuss their needs and identify women's projects, the so-called women's *shura*. But just as women needed men's permission to vote, most women also needed their permission to participate in women's *shura* or women's committees as representatives. In several villages the female representatives elected were not allowed by their husbands to participate or women were afraid to participate in the meetings due to fear of their husband's anger. Some had been told by the men that the staff of the

---

74 BOESEN, *ibid.,* 53.

75 BOESEN, *ibid.*

76 To respect local traditions separate elections were organized for women, usually in a private home. Men voted in public, usually the mosque or a public square. Although the idea was to have men and women collaborate on the local committees, this often turned out to be impossible in practice: 'here, men do not like that women are members of the *shura'.* BOESEN, *ibid.,* 38. See on the stronger conservatism of men compared to women also W. PROHL, supra n. 48, 6, who reports a survey in which 42% of the Afghan women consider gender equality 'important' compared to only 15 % of the male respondents.

NGO would then take them away to Kabul to make them 'like Kabul women or even like foreigners' who would forget 'how to behave properly as Afghan women'.[77] Generally only older women (who had grown-up children, especially sons) were accepted as partners in the discussions with men. Yet older women were also the ones who regularly stated that their daughters-in-law should not participate and stay at home. In effect the male *shura* often prioritized their projects at the expense of projects that were more sensitive to women's needs.[78]

7. HUMAN RIGHTS, ISLAMIC LAW AND CULTURAL LEGITIMACY

'Human rights is to have men and women in a family eat around the same table (laughter). Yes, it is. I have heard that it is for men and women to be equal'. Male villager, Nangarhar Province, Afghanistan.[79]

In a state that presents itself as bound by Islamic law as well as international human rights and anti-discrimination treaties, we face serious obstacles for the realization of gender equality and protection of women against gender based violence. What can human rights mean in an Afghan legal and social context that has many traditions that are directly in conflict with international human rights standards? This touches directly on the much debated question of universality versus cultural relativism in human rights.[80] The Afghan situation illustrates a wider issue: What can human rights mean in a judicial context that is bleak when it comes to adherence to the rule of law and to women's rights in particular?

---

77 BOESEN, supra n. 14, 38.

78 OESEN, *ibid.*

79 CERS, supra n. 11, 25.

80 See for a range of positions on this issue, CHARLES TAYLOR, 'A world consensus on human rights?', in: P. HAYDEN (ed.), *The philosophy of human rights* (St Paul: Paragon House, 2001) 409-422; DAVID KENNEDY, 'The international human rights movement: part of the problem?', in: *Harvard Human Rights Journal*, Vol. 15, 2002, 101-125; JOHN DONNELLY, 'In defense of the universal declaration model', in: GENE M. LYONS AND JAMES MAYALL (eds.), *International Human Rights in the 21st century. Protecting the rights of groups* (Lanham/Boulder/New York/Oxford: Rowman & Littlefields Publ. Inc.) 20-45; BERTA E. HERNANDEZ-TRYOL, 'Human rights through a gendered lens: Emergence, evolution revolution', in: KELLY D. ASKIN AND DOREAN M. KOENIG (eds.), *Women and international human rights law*, Vol. 1 (Ardsley: Transnational Publishers Inc., 1999) 3-39; ABDULLAHI AN-NA'IM, 'Toward a Cross-Cultural Approach to Defining International Standards of Human Rights: The Meaning of Cruel, Inhuman or Degrading Treatment of Punishment', in: ABDULLAHI AHMED AN-NA'IM (ed.), *Human Rights in Cross-Cultural Perspective: A Quest for Consensus* (University of Pennsylvania Press, 1992) 19- 43.

The glaring disparity between an apparent commitment to human rights
in theory and poor compliance in practice is unfortunately a common
problem. An Na'im has called this *'the paradox of human rights'*. Precisely
because no government in the world today can openly reject them any
longer, human rights are increasingly formally endorsed yet consistently
violated in all parts of the world because they lack *cultural legitimacy* in
that particular country.[81] This certainly seems to hold true for
Afghanistan - as in many other countries, including Western countries -
where much of the violence committed against women is deeply rooted
in cultural traditions that are still endorsed by large parts of the
community. An Na'im addresses explicitly what he calls 'the legitimacy
dilemma in the Muslim context'. While acknowledging the vast
differences between Muslim cultures across the world, he underlines
that the basic principles of *Shari'a*, even from a reformist modernist
interpretation of the Qu'ran and the Hadith (the two basic sources of
sacred Islamic texts), are not easy to reconcile with current standards of
human rights.

It is important to note that there is a range of scholarly positions on this
subject, from orthodox fundamentalist to reformist and modernist,
which goes beyond the scope of this article to fully address. It is
important to note that positions in this debate ultimately depend on the
approach toward the exegesis of the Qu'ranic texts and whether there is
a right to re-fashion the medievalist interpretative tradition of the Qu'ran
in the light of modern society's needs.[82] These different positions can also
be seen among Islamic feminist scholars on the question whether or not
Islamic law could eventually operate as a legal framework that would
allow gender equality, given its current emphasis on gender differences
and firm rejection of the notion of 'sameness'.[83] Note, however, that there
is a doctrinal diversity in feminist Islamic theory that is compounded by
great cultural and regional differences among Muslim countries.[84] For

---

81 ABDULLAHI AN NA'IM, 'Islam, Islamic law and the dilemma of cultural legitimacy for
universal human rights', in: C. WELCH JR. AND V. LEARY (eds.), *Asian perspectives on
human rights* (Oxford: Westview Press, 1990) 31-54, 32-33.

82 See the debate as summarized in the article of ABDULLAHI AN NA'IM, *ibid.*, 37. For an
example of a radically new interpretation of Qu'ranic texts on women, see AMINA
WADUD (1999), *Qu'ran and Women*, Oxford University Press. See also: REZA ASLAM
(2005), *No good but God. The origins evolution and future of Islam*, New York: Random
House.

83 See B. STOWASSER, 'Gender issues and contemporary Quran interpretation', in:
HADDAD AND ESPOSITO, supra n. 16. See also, SARDAR, supra n. 34; MIRZA, supra n. 16.
HAIDEH MOGHISSI, *Feminism and Islamic fundamentalism. The limits of postmodern analysis*
(London/New York; Zed Books, 1999).

84 See MIRZA, *ibid.*, 112.

the purpose of this paper it is important to note that there is a general agreement that if a modernist liberal interpretation of *Shari'a* law would allow for gender equality, it is currently not practiced yet in Muslim countries.[85] Modernist and feminist Islamic reformers agree that *Shari'a* law is in need of profound reform to do justice to women and that a contextual locally based approach is crucial to achieve cultural legitimacy of any reform.

From the perspective of this reformist modernist position there is a particular problem with discrimination of women under *Shari'a* law.[86] Despite formal legal changes that gradually and formally will enable more legal gender equality, throughout the Muslim world, *Shari'a* constitutes the personal law of Muslims even if it is not the formal legal system of the country. It will profoundly influence cultural traditions and customary law in particular. Is it possible to adhere to international human rights standards and not have it imposed as a neo-colonial Western project?[87] Is it possible to overcome the dilemma to remain *within* an Islamic tradition and change law and more importantly, change its implementation in legal and social practice toward gender equality? Is it possible to achieve a cultural legitimacy of the rule of law and gender equality based on international human rights standards while respecting Afghan legal and social traditions?

Looking specifically at Afghanistan, it is in theory, constructive to try to overcome this dilemma in building towards a justice system that links formal and informal justice systems. The latter is an age old system that culturally speaking one cannot discard, since it plays an important role in maintaining social cohesion and stability. Yet, it is imperative to question the compatibility of the underlying principles of *Shari'a* and Afghan customary law with human rights principles like gender equality and protection of women's safety against violent abuse, to avoid building a system that would provide *de facto* and *de jure* impunity to perpetrators of severe violent crimes against women. If we want to

---

85 Note that some feminist authors reject the idea that Islamic law would enable gender equality. See for example, MOGHISSI, supra n. 83.

86 AN NA'IM, supra n. 81, 38. See also SARDAR, supra n. 34; An Na'im also points to the discriminatory impact of *Shari'a* for non-Muslims since it imposes restrictions of the freedom of religion and belief. For example, men can divorce the wife at will, women can only seek divorce on very strict grounds, women can only receive half a share in the inheritance and they receive less compensation for criminal harm.

87 See CHANDRA TALPADE MOHANTY, 'Under Western eyes: Feminist scholarship and colonial discourses', *Boundary* 2, 12 (3), 1986, 333-358. She is one of the first feminist scholars who emphasises that a colonial project inevitably underlies western based international human rights standards.

achieve a system that upholds basic international human rights standards, it is necessary to address the specific obstacles rooted in both cultural and religious traditions.[88] In other words: it is necessary to find a way to materialize a 'gender component' in Afghan legal reform that provides effective legal protection to women.

From an Islamic legal reformist perspective it is crucial to find reforms of the conflicting aspects in *Shari'a*, with human rights principles without losing its religious legitimacy. According to a reformist and human rights scholar like An Na'im, it takes 'a theoretically possible enlightened construction' of fundamental Islamic sources to achieve legal equality between men and women under Islamic law, based on 'internally coherent Islamic arguments'.[89] This is possible if reform is coming from *within* the Islamic religious community, undertaken by reform oriented scholars and practitioners, and supported by enlightened reconstruction of cultural traditions that so far have excluded and subjugated women. This reform is not only possible but 'unavoidable' according to An Na'im in the face of 'the realities of modern life facing the Muslims throughout the world'.[90] Recent radical changes in Morocco's family law that improved woman's legal position profoundly can be considered as an example of reform from within that has achieved legitimacy.[91]

At this point in time, however, with a growing polarisation and stigmatization between Islamic and Western cultures after the terrorist attacks on the World Trade Centre in New York in 2001, reformist voices in Islam are increasingly accompanied, if not threatened by growing fundamentalist discourse. This is currently happening in Afghanistan regarding women's rights. Local women's organizations in Afghanistan emphasise the need for foreign support in their endeavours.[92] However, ultimately the challenge for the international community of donor

---

[88] Note that cultural and religious rules are often collapsed. Many restrictions on Afghan women are legitimized by referring to Islamic rules where it is in fact a culturally based tradition. An example is the taboo on Afghan women initiating divorce, that however, is allowed under certain conditions in *Shari'a*.

[89] AN NA'IM, supra n. 81. On the subject of 'enlightened ethnocentrism' as a necessary element to allow different cultures different perspectives on 'cruel behaviour' while simultaneously submitting themselves to international human rights standards, see also AN-NA'IM, supra n. 80.

[90] AN NA'IM, supra n. 81, 47.

[91] GILES TREMLETT (2004), 'Morocco boosts women's rights', *The Guardian*, 21 January 2004. Available at: <http://www.amanjordan.org/english/daily_news/wmview.php?ArtID=3782>.

[92] Personal communication with representatives of women's grass roots organizations in Kabul, July 2004.

countries, feminist organizations and NGOs is to play an active role in supporting internal Afghan reformist projects, without re-enacting and discursively constructing an opposition between the civilised West and the barbarous Islamic culture.[93] It is therefore crucial to engage and support Afghan women at a grass-roots level, who are willing to work toward gender equality and protection of women's basic human rights, in order to avoid interventions that are considered 'foreign' and would not gain cultural legitimacy. In this respect, Afghanistan poses a fundamental challenge to the homogenizing tendency that we often find both in many Western as in Islamic feminisms.[94]

Gaining cultural legitimacy of foreign support for Afghan reformist projects in the legal domain also requires an ongoing critical self reflection and modification of the concept of 'right'. The liberalist individualist legacy that has shaped international human rights law and that nominates the individual as the ultimate rights-holder, is at times at odds with the cultural-legal tradition that is based on group rights in Afghanistan as it is in many Asian Muslim countries.[95]

'The developed countries of the world should not expect other peoples of the world, including the Muslim peoples, to examine and re-evaluate their cultural and philosophical traditions in the interest of a more genuine respect for and greater compliance with international human rights unless they (the developed countries) are willing to examine and re-evaluate their own cultural traditions'.[96]

8. OUT OF THE SHADOW: TOWARDS JUSTICE AND LEGAL SUBJECTIVITY FOR WOMEN

Violence against women has become a topic that has mobilized political support in the 21st century, if sometimes only rhetorically, from governments, NGOs and feminist activist groups. It comes as no surprise that violence against women in Afghanistan and the need for human rights protection has figured prominently in the recent international efforts to support Afghan women's struggle for emancipation. Precisely now, at a time when Islam and Islamic culture is under siege, the need is more urgent than ever before to be aware of the larger political context in

---

93 JACQUI ALEXANDER AND CHANDRA T.MOHANTY, 'Introduction. Genealogies, violence and identity', in: JACQUI ALEXANDER AND CHANDRA T.MOHANTY (eds.), *Feminist genealogies, colonial legacies, democratic futures* (New York: Routledge, XII-XLII).

94 See MIRZA, supra n. 16, 120.

95 C. WELCH (1990), 'Global change and human rights: Asian perspectives in comparative context', in: C.E. WELCH JR. AND V. A. LEARY, supra n. 81, 3-12.

96 AN NA'IM, supra n. 81, 49.

which this struggle is situated and the cultural and social traditions that
are at stake in Afghanistan when pushing for legal reform to protect
women. Legal reform can never be effective without local social and
cultural legitimacy. This poses a challenge when the political agenda of
'liberation and modernization' is primarily based on straightforward
Western liberalist norms as documented in international human rights
law, that grow out of a modernist understanding of the self and its
capacity to act autonomously. Discrimination against and exploitation of
women and girls will not disappear overnight and the rapid imposition
of reforms from outside could itself cause new problems for women.
Outside pressure can provoke a backlash from men and increase the risk
of violence against women, particularly in the home.[97] In that respect we
have to be aware that human rights law does not blend well into pre-
existing cultural systems. Their power is indirect in that it can help
change cultural practices.[98] But it does require careful navigating,
because if international human rights law is simply used as a standard to
judge Afghan legal practice, it might lose its potential to foster social
change as its categorical condemnation of violence against women will
be perceived as yet another moralistic intervention through an institute
of Western culture.

Ultimately we want to create tools for women as the targeted right-
holders, which they can use to achieve protection in a context that so far
in many respects denies women's legal subjectivity. This confronts us
with various challenges. Communication for example is a crucial
variable in a context of transitional justice and changes towards
democratic governance. Female and male citizens can only be
empowered as legal subjects when rights are known to them and
accepted by their polity. One could view the current Afghan democratic
developments as an example how both constitutional and international
human rights law operates at times as largely symbolic legislation but in
a positive sense in that it communicates a set of aspirational norms that
do aim to influence what people actually will do. This also requires
interpretation and elaboration by the members of the community in
which the laws ultimately will be given meaning.[99] This requires creative

---

[97] UN COMMISSION ON HUMAN RIGHTS, *Other human rights issues. Women and human rights,*
Report of the Secretary-General on the situation of women and girls in the territories
occupied by Afghan armed groups, 2002, UN Doc. E/CN.4/Sub.2/2002/27.

[98] SALLY E. MERRY, 'Women, violence and the human rights system', in: M. AGOSIN (ed.),
Women, Gender and Human rights (New Brunswick/New York/London: Rutgers
University Press, 2001), 83-97.

[99] BART VAN KLINK (1998), *De wet als symbool. Over wettelijke communicatie en de Wet gelijke
behandeling van mannen en vrouwen bij de arbeid,* Zwolle: Tjeenk Willink.

campaigns to reach and inform the intended female subjects as rightsholders in a way that will create enough support so that the constitutional provision will lead to effective social and discursive practices toward gender equality. In that context it remains another challenge how to contribute and support that process as western socio-legal scholars without falling into the trap of a universalizing and culturally essentialist discourse that positions Islam, patriarchy, violence and oppression as inevitably linked?[100] These are difficult and complex questions that we ultimately have to address if we want to engage in a socially and strategically effective and culturally meaningful way. I do not think that these are the kind of questions that will ever lend themselves to any simple nor definite answers. Dilemmas do not lend themselves to easy solutions to begin with. But in laying them out we can achieve a richer understanding of the challenges that lie ahead when engaging in a dialogue from an international human rights perspective with Afghan women and more generally women in Islamic cultures. We have to find a way to engage in a discourse on women's rights that is not based on the orientalist opposition between a refined Europe and an inherently violent Islam that is inert and fixed on the oppression of women.[101] Keeping an eye on the violence against women that is happening on a large scale every day behind closed doors in virtually all Western cultures is one way to avoid an essentialist cultural stigmatization of violence against women in Islamic cultures.

It will remain necessary to navigate between a universalistic discourse on human rights and women's rights on the one hand and strategising in a local context to achieve acceptance and cultural legitimacy of these rights. This is a delicate process that takes time and most importantly, requires the engagement of Afghan women. A national human rights campaign that explicitly addresses women and women's rights is one necessary step towards empowering women in developing a sense of entitlement to justice. Furthermore, we need more research that literally

---

[100] ABU-LUGHOD, supra n. 3; UMA NARAYAN, 'Essence of culture and a sense of history: A feminist critique of cultural essentialism', in: UMA NARAYAN AND SANDRA HARDING (eds), *Decentering the center. Philosophy for a multicultural, postcolonial, and feminist world* (Bloomington and Indianapolis: Indiana University Press, 2000) 80-100. See also, VOLPP, supra n. 7, who points to the tendency to overread culture as an 'explanation' for violence among non-western minority cultures in the United States while ignoring the cultural dimensions and legitimate reasons for violence in dominant white American culture.

[101] EDWARD SAID, *Orientalism* (London: Penguin Books, 1995).

gives voice to Afghan women's concerns, needs and desires regarding their rights. Women are under represented in studies done so far.[102]

The existence of a gap between human rights standards and local women's rights should not necessarily be seen as a failure but as an inevitable yet challenging paradox. Human rights standards should in this context be viewed more as a regulatory normative goal, something to *strive towards*, than as something to *be had* by the individual rights-bearer.[103] From this point of view, the law and its judicial system are one of the many ways to achieve justice while acknowledging the need of simultaneously deploying other non-legal means and strategies as well. There is a long way to go in Afghanistan to rebuild a democracy that is truly respectful of the rule of law. Given the virtual absence in day to day life of legal subjectivity for women and subsequently a very fragile legal consciousness of themselves as rights-holders, much of the negotiations on rights for women and social change seem to take place in the absence of any law, in the shadow of no law. Yet, it is precisely the presence of international human rights law in the background, which casts a shadow that may become a transformative force toward social justice for women.

---

[102] The field study conducted by CESR, supra n. 11, 18, is one of the few that addresses the issue that it takes extra efforts to literally give voice to women.

[103] JOAN SCOTT, *Gender and the politics of history* (New York; Columbia University Press, 1999) (Revised edition).

FEMALE GENITAL MUTILATION: A MATTER FOR CRIMINAL JUSTICE?

Renée Kool

1. INTRODUCTION

As a result of immigration, Dutch society is increasingly being confronted with many kinds of practices from other cultures. Usually this is not a problem and familiarisation develops gradually in the course of time. In some cases, however, a cultural practice may be at odds with the standards and values which are seen as fundamental to Dutch society. Moreover, if practising a cultural custom results in a punishable offence, the question arises as to how this cultural tradition is to be evaluated by law; is prosecution of the offence expedient? In recent years cultural defence has been increasingly employed as justification for apparently illegal practices. In some instances manslaughter has been justified by the offender, due to a cultural necessity of revenge.

Another cultural tradition which has recently been perceived as a problem in the Dutch political debate is the circumcision of girls and women, termed female genital mutilation (FGM).[1] It is estimated that 130 million women and girls worldwide have been circumcised and 2 million circumcisions are performed annually.[2] Although the type of circumcision may vary, as well as the age at which it occurs, the procedure results in the irreparable mutilation of the female genitalia. In the Netherlands the custom is practised within several population subgroups, on girls between the ages of eight and thirteen years.

Practically all organizations, national and international, condemn FGM. In 2001 the European Council designated it as an 'inhumane procedure' as defined by Article 3 of the European Convention on Human Rights and Fundamental Freedoms (ECHR). It is important to note that not only Western countries have condemned FGM, but that this condemnation is also supported by international organizations and governments in the

---

[1] The term female genital mutilation is employed by the World Health Organization (WHO) and the UN Committee for Children's Rights, among others. The purpose of the term is to express that in addition to the physical aspect of circumcision, the socio-economic context must also be examined.

[2] EUROPEAN PARLIAMENT, *Verslag over verminking van de geslachtsorganen bij vrouwen (Report on mutilation of the sexual organs of women)* (Strasbourg, 2001) A5-0285/2001, 8/33.

countries this tradition originates from.[3] A number of these countries has adopted legislation regarding this issue, even though it may not be enforced. The same is true, however, of Western European countries; here too, penalisation – whether of a specific or general nature – may not be enforced. Until now France has been the only country where FGM cases have been actively prosecuted.

This difference in enforcement raises questions. Clearly, penal statutes are intended to be enforced, certainly when such serious punishable offences as FGM are involved. In recent years the Dutch Parliament has raised questions concerning the policy of the Dutch Government on FGM. Because in the Netherlands as well, FGM is punishable under assault and child abuse laws, but up till now not a single case has ever been brought before a court. This parliamentary pressure, in combination with the increasing international attention for FGM and the responsibilities of the courts, has recently resulted in the establishment of a State commission (the Sanders commission) which has been given the task of making recommendations on how to improve efforts to combat FGM. The report of the Sanders commission was published March 2005.[4] The basic premise of the commission is that any form of FGM should be prohibited, a premise that is consistent with the viewpoint of the Dutch Government. Starting from that viewpoint, the question to consider is how to improve the criminal investigation and prosecution of FGM; the option of introducing a specific provision is one of the points of discussion.

In this paper I will answer the question of whether such a specific provision is desirable. First, however, for the sake of clarity, a short description of FGM and its cultural background is laid out (section 2). Thereafter I pose the question of whether criminal enforcement is desirable (section 3). In the scope of that discussion, the meaning of a cultural defence is also considered as a possible justification for FGM as well as a mitigating factor in respect to sentencing. This will be followed by an inventory of advantages and disadvantages (section 4) and a brief

---

3   M. MASCLEE AND S. MEUWESE, 'Genitale verminking bij vrouwen en meisjes' ('Genital mutilation in women and girls'), in: *Ars Aequi*, 49, 2000, 7/8, 538. Also Art. 21 of the African Charter on Human and Peoples' Rights, 27 June 1981, forbids such practices; see also 'What's culture got to do with it? Excising the harmful tradition of female circumcision', in: *Harvard Law Review*, 106, 1993, 1954-1956.

4   The legal part of this investigation has been carried out by the Willem Pompe Institute, Utrecht University; R.S.B. KOOL, A. BEIJER, C.F. VAN DRUMPT, J. EELMAN EN G.J. KNOOPS, *Vrouwelijke verminking in juridisch perspectief (A judicial perspective on Genital Female Mutilation)*, Zoetermeer, maart 2005.

legal comparison based on relevant Dutch and Belgian penal provisions (section 5).

2. FORMS OF CIRCUMCISION AND CULTURAL BACKGROUND

As mentioned above, FGM is a widespread practice. The origin can be found on the African continent, in some parts of Asia (Indonesia, Malaysia) and in the Middle East (Egypt, Yemen).[5] It is an ancient custom, which was already in practice around 2,500 years ago. Although on a global scale it is a relatively rare occurrence, the number of estimated circumcisions performed annually is large enough to be considered a serious social problem.[6]

2.1. Types of circumcision

The moment of circumcision varies according to the interpretation of the ritual in which it is involved. Sometimes circumcision is performed on infants,[7] whereas at other times circumcision takes place at puberty as a sign of the transition to another phase of life, or at the beginning of pregnancy in protecting the foetus against supposedly detrimental influences of the clitoris.

In addition to the time at which it takes place, the form of the circumcision may also vary. The following forms are to be distinguished:[8]

---

[5] GODELIEVE VAN GEERTRUYEN, *Vrouwelijke genitale verminking: de sociaal-culturele context (Female genital mutilation: the social-cultural context)*, Afrika Vereniging (African Society) van de Universiteit van Gent, Text 1; available at: <http://cas1.elis.rug.ac.be/avrug/vrouwell.htm>.

[6] J.A. LIU, 'When law and culture clash: female genital mutilation, a traditional practice gaining recognition as a global concern', in: *New York International Law Review*, Fall 1998, 1; T. VEERMAN, A. HENDRIKS & J. SMITH, 'Recht doen aan de gezondheid(sbelangen) van kinderen' ('Asserting children's health rights'), in: *Recht en kritiek*, 21, 1995, 140.

[7] The desire of mothers to spare their daughters from a painful memory is given as an explanation for this type of extremely early circumcision. Such early circumcision is common amongst Malinese immigrants living in France, amongst others. Infant examinations have created an opportunity for monitoring and prevention.

[8] M. VAN DER LIET-SENDERS, 'Inbreuken op seksuele en reproductieve rechten' ('Infringement on sexual and reproductive rights'), in: I. BOEREFIJN, M.M. VAN DER LIET-SENDERS AND T. LOENEN (eds.), *Het voorkomen en bestrijden van geweld tegen vrouwen (The prevention and combating of violence against women)* (The Hague: SZW, 2000) 238-239.

- Circumcision (or clitoridectomy). This procedure removes the foreskin or the top of the clitoris. The procedure has been compared to the circumcision of boys and is reported to be performed only via modern surgical procedures on adult women.
- Excision. This surgical procedure removes the clitoris as well as the *labia minora*.
- Infibulation. This is the most extreme procedure. The clitoris and both the *labia minora* and *majora* are cut away, after which the wound is fully stitched; healing occurs by holding the legs pressed stiffly against each other for a time. A small incision is left to allow the discharge of urine and blood. At marriage the wound is reopened, as well as at the birth of a child. As a rule re-infibulation follows.

It should be remembered that such circumcisions, with the exception of surgical circumcision, are usually performed without anaesthesia in unhygienic conditions, which may be fatal to the girl or woman. *Van der Liet-Senders* reports that 85% of the women and girls who are circumcised undergo circumcision or excision; 15% undergo infibulation. This last custom is practised, among other practices, within the Somali community in the Netherlands.[9] It should be clear that this concerns an irreversible form of severe physical damage, paired with psychological trauma. Healthy, sexually functional parts of the female body are removed without any medical indication whatsoever; restorative plastic surgery can only partially repair the damage.

2.2. Cultural motives

The disadvantages for girls and women are evident, but what benefits are offered in exchange? Why do women assent to their own circumcision as well as to that of their daughters? Viewed from a Western vantage point, such a 'voluntary' form of mutilation cannot be easily explained. Although Western women also may practise extreme forms of mutilation, such as branding or some forms of piercing, these are not nearly as drastic as the forms of genital mutilation named above.[10]

---

9   VAN DER LIET-SENDERS, supra n. 9, 239.

10   The only systematic exception that can be thought of here is the circumcision of boys, which is practised on a large scale in the Western world (and elsewhere). While this form of circumcision in its outer form is comparable to the lightest form of FGM, the underlying reasons for it significantly differ. Recently the circumcision of boys has also been called into question by the Dutch member of parliament A. Hirsi Ali.

A number of cultural foundations can be claimed. First is the claim of religion: circumcision is said to be prescribed by the Koran or the Bible. However, such texts are not to be found in these scriptures, although they do exist in some authoritative interpretations.[11] A second basis lies in the mythical belief that the female sexual organ, in particular the clitoris, has a detrimental effect on male sexuality, or even on the baby. It is self-evident that no valid foundation exists for such a superstition. A third reason is the necessity to control the sexuality of the woman. It is believed that without circumcision, the woman may become promiscuous and will no longer be under her husband's control. Circumcision purges the woman of her overabundant sexuality and ensures that the man is able to adequately respond to his wife's sexual demands. This image of purity is specifically expressed by the practice of infibulation, where the (potential) wife, remains, as it were, sealed until the moment that her husband can make his rightful claim on her sex. A corollary of this is the argument that circumcision enhances the beauty of the woman, but – given the horrific mutilation which results from the more severe forms of circumcision – little significance can be attached to this argument. Finally, circumcision also serves as an initiation ritual, in the transition from girl to woman. This argument, however, is meaningless in cases where circumcision is performed at an extremely young age.

2.3. Gender perspective

The foundations stated illustrate in many regards a gendered approach to female sexuality. The sexual autonomy of the girl/woman in such a cultural setting does not stand on its own, but derives its meaning from the sexuality of the man.[12] The key to female sexual integrity within such a cultural context is contained in her circumcision.[13] However, gender is of importance from a broader perspective as well; female sexuality derived from a male perception must also be examined against the background of marriage as a socio-economic necessity for the woman. In the countries where female circumcision is common, for women marriage is often one of few options for survival. Those who do not allow themselves to be circumcised are excluded from the community; in any case they are not considered to be marriageable and thus are forced

---

[11] L-J. LEUSINK, *Een huis is niet mooi zonder toegangsdeuren. Over vrouwenbesnijdenis*, Ph.D. Thesis, Law, Utrecht University, December 2003.

[12] K. BOULWARE-MILLER, 'Vrouwenbesnijdenis' ('Female circumcision'), *Nemesis*, 1988, 139.

[13] A. FUNDER, 'De minimis non curat lex: the clitoris, culture and the law', in: *Transnational Law and Contemporary Problems*, Fall 1993, 10; see also, supra n. 4, 1952.

to sacrifice a certain level of financial and social security.[14] The consent of adult women to circumcision must be put into perspective against this background. As far as minor-aged girls are concerned, Western standards of legally valid consent are nonexistent and in any case parents or others take the decision on their circumcisions.

3. CRIMINAL ENFORCEMENT AND CULTURAL DEFENCE

The question of whether cultural tradition can be cited as a defence for inflicting serious physical damage, which in the worst case may even be fatal, quickly leads to a polarisation of the debate. The Western human rights tradition emphasises the universal character of human rights and within it the protection of the physical and emotional integrity of the individual. Others, on the contrary, dismiss such an individualistic approach and see in this, the unjust domination of 'enlightened' Western thinking.[15]

The question is whether this apparent division can be put into perspective. Clearly, a universal orientation towards human rights with the individual as its centre does not preclude an endorsement of the cultural context in which a violation of human rights must be judged.[16] In other words, claims on physical and emotional integrity need not be incompatible with the right to a specific religious or cultural identity; neither of the two can pre-emptively be claimed with absolute validity.[17] In a democratic State under the rule of law all parties must initially be granted the same latitude, in order that respect can be shown for the underlying social and cultural structures from which individuals derive their self-image.[18] Again and again, both should be measured against each other, within the context in which the rights are enforced, whereby care must be taken to adequately reflect on one's own presuppositions embedded in the human rights discourse. Obviously, the strongly

---

14 VAN GEERTRUYEN, supra n. 6; BOULWARE-MILLER, supra n. 13, 141; FUNDER, *ibid.*, 9.

15 See for these, summary, among others, M-C. FOBLETS, 'De Parijse besnijdenisprocessen' ('The Parisian circumcision suits') in: *Recht der Werkelijkheid*, 1992, 107-117 resp., 'Vrouwenbesnijdenis. Over handhavingsmodellen van mensenrechten' ('Female circumcision. On enforcement models of human rights'), in: *Recht der Werkelijkheid*, 2, 1993, 201-206.

16 L.BIBBINGS, 'Human Rights and the criminalisation of tradition: the practices formerly known as "female circumcision"', in: P. ALLDRIDGE AND C. BRANTS, *Private Autonomy, and the Law* (Oxford: Hart Publishing, 2001) 139-161; FUNDER, supra n. 14, 12.

17 See supra n. 4, 1958.

18 J. E. GOLDSCHMIDT, 'Het grotere gelijk: alternatieven voor een destructieve verabsolutering van het gelijkheidsbeginsel' ('The greater good: alternatives to the destructive process of making the equality principle absolute'), in: *Nederlands Juristen Comité Mensenrechten*, 29, 2004, 786; FUNDER, supra n. 14, 17; BIBBINGS, supra n. 17.

individualistic, 'enlightened' Western image of humanity is also an historic construction, formed under the influence of cultural and socio-economic circumstances.

Does this mean that in the judgement of FGM as an alleged violation of human rights, a punishable offence, there should be allowance for a cultural defence, derived from the right to cultural self-determination or the right of religious freedom? In principle yes, certainly the right of cultural determination is also a legitimate human right. At the same time, however, care must be taken to avoid cultural relativism, where the constitutional State's own values threaten to become undermined; where the openness of the constitutional State is pushed to its limits.[19]

This is also the case concerning acceptance of a cultural defence as justification for FGM. In the context of the modern Western constitutional State, numerous arguments can be given within criminal enforcement for the rejection of this defence.

3.1. Irreversibility

The first argument which can be made is due to the irreversible character of the act. The damage to the female body and its reproductive capacity caused by circumcision is disproportionate and for this reason cannot be justified by a claim of cultural determination.

3.2. Inequality

A second, corresponding argument is the gendered character of the socio-economic relationships in which this cultural justification is rooted. Within the international debate on FGM, much attention has been paid to the gender aspect and the corresponding inequality. In line with Article 2 of the Convention for the Elimination of All Forms of Discrimination Against Women (the Women's Convention), the objective is to realize equitable claims to human rights for men and women. It is generally accepted that such equal rights may not be denied on the basis

---

[19] K. MEERSCHAUT & A. BACKS, *Vrouwenbesnijdenis en recht (Female circumcision and law)*, Afrika Vereniging (Africa Society) of the University of Gent, Text 4, available at: <http://cas1.elis.rug.ac.be/avrug/vrouwel4.htm>; A.C. 'T HART, *Hier gelden wetten! (There are laws here!)* (Deventer: Gouda Quint, 2001) 212. See also H. WILLEKENS, 'Culturele conflicten en vrouwenonderdrukking' ('Cultural conflicts and the oppression of women'), in: *Recht der Werkelijkheid*, 13, 1992), 169-174 and H. IETSWAART, 'Waar moet dat heen? Over wetenschap en politiek' ('Where is it going? On science and politics'), in: *Recht der Werkelijkheid*, 14, 1993, 195-201, both in reaction to FOBLETS, supra n. 16; E. VAN MIDDELKOOP, 'De rechtbank als Spiegel van de multi-culturele samenleving' ('The court: reflecting the multicultural society'), in: *Trema*, 7, 2004, 295-298.

of a public/private dichotomy, but can these rights then be denied where a claim is made to the right of practising cultural traditions? In that case does government protection of equal rights for women cease to exist?[20]

Here we must proceed with caution. Obviously, some discretion concerning the validity of the discourse on equality is appropriate, as Holtmaat has stated.[21] First of all this idea only gained legitimacy within Western thinking in the recent past, while the claim of legitimacy is not unequivocally accepted universally. And it is certainly not accepted without question where it implies a criticism of non-Western-oriented sexual cultural practices.[22]

In addition, as Saharso and Römkens have noted, the Western world may be trying to relieve its own guilty conscience in this way.[23] Many Western forms of 'everyday' violence quickly seem less problematic when compared to a 'bizarre' form such as FGM. The problematization of FGM as a theme in the multicultural debate is, they propose, a sign of a certain ethnocentrism and distracts us from the central theme: care for women.[24]

Although this appeal for reflection on and tempering of specific cultural convictions is pertinent, it does not reduce the necessity of taking measures against FGM. However, I would like to introduce a 'territorial' limitation at this point, in the sense that I believe that a criminal justice approach relating to FGM must be differentiated to match the region in which the efforts to combat it take place. When circumcisions have a direct contiguity with Western society, I have, with due consideration, no difficulty accepting that the Western discourse on equality should prevail. The cultural argument simply offers insufficient scope for this

---

[20] J. TIGCHELAAR, 'De politieke partij, de trouwambtenaar en de imam' ('The political party, the marriage registrar and the imam'), in: *Nemesis,* 2002, 72-63; Tigchelaar indicates the social vulnerability of the minority group as a factor in the decision-making in jurisprudence on equity.

[21] R. HOLTMAAT, 'De meerwaarde van het VN-verdrag in de multiculturele samenleving' ('The additional benefit of the UN convention in the multicultural society'), in: R. HOLTMAAT (ed.), *Een verdrag voor alle vrouwen (A convention for all women)* (The Hague: E-quality, 2002) 130-133.

[22] GOLDSCHMIDT, supra n. 19, 790 emphasises the importance of a material approach to the equality foundation and indicates its accessory character.

[23] S. SAHARSO, 'Over de grens: zwarte, migranten en vluchtelingenvrouwen in het debat over multiculturaliteit' ('Over the border: black, migrant and refugee women in the debate on multiculturality'), in: R. HOLTMAAT, supra n. 22, 41-57; R. RÖMKENS, 'Geweld tegen vrouwen en het debat over multiculturaliteit' ('Violence against women and the debate on multiculturality'), in: R. HOLTMAAT, supra n. 22, 57-71.

[24] RÖMKENS, *ibid.,* 23, 47; she discusses *'ambiguïteit in politieke overwegingen' ('ambiguity in political considerations').*

claim on equality with its claim of sexual self-determination of girls and women contained within it.[25]

When intervention on FGM outside the Western world is concerned, the legitimacy of such claims on equality should be judged within that context.[26] But then too, as Funder observed, the debate should centre on the dichotomy between the sexes and not be phrased in terms of sexually neutral comparisons:

'The outcry against stopping the practice, however, is a plea in the name of culture, not of women's moral fiber. The reason is that women's morality (that is, the control of men over women's sexuality, or measures taken uphold the notion that a "less sexual woman is more moral") is a barometer of cultural integrity: the extent of control over women measures the extent of control of the men, of traditional values, in the face of a potentially liberatory (and to that extent invasive) Western tradition'.[27]

3.3. In the best interest of the child?

There is also a third argument that calls for judicial intervention. From the perspective of human rights, restraint is normally observed regarding the domain of the family; the government's stance on this is to

---

25 GOLDSCHMIDT, supra n. 19, 788-790; Goldschmidt identifies the gravity of the violation as one of the factors which can form a limit for adjudication of a right to cultural self-determination as a consequence of equality.

26 Incidentally, my intention is not a territorial restriction of jurisdiction, but only a limitation of political intervention into circumcision elsewhere, particularly in non-Western countries. Not only would such a limitation of national jurisdiction not be in accordance with the foundation of judicial authority (Arts. 2-5 Dutch Penal Code (DPC)), at the same time it would impede effectively combating FGM in the country of origin. In any case, the circumcisions of many girls who reside in the Netherlands are commonly performed in other countries. A liberalisation of the national judicial authority via decline of the demand for double punishability, as pending in parliament, would seem more likely (Tweede Kamer (Dutch Lower House) 2003-2004, 29451, n. 2). Moreover, further liberalisation of judicial authority, analogous to Art. 5a DPC could be considered.

27 FUNDER, supra n. 14, 10. See also 11, *'The link between cultural autonomy and the autonomy of men over women is rarely drawn, but it has detrimental effects. Not the least of these is the reluctance of Western human right writers, for fear of claims of cultural imperialism, to criticise a cultural practice (for example, female genital mutilation). This is strategic misnaming: a cultural practice is in fact a culturally specific variant of the universal exercise of autocratic (that is patriarchal) power which holds sway in spheres of life where civil and political rights and equivalent standards of justice to those in civil society, do not apply'.* See also for the Dutch discussion H.WIERSINGA, 'Het beschavingsoffensief van de wetgever' ('The civilisation offensive of the legislator'), 2 *Recht en kritiek*, 2, 1997, 128-154 and from the same author: *Nuance in benadering* (*Nuance in approach*) (Deventer: Kluwer, 2002), dissertation Leiden University.

maintain a reserved distance (Article 8, paragraph 1 ECHR). When the circumcision of girls as requested by the parents or family members is concerned, however, another argument pertains; the best interest of the child. The actions of the legal representatives, the parents, must be measured by objective criteria, in service to that interest, in particular in the interest of health (Article 24, paragraph 3, Convention on the Rights of the Child).[28] The basic assumption is that the child is an autonomous legal subject that requires representation under the law so that its right to self-determination is respected.

In light of the mutilation, it cannot be argued that the irreversible character of FGM is beneficial to the health of the girl. As far as the right to self-determination is concerned, the situation is more complex. Clearly, the right to self-determination applies not only to sexuality but also to cultural identity. In fact, neither is respected in the case of FGM; the minor-aged girl is unable to adequately judge such consequential decisions.[29] What prevails is the parent's desire to transmit their right to cultural self-determination. This 'intrinsic interest', however, is not the same as the interest of the child; viewed objectively, such advocacy cannot be defended.

Moreover, here too the inviolability of the body, contained in law on physical and psychological integrity, should prevail over the right of cultural self-determination.[30] This is especially true where this cultural identity is based on a gendered standpoint, as in the case of a child of female sex. There can be no question of actual freedom of will or the self-determination to follow religious practices or cultural norms given the position of the girl, who is dependent in a number of ways. When assessed against the relevance criterion formulated by Veerman c.s., the results do not favour a cultural defence: the nature and scope of damage or potential damage to health, in conjunction with the effects of the adopted strategy in relation to the objective (safeguarding health) and the possibility of employing alternative means to attain the objective, impede due protection under the law.[31]

It may be observed that this does not exclude decriminalisation of the least harmful form of FGM.[32] Consistent with current opinion, however,

---

[28] VEERMAN, HENDRIKS & SMITH, supra n. 7, 151.

[29] VEERMAN, HENDRIKS & SMITH, *ibid.*, 150, where they refer to the *Nielsen v. Denmark* case, ECtHR 28 November 1990.

[30] Hoge Raad (Dutch Supreme Court), 1 July 1982.

[31] VEERMAN, HENDRIKS & SMITH, supra n. 7, 153-154.

[32] VEERMAN, HENDRIKS & SMITH, supra n. 7, 162; LIU, supra n. 7, 7. See also in this respect FUNDER, supra n. 14, 5, which points out that for minorities the right to cultural self-determination is coloured by an imperialistic past, which may provide occasion for a certain relaxing of the prohibition on FGM. See also K. BARTELS & I. HAAIJER, ''s Lands

the Dutch Government contends that this type of circumcision must also be considered indefensible; this viewpoint gives circumcision a sexually discriminatory character. Although the principle of this viewpoint can be supported, a different approach appears to undermine that support; other results are also plausible. That, however, leaves the conclusion intact, that the Dutch Government is prepared to take action against FGM on a number of grounds.

4. GENERALIS OR SPECIALIS?

Now that it has been established that the efforts of the Dutch Government to combat FGM are legitimate, the question arises as to what role a criminal procedure might play. In fact criminal justice already has jurisdiction here; FGM is punishable as (aggravated) physical abuse (Articles 300-303 Dutch Penal Code (DPC)). Where parents or legal guardians are involved, the penalty is increased (Article 304 DPC). Moreover, should the girl die as the result of circumcision, a case can be made for culpable homicide versus serious bodily harm (Articles 307-309 DPC).[33]

In any case, FGM is a punishable offence. However, enforcement is not an easy matter. The offence is committed in a closed family circle, to which police and criminal justice authorities do not have easy access. Those directly involved are unlikely to report violations to the police. The only chance of success would seem to be reports of violations from the medical and/or social service sectors, at least as far as professional codes of ethics do not prohibit this.[34] In addition it can be noted that

---

wijs, 's lands eer? Vrouwenbesnijdenis en Somalische vrouuen in Nederland' ('A country's way, a country's honour? Somali women in the Netherlands) (The Hague: Pharos, 1992) 113 and G. NIENHUIS, Knagen aan een oude traditie (Gnawing away at an old tradition) (The Hague: Pharos, 2004); the author refers to the recent evaluation of the prevention project 'Van beleid naar praktijk' ('From policy to practice'), from which it appears that many parents would like their daughters to undergo a lesser form of circumcision.

[33] The translation of the terms used in Arts. 300-304 and 307-309 DPC has been taken from LOUISE RAYAR AND STAFFORD WADSWORTH, The Dutch Penal Code, The American series of Foreign Penal Codes, vol. 30 (Littleton: Fred B. Rothman & co, 1997), ISBN 0-827700507.

[34] While most professional groups, including de Koninklijke Nederlandsche Maatschappij tot Bevordering der Geneeskunst (Dutch Society of medical practitioners), take the position that reporting is not compatible with the confidentiality of the therapist or care professional relationship, there are exceptions. See regarding these, Geneeskundige Hoofdinspectie van de Volksgezondheid, 'Informatie over vrouwenbesnijdenis' ('Information on female circumcision') (Rijswijk: GHIbulletin, 1994), where reporting is required.

reports are made on a voluntary basis, and as a rule come through the intermediary Advies- en Meldpunten Kindermishandeling (ChildLine).[35] Yet imagine that the police and the public prosecutor were to become aware of a circumcision or the likelihood of one. Would a specific provision for FGM ease their task? Opinions regarding this are divided. In its resolution on genital mutilation of women, the European Parliament has requested its Member States to regard FGM as *an offence*, a term which reveals no specific preference.[36] Neither does the need for supplementary legal measures referred to in the same resolution offer concrete criteria for the method of prosecution.

In the meantime, a number of Member States (such as Sweden, Austria, Belgium and the United Kingdom) have passed specific criminal provisions. An appeal for this has also been heard in other countries, specifically in the Dutch Parliament.[37] Conversely, the Dutch Government (as a whole) has taken the position that such a specific provision is not desirable.[38] However, considering the legitimacy of introducing a specific provision regarding FGM, an awareness of the different types of specific provisions is required. One can create a new legal provision, or prefer to attach a new paragraph to a regular legal provision qualifying FGM as a specific variant of (child) abuse, justifying increased maximum sentences. As the current debate concentrates on the question whether or not the introduction of a new legal provision is legitimate, alternatives should also be taken into account. Bearing this in mind, what are the arguments for and against such a specific provision?

---

[35] Here there is a significant difference to the French practice, where pursuant to Art. 434-3 Code Penal it is a *duty* to report violations, also for the medical sector. At the same time an exception to professional secrecy is made (Art. 226-13 Code Penal). For comparison: Art. 458bis Belgian Penal Code specifies the *right* to report violations, in which the report should be made directly to the public prosecutor.

[36] European Parliament, *'Resolutie van het Europese Parlement over genitale verminking van vrouwen'* ('Resolution of the European Parliament on the genital mutilation of women') (2001/2035(INI) (Strasbourg, 20 September 2001), consideration 11.

[37] See regarding this, Tweede Kamer (Dutch Lower House) 2003-2004, 22894, 23, motion Arib. Furthermore: TK 2003-2004, 29200 XVI, 231, 10; A. HIRSI ALI, *Voorstel tot het invoeren van een controlesysteem ter bestrijding van genitale verminking (Proposal for the adoption of a monitoring system to combat genital mutilation)* (The Hague: VVD political party, 2004) and B. DITTRICH, 'De strafbaarstelling van vrouwenbesnijdenis' ('Penalisation for female circumcision'), *Proces*, 4, 2003, 202-204.

[38] Tweede Kamer (Dutch Lower House) 2003-2004, 29200 XVI, 231, 8. The Government comes to this conclusion on the basis of the investigative report by VAN DER KWAAK, C.S.; A. VAN DER KWAAK, E. BARTELS, F. DE VRIES AND S. MEUWESE, *'Strategieën ter voorkoming van meisjesbesnijdenis, inventarisatie en aanbevelingen' (Strategies for the prevention of girls' circumcision, inventorisation and recommendations)* (The Hague: Ministry of Health, Welfare and Sport, 2003).

4.1. Arguments against a specific provision

4.1.1. Subsidiarity and symbolic legislation

The basic premise is that criminal justice is *ultimum remedium*. That necessitates a critical attitude in regard to the adoption of specific provisions; if general provisions are adequate, specific provisions should not be set. Care must be taken to avoid the expansion of criminal justice, certainly where insufficient efforts have been made to enforce existing provisions.[39] It is clear that FGM falls under the designation of the general provisions regarding (premeditated and/or aggravated) physical abuse (Articles 300-303 DPC). The adoption of a specific provision, therefore, would not seem self-evident. Taken together with the problem of detection discussed above, a specific provision is likely to be seen as symbolic legislation.[40] Thus, criminal law will miss the mark. Moreover, while the symbolic function of specific provisions cannot be denied, the purpose of such provisions is enforcement. From this rationalistic viewpoint, symbolic legislation is to be avoided.

Another corresponding objection is that a criminal, repressive reaction can only be the last resort in a nuanced approach, aimed at education and prevention. A specific provision will emphasise the criminality of FGM and may thus trigger criminalisation and stigmatisation of the target group, which is likely to lead to the practices 'going underground' and decrease the chance of prevention.

4.1.2. The exception needs no rule?

Another question concerns the defence for such a specific provision; is it necessary to make such an exception? A good interpretation of the purpose of criminal justice implies an allowance for minority opinions. The purpose of criminal law and the law in general is of course to serve the emancipation of the individual, which also includes the right to one's own cultural identity. From the perspective of equality and the respect associated with it, criminal law recognises a principle of openness from which justice can be done to the cultural identity of the individual.[41] Assuming that the general provision is formulated in such a way that it

---

[39] E. BARTELS, A. VAN DER KWAAK AND H. BARTELS, 'Meisjesbesnijdenis in justitieel perspectief' ('Girls' circumcision from a judicial perspective'), in: *Proces*, 2002, 52.

[40] See for the finding that a specific provision leads to problems of evidence, WHO, Department of Women's Health, Health System and Community Health, Female,*'Genital Mutilation. Programmes to date: What works and what doesn't. A review'* (Geneva, 1999).

[41] 'T HART, supra n. 20, 205.

makes allowances for such open interpretation, it is neither the specific nor the general character of the provision, but the basic attitude in which this is applied, which determines the degree to which justice is done in regard to minority opinions.[42] From this viewpoint the adoption of a specific provision cannot be defended, nor is it necessary. That implies no misunderstanding of the right to cultural self-determination, but is the logical result of a *consequent implementation of the individual approach of the law*[43] within which the interest of the individual is weighed against that of society. The interests of society, however, demand a certain defining of the limits of the principle of openness practised within criminal law.[44] The boundary lies where – as in the case of FGM – damage is done to the equality of individuals, specifically where there is evidence of a misunderstanding of human rights.

Another corresponding argument against the adoption of a specific provision is the accompanying risk of fragmentation of society. Who determines whether and why a specific provision is justified in a particular case? What will prevent other groups with just as many justifiable minority positions to negotiate specific provisions in criminal law? Here an unacceptable risk of the erosion of legal protection arises.

4.2. Arguments in favour of a specific provision

4.2.1. Legality: signalling function and fitting retribution

Judged by the criteria of the Criminal Penal Code, FGM is child abuse. However, parents who allow their daughters to be circumcised would not term it so. To the contrary, they experience circumcision as being in the best interests of their daughter. Here, two judicial options present themselves. First one could state that the parents' behaviour is not unlawful. It does not respond to the tenor of the legal provision, therefore the so-called *Typizität* is missing. The cutting of the female genitals symbolises a positive action aimed at the transmission of the girl towards adulthood enabling her to become a full member of the group. In this respect, the circumcision does not correspond to the legal concept of physical abuse, which implies intent to violate the physical integrity. Therefore, the circumcision cannot be qualified as an assault, as a result of which an acquittal should follow. However, as such an appeal reflects personal cultural beliefs, it is not likely to be accepted.

---

[42] 'T HART, *ibid.*, 217-218.

[43] 'T HART, *ibid.*, 247.

[44] MEERSCHAUT & BACKS, supra n. 20; 'T HART, *ibid.*, 242.

A second option is to appeal for a miscarriage of justice. The parents have erred concerning the criminality of the circumcision, something which is understandable, given that against their cultural background they do not experience this as physical abuse. There is no evidence of acting in an unlawful manner in the sense of Article 300 and according to the Dutch Penal Code of Procedure (DPC). According to Article 350, Dutch Penal Code of Procedure such an appeal should result in a discharge from prosecution.

Now one can push such a defence aside with the argument that the provisions are clear enough; the parents' ignorance of the unlawfulness of FGM is no excuse. However, that argumentation would seem to be too simple; the target group are after all immigrants. Can the same demands be made on the legal consciousness of the citizen, where *imported crimes*[45] are concerned as when regular crimes are concerned? Specific provisions should send a clear signal, whereby justice is done to the responsibility of the legislator to set clear standards (*lex certa*-principle, Article 1 DPC).

Connected to this is the question of where such a specific provision for FGM should be placed in the Penal Code. Looking at the current legal system, placement in title XX, concerning 'Physical abuse', would seem the most appropriate place. But another option would be the placement in title XIV, dealing with 'Indecency'. The argument that the target group (members of an ethnic minority) do not experience FGM as an act of abuse, lends support to this idea. Classification of the act as assault or infliction of grievous bodily harm can be seen as an attack on that particular group, something which may increase the appeal for a specific cultural identity and the associated practices may thus be driven further into illegality. Placing specific provisions on for example, title XIV could contribute to the prevention of such undesirable stigmatisation. The 'Indecency' cited there, after all, has to do with standards of moral decency, which is understood also as proper care for the child (Articles 252 and 253 DPC).[46]

4.2.2. Subsidiarity from the other side

It has been stated above that a specific provision brings the risk of fragmentation of society or of criminal justice. But is this really the case? After all, a specific provision for FGM does not imply any impunity; it

---

[45] Tweede Kamer (Dutch Lower House of Parliament) XVI, 231, 7; the term comes from Minister Hoogervorst.

[46] KOOL, Tekst en Commentaar Strafrecht, Titel XIV, 'Inleidende opmerkingen', aantekening 1 (Text and Commentary on Criminal Law, Title XIV, 'Introductory remarks', note 1).

only creates a shift of emphasis engendered by meeting the need of minority groups for the right of cultural self-determination. Now that the views of minority groups do not justify impunity, should we not consider from the principle of open-mindedness, whether the cultural dilemma faced by minority groups due to the general provision can be solved in another way or at least eased? In the case of FGM, although a specific provision may not bring the desired impunity, it may be able to remove the stigma of abuse and perhaps create a lesser punishment.

An associated argument is that by doing so a *more fitting reprisal* right will be offered.[47] After all, if the provision can be formulated in a way that is acceptable to the target group, the moral appeal embedded within it is more likely to serve its purpose and in the process, a certain acceptance of the provision and its enforcement can be created within the minority group. Such an endorsement of the penal standard does require an accompanying policy aimed at the education of the target group. If this is missing, the foundation for legitimacy has been officially fulfilled, but the material implementation will remain inadequate.[48]

4.2.3. Reduced scope for pursuing a cultural defence?

An 'accompanying' advantage is also that the process appears to place limits on the pursuance of a cultural defence. By formulating a clear provision, leaving no place for cultural considerations, the scope for a cultural defence and with it psychological circumstances beyond one's control, becomes limited. This offers the potential offender, with the enlistment of the aid of the legal standard, an instrument to resist the culturally-determined appeal to allow FGM to be performed. It is then, after all, not one's personal moral judgement that influences the decision against the circumcision, but the penalty and the accompanying threat of sanctions by the Dutch legislator.

In the process, a counter-balance is also offered to the increasing use of justification due to psychological circumstances beyond one's control (Article 40 DPC), as a legal interpretation of cultural defence. In practice, such a defence is hardly ever accepted; the accused is nearly always viewed as having had the opportunity to abstain from the challenged acts, or at least to have been able to devise a less-intrusive alternative.[49] Regarding the circumcision of girls there would seem to be no other test

---

47 BARTELS, VAN DER KWAAK AND BARTELS, supra n. 40, 52.

48 See among others DITTRICH, supra n. 38, in which he proposes the use of paid Somali confidential advisors.

49 C. KELK AND R.S.B. KOOL, '(Psychische) overmacht' ('Psychiatric circumstances beyond one's control'), *Delikt en Delinkwent*, column on Rechtspraak (Jurisprudence), 2004, 8, 100-109.

possible; the pain and suffering of the parents as the result of their inability to fulfil the cultural demands of the group clearly cannot prevail over the unlawful, sexually discriminating violation of the physical and emotional integrity of their daughter, along with the attendant pain and suffering.

5. A VIEW OF THE PRACTICE: A BRIEF LEGAL COMPARISON

Apart from the considerations of legal theory and legal politics described above, the question can be posed as to whether the adoption of a specific provision will benefit enforcement. In order to formulate an initial answer to this question, a short legal comparison follows. What can a comparison of the generally-formulated Article 303 DPC and the *specialis* formulated in Article 409 of the Belgian Penal Code (BPC) generate? For the scope of this paper, I will limit myself at least as far as possible, to a few sections/paragraphs from both provisions.

Article 303 section 1 DPC states:

Premeditated aggravated physical abuse is punishable by a term of imprisonment of not more than twelve years or a fine of the fifth category

Article 409 paragraph 1 Belgian Penal Code (BPC) states:

(S)he that performs, enables or facilitates any form of mutilation on the genitals of a person of the female sex, with or without her permission, is punishable by imprisonment of three to five years

5.1. Rationale and scope

The aim of Article 409 BPC is to make FGM an offence in *an unambiguous manner*.[50] Given the consequences of FGM for the emotional health and development of the girls and women who would be circumcised, such a specific provision is considered appropriate. The case is strengthened because it not only concerns a single circumcision but also has influence on the surrounding group. Thus Article 409 BPC also pertains to *those in the circuit* who organize the performance of FGM on a relatively large scale, when necessary in other countries. In the fifth paragraph, a broad statement of responsibility is formulated resembling that which is

---

[50] Belgian House of Representatives, *Wetsontwerp betreffende de strafrechtelijke bescherming van minderjarigen (Bill on the criminal protection of minors)*, 1907/1-98/99, 4 January 1999, explanatory memorandum, S- 5372, 15, Art. 21. It should be noted that this amendment constituted a direct reaction to the Dutroux affair and therefore was sharply focussed on the protection of juveniles.

formulated in Article 249 DPC. Both statements express the spirit of care for the minor child, or of a person dependent on the offender. The scope of the functional responsibility laid down in Article 409 BPC is quite broad. Thus the dependence required does not need to have a judicial foundation; evidence of a concrete dependent relationship – even if of short duration – is adequate.[51]

Article 303 DPC makes the deliberate infliction of serious bodily harm a punishable offence. In Article 82 DPC, harm is taken to mean that which cannot be fully recovered or that which causes incapacity for work; purely psychological damage does not meet this requirement.[52] It is up to the judge to determine what can be understood as serious bodily harm; it is likely that the most severe forms of FGM would fall into this category. Of further relevance is the relation between 303 and the aggravated circumstances formulated in Article 304 sub 1 DPC; if the crime is committed against a child, the punishment may be increased by one-third. Here, the legislator has formulated functional responsibility in a way similar to Article 409 paragraph 5 BPC, however, with the provision that this is limited to offenders who are legally related to the child.

5.2. Mutilation vs. aggravated physical abuse: illegality as a component

A second point of comparison is offered by the component *mutilation* ex Article 409 BPC and the component *aggravated physical abuse* ex Article 303 DPC. In both provisions, the legislator has not found it necessary to explicitly exempt medical procedures.[53]
In both descriptions of the offence, illegality is expressed in the level of the components and must therefore, be proven by the public prosecutor. For Article 409 BPC, this is derived from the component *mutilation*; the component does not refer to *minor damage* of the genitals, but to more severe forms of damage. The same normative connotation is expressed

---

51 Art. 409 para 5 Belgian Penal Code states:
  'In para. 1 if the intended mutilation of a minor or a person that by reason of his/her physical or emotional condition is incapable of providing for him/herself, is carried out by his/her father, mother or other blood relation in the ascending line, or by any other person who has authority over the minor or incapable person, or by a person who has him/her under remand, or by a person who occasionally or habitually resides with the victim, the minimum punishment listed in para. 1 to 4 is doubled in the case of imprisonment and extended by two years in the case of confinement'.

52 WEMES/CLEIREN AND NIJBOER, *Tekst en Commentaar Strafrecht (Text and Commentary on Criminal Law)*, Article 82, notes 1 and 2.

53 Belgian House of Representatives, supra n. 51, 16; NOYON/LANGEMEIJER/REMMELINK, *Het Wetboek van Strafrecht (Criminal Law Statute Book)*, Article 300 DPC, note 1a.

by the component *aggravated physical abuse* stated in Article 303 section 1 DPC: it must be proven that the act, one is accused of, is in conflict with the objective law.[54]

A difference can be seen in Article 409 para.1 BPC, which expressly determines that consent of the woman or girl to undergo FGM does not lead to impunity; the act remains unlawful. In the Dutch legal system, consent may lead to acquittal as the behaviour is not unlawful for reason of not responding to the tenor of the legal provision (*Typizität*).

The question is whether the woman has been able to give her consent freely or whether she is in a position of dependence. In the case of a child, consent is legally irrelevant, due to her lack of legal capacity to act. At the utmost, consent of the child might be seen as a basis for reduced sentencing, but even this seems doubtful. The same observation can be made regarding the consent of the woman; if the judge is of the opinion that this consent does not negate the illegality, he or she can take this into consideration in determining the sentence.

5.3. The nature of the damage

Another significant difference is that the *mutilation* ex Article 409 BPC would seem to encompass a less serious form of damage than the *aggravated physical abuse* in ex Article 303 DPC. Clearly, if the mutilation results in an apparently incurable illness or incapacity for work, the sentence may be increased on the basis of the third paragraph.[55] There is no evidence of such exceptional circumstances allowing increased sentencing in Article 303 DPC. Although the article refers to *aggravated physical abuse* and not to *serious bodily harm* the meaning of Article 82 DPC can be applied here too; Article 303 is after all a graver variant of Article 302 DPC.[56] The component *aggravated physical abuse* therefore demands the incurable (appearing) illness and incapacity for work already mentioned in Article 409 paragraph 3 BPC as a circumstance for increased sentencing. What does this difference in wording mean with regard to the burden of proof for the public prosecutor? There can be no argument concerning the mutilating nature of the most severe forms of FGM; it concerns irreversible procedures that lead to severe damage of the female sexual organs. It is sufficient for the Belgian public prosecutor

---

[54] J. DE HULLU, *Materieel strafrecht (Material penal law)* (Deventer: Gouda Quint, 2003) 183.

[55] Art. 409 para. 3 BPC states:
If the mutilation has caused an apparently incurable illness or chronic incapacity to work, the punishment is five to ten years.

[56] CLEIREN AND NIJBOER, *Tekst en Commentaar Strafrecht (Text and Commentary on Criminal Law)*, Article 303, note 1.

to produce a medical report showing evidence of such damage.[57] If there is such damage, an increase in sentencing listed in paragraph 3 can be charged and the evidence for this should be presented. That is not the case for the Dutch public prosecutor, who must prove that there is evidence of *aggravated physical abuse*: there must be evidence of such severe damage, that there is no chance of full recovery or similar serious harm. The burden of proof on the grounds of generic provisions therefore would seem to be heavier for the Dutch public prosecutor in comparison to the Belgian variant.

Incidentally, as regards both provisions it is unclear whether they pertain to the lesser form of FGM, the circumcision. That procedure involves only a small incision of the clitoris, something which would not appear to be categorised as *mutilation or aggravated physical abuse* ex Article 303 section 1 DPC.

5.4. Mutilation vs. premeditation

There is rather a difference in wording, particularly in the requirement of intent. In the Belgian definition this is contained in the component *mutilation*, whereas in the Dutch definition the intent is stated separately in the form of *premeditated*. In both cases, there is evidence of acting with intent in the sense that a conscious, intentional act is committed. For the appropriateness of Article 303 DPC, however, it is relevant that this should be in the form of a malicious plan; it must be proven that the suspect deliberately and knowing, in conflict with objective law has caused serious bodily harm in the form of FGM. According to Art. 409 BPC, it is sufficient to show likely cause that the accused at least had accepted that there was a considerable chance of mutilating the victim. In other words, conditional intent is sufficient. Clearly, here too the burden of proof weighs heavier for the Dutch public prosecutor.

5.5. Another comparison: Article 303 DPC vs. Article 409 BPC

One could dispute the comparison above, by observing that it is not Article 303 DPC, but Article 302 DPC that would seem to be the most likely rule to compare to Article 409 BPC. My choice for Article 303 DPC, however, is prompted by the relationship with Article 304 DPC in which conditions for heavier sentencing are included if the circumcision is performed on a child. In view of *Cleiren* and *Nijboer* there is evidence of a

---

[57] It is evident that there are problems linked to collecting evidence, but that can remain peripheral consideration in the scope of this legal comparison directed toward penalisation.

mutual bond, which justifies the primary choice for Article 303 as a comparative article.[58]

Nevertheless, a comparison between Article 302 DPC as the most appropriate article for the prosecution of FGM, and Article 409 BPC is also an option. Therefore, a brief legal comparison between the two definitions follows, so that it can be determined whether an indictment based on Article 302 DPC removes a number of the objections listed above as regards Article 303 DPC.[59] The text of the law is stated below for review.

Article 302 paragraph 1 DPC states:

A person who intentionally inflicts serious bodily harm on another person is guilty of aggravated physical abuse and is liable to a term of imprisonment of not more than eight years or a fine of the eighth category.

5.5.1. Presumption of illegality

The drawback of the public prosecutor having to prove the unlawfulness stated in Article 303 DPC is irrelevant here (*Typizität*). There is no question of abuse, the task is to objectively determine the deliberate infliction of serious bodily harm; illegality is presumed. If the suspect believes to have acted in a warranted manner it is his/her responsibility to produce evidence of such. Other than is the case for Article 303 DPC in relation to Article 409 BPC, the public prosecutor here has no burden of proof. Compared to the Belgian definition, there is thus a lighter burden of proof for the Dutch public prosecutor.

5.5.2. The nature of the damage

Concerning the nature of the damage the comparison is on level-pegging. The damage denoted in Article 302 DPC, just as that in Article 303 DPC, should be viewed in relation to Article 82 DPC. The difference in both definitions does not lie in the nature of inflicted damage, but in the intention of the act. Therefore, it remains true that the burden of proof for the Dutch public prosecutor on the basis of the generic definition weighs heavier than that of his Belgian colleague on the basis of the specific provision.

---

[58] CLEIREN AND NIJBOER, *Tekst en Commentaar Strafrecht*, Artikel 303, aantekening 1 (*Text and Commentary on Criminal Law*), Article 303, note 1.

[59] Actually, no choice is necessary. The public prosecutor can choose a principle/alternative indictment based on Art. 303 or Art. 302 DPC.

5.5.3. Intent as key argument

As stated, the difference between Articles 302 and 303 DPC lies in the requirement set for intent. For Article 302 DPC, proof that the accused has acted deliberately is sufficient, in the sense of a minimal awareness of the acceptance of a considerable likelihood. As we know, this requirement for intent does not correspond to the intention of the offender; the criminal intent is neutral. The situation is different in Article 303 DPC. The committing of *premeditated aggravated physical abuse* cannot be other than intentional; one acts in full awareness of the 'wrongfulness' of his/her act. The full awareness of the unlawful character of the action that is expressed in the premeditation, in conjunction with the 'wrongfulness' of the act, must be proven by the public prosecutor. For Article 409 BPC the same demand pertains, though to a lesser degree: the Belgian public prosecutor must prove that there is evidence of *mutilation*, which implies a deliberate unlawful act. The difference in the burden of proof pertaining to Article 302 DPC therefore does not lie in the intent alone, but in the direct relation between the intent and the unlawfulness that is expressed in the component *mutilation*. For that reason, on the basis of Article 409 BPC, a heavier burden of proof lies on the Belgian public prosecutor as far as intent is concerned, than for his/her Dutch colleague on the basis of Article 302 DPC. However, this advantage on the Dutch side should be somewhat qualified. In light of that, which in the sense of Article 409 BPC must be understood as *mutilation of the person of the female gender*, there would appear to be little argument as to the required intent on the basis of the facts. The nature of the procedure performed is such that any misinterpretation of the intent would be difficult to imagine.

6. CONCLUSION

It is time for a conclusion. What can the above teach us? Concerning the legal comparison made in section 5, the conclusion must be drawn that no definitive answer can be given to the question as to whether a specific provision offers sufficient practical advantages to warrant its adoption on those grounds. Prosecution relevant to FGM could be principally based on Article 303 DPC and alternatively as a violation of Article 302 DPC, both in connection with Article 304 sub 1 DPC, if appropriate. The weight of the burden of proof for the first definition and the possible failure in this matter can be overcome by an alternative indictment. Compared to the Belgian definition, when the advantages and disadvantages in such a case are weighed against each other, a specific provision offers no clear judicial advantages. However, this does not exclude the possibility of adding a new paragraph to Articles 300-303 DPC, justifying increased maximum sentences in the case of FGM.

Moreover, if the normative, symbolic function of criminal justice is considered, the adoption of a specific provision is desirable. It has been argued that FGM seriously violates the equality between the sexes, substantiated in severe damage to physical and psychological integrity. From a Western perspective, the protection of this integrity should prevail over claims of cultural self-determination, certainly where there is evidence of gendered cultural traditions.

This does not mean, however, that criminal law should be insensitive to the cultural dilemmas placed before minority groups arising from provisions. Such considerations, however, should not lead to an erosion of the moral values which are fundamentally respected within Western society and elsewhere, expressed in criminal provisions which are supported by majority opinions. It is here that the adoption of a specific provision may be able to provide a degree of latitude to soften the pain of the cultural dilemma. Doing so, admittedly, will not remove its penal nature, but by no longer defining FGM as 'ordinary' physical abuse and perhaps even to categorise it as a moral offence, one reduces the stigma attached to the act. Moreover, penalisation as a moral offence offers those involved a certain egress to defend their opposition to the moral values of their own group, while enlisting the aid of the 'Dutch' norm. This, admittedly, implies short-term thinking. What we in fact are trying to achieve is that minority groups arrive at a rejection of FGM on the basis of their own convictions. This, however, requires long-term thinking, with an accompanying policy aimed at education and prevention. As far as criminal law is concerned 'for the time being' we may be content with less and take satisfaction from the introduction of a specific provision, preferably by adding a new paragraph to Articles 300-303 DPC.

IF HOME IS NO HAVEN: WOMEN'S RIGHT TO ADEQUATE HOUSING IN CASES OF DOMESTIC VIOLENCE

Ingrid Westendorp

1. INTRODUCTION

In theory, the right to adequate housing and the right to privacy are individual rights. In practice, however, these rights may be regarded and dealt with as rights of families in spite of the fact that worldwide, numerous cases of domestic violence occur, affecting the enjoyment of these rights for women (and children).[1]

In this chapter firstly, the elements that constitute an adequate housing situation, will be discussed. One of the elements determining adequacy is security. International protection of the right to housing focuses on threats from outside, particularly with respect to forced evictions by States and third parties. In cases of domestic violence, however, the threat comes from inside. The effect of domestic violence on the adequacy of the housing will be looked into as well as the rules that protect the privacy of the home, that withhold the authorities to interfere. The question 'why many women stay in situations of domestic violence and why they need help' will be answered.

Furthermore, the responsibility of the State in situations of domestic violence will be dealt with. States have a duty to uphold individual human rights and to prevent violations. If prevention fails and domestic violence has occurred, States must interfere. As far as protection of the right to adequate housing of the victim is concerned, there are two possibilities for immediate relief; eviction of the perpetrator from the family home or temporary shelter for the victim. Advantages and disadvantages of both possibilities will be discussed. Finally, the duty to award reparations will be examined.

2. ADEQUATE HOUSING CONDITIONS

Within the context of international human rights protection, the most pertinent provision dealing with the right to adequate housing is Article

---

[1] Although I acknowledge that children, too have a right to adequate housing and therefore are entitled to live in safety and dignity just like adults, the focus of this paper is solely on the housing rights of women.

11(1) of the International Covenant on Economic, Social and Cultural Rights (ICESCR).[2] The Committee on Economic, Social and Cultural Rights (CESCR) has further interpreted this Article and clarified the meaning of adequate housing in its General Comment no. 4.[3] According to the CESCR, the adequacy of a housing situation is determined by security of tenure, availability of services, habitability, affordability, accessibility, location and cultural adequacy. That this right is meant to be an individual right for women and men may be inferred from the fact that Article 11(1) accords the rights contained in this provision to *everyone* while Articles 2(2) and 3 deal with the prohibition as to discrimination based on sex and equality between women and men respectively.[4] In addition to these aspects that determine the adequacy of a housing condition, it is understood that home should be a safe haven; a place where a person can live in security and dignity. The element of security of tenure is focused, however, on threats and dangers from the outside; emphasis is placed on being protected against forced evictions and harassment both by the authorities and by third parties.[5] Moreover, tenants are to be protected against landlords who demand exorbitant rents that might exceed the affordability of the housing.[6]

A right that is closely connected to the right to housing is the right to privacy. This right belongs to the category of civil and political rights. It is a right that imposes a negative obligation on the State because it entails the right of citizens to be let alone and thus the authorities should back off and not interfere with the private sphere of individuals.[7]

---

2   Art. 11(1) of the International Covenant on Economic, Social and Cultural Rights recognizes that everyone has the right to an adequate standard of living [...] including [...] housing.

3   General Comment no. 4, the right to adequate housing (art. 11(1)), 1991, UN Doc. E/1992/23.

4   Art. 2(2) of the ICESCR reads: 'The States Parties to the present Covenant undertake to guarantee that the rights enunciated in the present Covenant will be exercised without discrimination of any kind as to [...] sex [...]'. Art. 3 determines: 'The States Parties to the present Covenant undertake to ensure the equal right of men and women to the enjoyment of all economic, social and cultural rights set forth in the present Covenant'.

5   Forced evictions are to be understood as the removal against their will of people from their homes and/or land without legal or other protection. The concept does not cover situations where forceful evictions are carried out in conformity with the provisions of the ICESCR, *i.e.* in cases of persistent non-payment of rent. General Comment no. 7, on the right to adequate housing; forced evictions, 1997, UN Doc. E/C.12/1997/4, paras. 4 and 12.

6   General Comment no. 4, supra n. 3, para. 8(c) on affordability.

7   Already in 1890 Samuel Warren and Louis Brandeis characterized the right to privacy as 'the right to be let alone'; they assumed that the right to isolate oneself from the

However, since the State should ensure respect for this right, it will also entail the positive obligation to protect individuals from interference of their privacy by third parties.[8] Besides operating vertically, *i.e.* in the relationship between the State and the individual, the right also operates horizontally, *i.e.* in relationships between individual citizens.[9]

The scope of the right to privacy is rather broad.[10] The exact contents may vary, but it comprises among other rights the right to respect the privacy of the home, family life, to live as one wishes, correspondence and telephone conversations, protection of honour and reputation, and the right to protection of personal data. In the framework of this paper the right to the privacy of the home and flowing from this, the right to live as one wishes are particularly important. That is why the focus will only be on these two aspects of the right to privacy.

The essence and the importance of privacy protection of the home is aptly put in an age-old English proverb that says that 'An Englishman's home is his castle'.[11] At home the individual is supposed to be free; saying and doing whatever she or he likes without running the risk of interference.

In most countries, both criminal and civil laws will ensure that individuals do not have to tolerate interference of their privacy either by the authorities or by third parties, unless in a restricted number of legally defined instances. Internationally, the right to privacy is protected by Article 12 of the Universal Declaration[12] and Article 17 of the

---

public sphere was 'sacred'. Later scholars called the right to privacy an 'inalienable right'. AMITAI ETZIONI, *The Limits of Privacy* (New York: Basic Books, 1999) 190.

8   HENRY J. STEINER, PHILIP ALSTON, *International Human Rights in Context; Law, Politics, Morals*, 2nd ed. (Oxford: Oxford University Press, 2000) 181-183. The Dutch Government *e.g.* declared in 1984 that in light of Arts. 8 European Convention on Human Rights and Fundamental Freedoms (ECHR) and 17 ICCPR it considered it her duty to protect the right to privacy of its citizens also against third parties. LUCAS VERHEY, *Horizontale werking van grondrechten, in het bijzonder van het recht op privacy* (Zwolle: Tjeenk Willink, 1992) 405.

9   As acknowledged for instance by the Human Rights Committee in its General Comment no. 16, the right to respect of privacy, family, home and correspondence, and protection of honour and reputation (Art. 17), 1988, UN Doc. A/46/38, para. 1.

10   The scope of what is considered to be a matter of privacy varies not only among countries, societies and cultures, but also changes during the course of time. ETZIONI, supra n. 7, 202.

11   At the same time it is also proof of age-old gender bias, since it reflects the cultural idea of the *pater familias* who is the master of his home and rules over wife and children, practically untouchable within his own four walls. Also see RHONDA. COPELON, 'Intimate Terror: Understanding Domestic Violence as Torture', in: REBECCA J. COOK (ed.), *Human Rights of Women, National and International Perspectives* (Philadelphia: University of Pennsylvania Press, 1994) 132-133.

12   Art. 12 Universal Declaration of Human Rights reads: 'No one shall be subjected to arbitrary interference with his privacy, family, home or correspondence, nor to attacks

International Covenant on Civil and Political Rights (ICCPR).[13] Similar to the provisions in the ICESCR, Articles 2(1) and 3 of the ICCPR prohibit discrimination based on sex and demand equality between women and men.[14]

3. THREATS FROM THE INSIDE

Regardless of the level of development or the cultural or religious background, domestic violence is prevalent in all countries around the world.[15] The adjective 'domestic' is not understood in a narrow way. It is not restricted to the home, but it encompasses the immediate environment of the victim.[16] Thus, the perpetrators may be parents, husbands, wives, in-laws, children, house friends, superiors or any other person who has an intimate relationship with the battered person. Victims may be children, women, men, parents, the elderly, the sick, the disabled, subordinates or any other person in a more or less dependent relationship. The most common of all these abusive relationships is, however, a man abusing his wife or female partner.[17] An explanation for the fact that this type of domestic violence occurs so frequently is that woman battering is common both in rich and poor countries, in all layers of society.[18] The UN Centre for Social Development and Humanitarian Affairs defines domestic violence as:

---

upon his honour and reputation. Everyone has the right to the protection of the law against such interference or attacks'.

13 Art. 17 of the ICCPR: (1) 'No one shall be subjected to arbitrary or unlawful interference with his privacy, family, home or correspondence, nor to unlawful attacks on his honour and reputation. (2) Everyone has the right to the protection of the law against such interference or attacks'.

14 Art. 2(1) of the ICCPR provides: 'Each State Party to the present Covenant undertakes to respect and to ensure to all individuals within its territory and subject to its jurisdiction the rights recognized in the present Covenant, without distinction of any kind, such as [...] sex [...]. Art. 3 reads: 'The States Parties to the present Covenant undertake to ensure the equal right of men and women to the enjoyment of all civil and political rights set forth in the present Covenant'.

15 CHERYL THOMAS, 'Domestic Violence', in: KELLY D. ASKIN, DOREAN M. KOENIG (eds.), *Women and International Human Rights Law*, Vol.1 (Ardsley, New York: Transnational Publishers, Inc., 1999) 219. Also COPELON, supra n. 11, 117. Also, Preliminary report submitted by the Special Rapporteur on Violence Against Women, Ms Radhika Coomaraswamy, UN Doc. E/CN.4/1995/42, paras 120-121.

16 RADHIKA COOMARASWAMY, LISA M. KOIS, 'Violence Against Women', in: KELLY D. ASKIN, DOREAN M. KOENIG (eds.), *Women and International Human Rights Law*, Vol. 1, (Ardsley, New York: Transnational Publishers, Inc., 1999) 185.

17 COPELON, supra n. 11, 120. Also, UN Doc. E/CN.4/1995/42, para. 118.

18 Research in the Netherlands into the risk factors has shown that woman battering cannot be linked with any specific social class. Comparison with other countries indicates that the situation in this country fits in the general picture. RENÉE RÖMKENS,

'[...] *the use of force or threats of force by a husband or boyfriend for the purpose of coercing and intimidating a woman into submission. The violence can take the form of pushing, hitting, choking, slapping, kicking, burning or stabbing'.*[19]

Besides physical mistreatment 'violence' may also consist of psychological abuse like uttering threats to harm either the woman herself, her children or other relatives, using abusive language, humiliating or belittling women, also in front of others, and thus undermining their self-esteem.[20]

In most States, domestic violence is not regarded as a separate crime, but is incorporated in general offences such as assault or abuse.[21] In many criminal systems, however, a procedural distinction is made between assault committed by a stranger and by a family member. In the first case, the crime is regarded as grave and the perpetrator, if known, will be prosecuted. In the latter case, however, the crime may not be regarded as a serious offence but merely as a lovers' tiff.[22] Mostly, prosecution will

---

'Geweld in de Huiselijke Sfeer', in: I. BOEREFIJN, M. VAN DER LIET-SENDERS, T. LOENEN (red.), *Het voorkomen en bestrijden van geweld tegen vrouwen; Een verdiepend onderzoek naar het Nederlandse beleid in het licht van de verplichtingen die voortvloeien uit het Vrouwenverdrag* (Den Haag: Ministerie van Sociale Zaken en Werkgelegenheid, juli 2000) 111.
It is estimated that in the Netherlands at least 40 children die every year because of child abuse, whereas the number of women who die of the consequences of domestic violence is believed to be between 60 and 80. Child abuse seems to occur more frequently (though certainly not exclusively) in the socio-economically weaker sections of society. Partij van de Arbeid, *Stop Huiselijk Geweld!*, Manifest aangeboden aan de Minister van Justitie en de Minister van Binnenlandse Zaken op 9 mei 2000.

[19] UNITED NATIONS CENTRE FOR SOCIAL DEVELOPMENT AND HUMANITARIAN AFFAIRS, *Strategies for Confronting Domestic Violence: A Resource Manual* 7, 1993, ST/CSDHA/20.

[20] For a recount of several kinds of physical and psychological abuse common in the framework of domestic violence see COPELON, supra n. 11, 122-126.

[21] Examples are the Czech Republic, Hungary, Lithuania, Macedonia and the Netherlands. In the Netherlands, however, woman battering and child abuse may be regarded as aggravating circumstances meriting more severe sanctions. See Art. 304 of the Dutch Penal Code (*Wetboek van Strafrecht*).

[22] The reasoning may be that after all family members love each other and will never seriously harm each other. Moreover, the (female) victim is often blamed as much as the (male) perpetrator, and in police reports they may speak about a 'violent couple'.

only take place if the victim has lodged a complaint.[23] Information by relatives or other witnesses may not result in an investigation.[24]

The Special Rapporteur on Violence Against Women enumerates several causes of domestic violence that have been analyzed by the United Nations. These include alcohol and drug abuse and/or an abusive childhood of the perpetrator, provocative behaviour of the victim and economic and social factors such as inadequate housing, cultural factors and structural inequality. Inadequate housing conditions induced by unfavourable economic circumstances or overcrowded living spaces, trigger violent behaviour because they cause stress and frustration. However, since woman battering also takes place in well-to-do families, inadequate housing is not considered so much as a cause, but rather as an aggravating factor for domestic violence.[25] The same holds true for alcohol and drug abuse or the psychological predisposition of the perpetrator.

What is considered to be the most important cause for domestic violence is the perception of women as subordinate to men. Unequal power positions facilitate men's dominance and lead to subjugation of and discrimination against women.[26] The man of the house is traditionally the usual breadwinner and in return he may expect his wife to carry out certain duties. If she fails to carry them out properly, or if she rebels against this unequal power position, it is thought that she might expect

---

[23] Often, this complaint must be backed up with testimonies by witnesses, and extensive medical and forensic evidence. Countries that legally approach domestic violence in this way are for example Bulgaria (where domestic violence is called a 'private character crime'), Croatia (domestic violence is known as 'kitchen-violence'), Russia, and Turkey. INTERNATIONAL HELSINKI FEDERATION FOR HUMAN RIGHTS (IHF), *Women 2000* (Vienna: Agens-Werk, Geyer & Reissen, 2000) 115, 130, 381 and 455.

[24] Though in some countries it is possible or even compulsory that in cases of suspicion of child abuse, others such as relatives, physicians, teachers, and neighbours report this to the police, this is nowhere possible as regards woman battering. Reporting suspicion of child abuse is compulsory for example in the USA, while in the Netherlands, reporting takes place on a voluntary basis. However, the willingness to report child abuse is not very great in the Netherlands because people respect each other's right to privacy and are reluctant to interfere in family situations. See JAN WILLEMS, *Wie zal de Opvoeders Opvoeden? Kindermishandeling en het Recht van het Kind op Persoonsvording (Who will educate the educators? Child abuse and the right of the child to become a person)* (Den Haag: T.M.C. Asser Press, 1998) 545-554, particularly on 546.

[25] UN Doc. E/CN.4/1995/42, para. 119.

[26] THOMAS, supra n. 15, 249. Also RÖMKENS, supra n. 18, 119 and COPELON, supra n. 11, 121, where she points out that most studies of domestic violence come from modern countries that are supposed to have done away with patriarchal systems like the US and the UK. Coomaraswamy concurs with the view that the male patriarchal ideology is the main cause for domestic violence in her report of 10 March 1999, UN Doc. E/CN.4/1999/68, para. 31.

him to become violent. In many parts of the world the woman herself is blamed if she is being battered. It is believed that she must be a bad wife, because men do not beat for nothing.[27]

3.1. Effects on the right to housing

If a woman is battered in her own home, many of her rights are infringed. Most obvious is perhaps the violation of her right to physical integrity, and in extreme circumstances maybe even, the very right to life itself. A woman's mobility rights may be violated in cases where she is policed by her husband and forbidden to leave the house without his permission. Some women are virtual prisoners within their own homes. Living in constant fear of being molested turns home into a hell. Every 'wrong' step may trigger a bout of violence, though many times it will be unclear why fault was found. Indeed the 'punishment' could be randomly meted out at the whim of the perpetrator.[28] Living in such unsafe conditions will render the housing situation inadequate, no matter how habitable or luxurious the premises, and how well fitted up with every modern convenience, since the basic notions of living somewhere in peace, security and dignity are obliterated.

If the abuse causes the woman to leave, she may also be faced with inadequate housing. If she is not able to finance adequate housing herself, she may have to live in a shelter, or find a host home. This entails that she loses her freedom and becomes dependent on others. Her home is no longer her own space where she can keep house as she pleases. She will have to adapt, perhaps for the rest of her life. If she has an income, she may be able to secure a place to live, but since women's incomes are generally lower than men's, it will be difficult to obtain adequate housing because there is a world-wide lack of affordable housing, also in developed countries. Generally there are long waiting lists for subsidized housing.

Some women who fear for their lives may leave without any alternative and thus become homeless, although they are aware of the fact that living rough also presents many dangers.

---

[27] Very insightful in this regard is a report carried out by Human Rights Watch in Uzbekistan, entitled: *Sacrificing Women to Save the Family; Domestic Violence in Uzbekistan*, HRW Publications, Vol. 13, No. 4(D), July 2001. Particularly 15-18.

[28] See for instance COPELON, supra n. 11, 116-152.

3.2. Effects on the right to privacy

Although the privacy of the home may in many States be well protected against outside interference, it is not always recognized that this right may also be violated from the inside.[29] Home is regarded as sacred as far as family life is concerned; a place where all family members equally enjoy their privacy and where all are supposed to be equally averse to outside interference.[30] That is why the police will much sooner enter a house if inhabitants are suspected of trafficking drugs or weapons than when they have received a report of domestic violence. Whatever happens behind the front door between family members may in many States be regarded as a private or family matter in which they do not wish to interfere.[31] The fact that domestic violence is often categorized or treated as an offence that is to be prosecuted only in case a complaint has been lodged, contributes to the reluctance of the police to interfere, since the odds are that a woman will be coaxed or coerced by partners or family to drop the complaint.

In many States, complaints may be withdrawn at any stage with the effect that prosecution is stopped immediately, so that all police work would have been in vain.[32] In some States the police will not even come to the rescue if the victim does not promise beforehand to maintain the complaint.[33]

---

[29] For example, as far as the situation in the USA is concerned, the right to privacy is rather well protected from violation by the State, but the defense is weak against violations by non-State actors. ETZIONI, supra n. 7, 10.

[30] Typically, out of respect for the right to privacy, the State will wait taking action until the results of the acts that have happened behind the front door have become visible in the public sphere and can be backed up with evidence. ETZIONI, supra n. 7, 196 and 211. Sometimes there may already be several reports of abuse but the authorities will wait until serious harm has been done. *E.g.* in Bulgaria there is a policy of non-intervention unless the case is extremely serious. In Hungary the attitude of the police is to intervene only if 'blood is spilled'. In Lithuania the police intervene only in cases of serious bodily injury or murder. In Uzbekistan, the police will not investigate domestic violence unless it results in the victim's death. See: IHF, supra n. 23, 115, 206, 288 and 503 respectively.

[31] The police will regard domestic violence as a private or family matter and will subsequently not intervene *e.g.* in Bulgaria, Croatia, Czech Republic, Hungary, Kyrgyzstan, Lithuania, Macedonia, Romania, Slovakia, Tajikistan and Uzbekistan. IHF, supra n. 23, 115, 130, 148, 205, 244, 288, 309, 363, 404, 437 and 503.

[32] States where withdrawal of the complaint will immediately stop the procedure are for example Armenia, the Czech Republic, Lithuania, Poland, Slovakia and Ukraine. IHF, supra n. 23, at 45, 148, 288, 336, 403 and 487.

[33] This is for instance the case in Ukraine.

Non-interference is turning a blind eye to the fact that not all family members are equally empowered and capable of fulfilling their rights.[34] In cases of domestic violence and child abuse, the victim, contrary to the perpetrator, will need and benefit from outside interference and may gladly waive her or his right to privacy in order to be protected against physical violence. Respect for the privacy of the home and a subsequent policy of non-interference comes down to respecting the right to privacy of the perpetrator, while violating the right to privacy of the victim.[35]

3.3. Why do women stay?

What induces women to stay in a situation where their most basic rights are violated? The reasons may be practical, sociological and psychological. Many women who want to leave an abusive relationship simply have nowhere to go. They are economically dependent on their husband or male partner and the only alternative they may have is to live in the streets, facing all the health and violence hazards involved in that.[36] In many countries around the world, single women and divorcees in particular, face discrimination if they try to gain access to land and/or housing.[37] In a country like China most married couples live in a house that has been allocated by the husband's employer. That is why it is the woman who has to leave after the divorce and faced with homelessness.[38] In many States there are no shelters or an insufficient number of them.[39] It may be an option to return to the parental home or

---

[34] UN Doc. E/CN.4/1995, 42, para. 54.

[35] Rebecca Cook maintains that the fact that States allow women's rights to be violated at home contributes to the total subjugation of women. The authorities should not only defend women's rights in the public, but also in the private sphere. REBECCA COOK, 'Accountability in International Law for Violations of Women's Rights by Non-State Actors', in: DORINDA G. DALLMEYER (ed.), *Reconceiving Reality: Women and International Law* (Washington D.C.: The American Society of International Law, 1993) 94.

[36] Economic dependency is frequently mentioned as a reason to stay in spite of the recurring violence. Examples are Croatia, Lithuania, and Turkmenistan, IHF, supra n. 23, 130, 288 and 469 respectively.

[37] *E.g.* in Kazakhstan it is impossible for a woman to rent or buy a house. IHF, supra n. 23, 229.

[38] LEILANI FARHA, 'Women and Housing', in: KELLY D. ASKIN, DOREAN M. KOENIG (eds.), *Women and International Human Rights Law*, Vol. 1 (Ardsley, New York: Transnational Publishers, Inc., 1999) 516.

[39] A few examples: in Albania there is just one shelter, situated in Tirana and financed by a Women's NGO. In Lithuania there are 5 shelters, 2 of which are financed by the Government. Women may stay there up to 6 months. In Russia there are shelters in St. Petersburg and in several provincial cities, but none in Moscow. In Tajikistan there are no shelters at all. In Malaysia there are three shelters. In Canada the number of shelters has been considerably decreased due to expenditure cuts. See IHF, supra n. 23, 30, 289, 382 and 437; Report on the Regional Consultation on the 'Interlinkages between

live with other relatives, but this is certainly not an ideal situation if it is at all possible. Many families already live in inadequate, cramped spaces and a woman will feel that she imposes upon her relatives if she lives with them indefinitely, especially if she is accompanied by her children.

In many cultures, domestic violence is seen as an acceptable method for a man to discipline his wife.[40] Therefore, parents, other relatives, the community or the church may urge battered women to stay with their husbands and endure the violence, particularly since the blame for the violence will be put on the woman herself; she must be a bad housewife.[41] In such societies, women face being ostracized when they leave their husbands. A woman who divorces her husband brings shame not only on herself, but also on the whole family.[42]

Women may also stay for emotional reasons; they love their husband or they have sympathy for him, they still hope that he will improve, or they want to keep the family together for the sake of their children.[43]
Some psychologists claim that women may remain in abusive relationships because they suffer from *Battered Woman Syndrome*. Their self-esteem will be almost non-existent and they start believing that they are indeed to blame for their husbands' violence. After some time they are emotionally drained so they stop thinking of a way out. Moreover, they may be too afraid to leave because they fear their husband will harm them, their children, or other relatives if they do and they assume

---

Violence Against Women and Women's Right to Adequate Housing in cooperation with UN Special Rapporteur on Right to Adequate Housing, Delhi, India 28th-31st October 2003; and FARHA, *ibid.*, 516 respectively.

[40] This is for instance true in Nigeria where the law, custom and practice sanction correcting a wife on the same footing as correcting children. PAT MAHMOUD, 'Patterns of Violence Against Women in Nigeria with Specific Focus on Domestic Violence', in: INTERNATIONAL LEAGUE FOR HUMAN RIGHTS, *Combatting Violence Against Women*, New York, March 1993, 7.

[41] See for instance HUMAN RIGHTS WATCH (HRW), *Sacrificing Women to Save the Family; Domestic Violence in Uzbekistan* (Human Rights Watch Publications, Vol. 13 No. 4(D), July 2001) 19.

[42] In Poland the plans to establish shelters (for a total of maximum 180 women and 360 children) with the help of the UN Development Programme (UNDP) were suspended by the Government because it was feared that helping women outside the family home would contribute to the family break-up; an unacceptable option. IHF, supra n. 23, 334-335.
Divorcing a husband in societies where marriages are arranged are particularly shameful for the family and the woman may even be killed by her own relatives. UN Doc. E./CN.4/2002/83, para. 36.

[43] This has for example been mentioned by battered women in Armenia, Bosnia, the Czech Republic, and Hungary, IHF, supra n. 23, 45, 96, 148, and 206 respectively.

that it is impossible to find a place where they can escape their husbands' wrath.[44]

Several of these reasons show that many women may be unable to help themselves either emotionally or financially. That is why they should be able to rely on the authorities to respect and protect their rights.

4. STATE RESPONSIBILITY IN CASES OF DOMESTIC VIOLENCE

International law today perceives domestic violence as a human rights violation. This has not always been the case. In fact, for many centuries, international law only dealt with the acts of States. Therefore, the only violence that fell under the scope of international law was violence between States or inflicted by States upon their subjects. Violence occurring in the home was considered to be a private matter, falling outside the scope of international law.[45]

The notion that the State is responsible even though the harm is inflicted by a third party was expressed by the Inter-American Court of Human Rights in the *Velázquez-Rodriguez* case.[46] The State and its organs have to exercise due diligence to prevent the violation or to investigate and

---

[44] *Battered Woman Syndrome* is a psychological reaction that occurs when normal people are exposed to repeated trauma. The syndrome is a subgroup of Post-traumatic Stress Disorder and has four general characteristics: 1) the woman believes that the violence is her fault; 2) she is unable to place the responsibility for the violence elsewhere; 3) she fears for her life (and for her children's lives); 4) she has an irrational belief that the abuser is omnipresent and omniscient so there is no possibility for escape. L. WALKER, *The Battered Woman Syndrome*, 1984, available at: < www.divorcenet.com/or/or-art02.html>, consulted on 17 September 2001.

[45] HILARY CHARLESWORTH, CHRISTINE CHINKIN, & SHELLEY WRIGHT discuss the dichotomy between public and private domains in international law in their article: 'Feminist Approaches to International Law', in: *American Journal of International Law*, Vol. 85, 1991, 613-645. See particularly 627.

[46] Inter-American Court of Human Rights in the *Velásquez-Rodriguez v. Honduras* case, IACtHR 29 July 1988, OAS/ser.L./V./III.19, doc. 13, where the Government was held responsible for the disappearance of individuals, although the actual abductions had been carried out by private persons. Also see Article 18 of the Maastricht Guidelines on 'Acts by Non-State Entities': 'The obligation to protect includes the state's responsibility to ensure that private entities or individuals, […] do not deprive individuals of their economic, social and cultural rights. States are responsible for violations of economic, social and cultural rights that result from their failure to exercise *due diligence* in controlling the behaviour of such non-state actors' (emphasis added). THEO VAN BOVEN, CEES FLINTERMAN, INGRID WESTENDORP (eds.), *The Maastricht Guidelines on Violations of Economic, Social and Cultural Rights*, SIM Special No. 20 (Utrecht: SIM, 1998) 9.

punish the crime.[47] With regard to the violence inflicted on women in the domestic situation, this means that when a State does not stop violence occurring in private relations, it tacitly condones this violence, and thus becomes an accomplice.[48] Since violence against women by their intimate partners is now believed to be a violation of human rights, international human rights instruments may be invoked to protect the victims.[49] CEDAW stated in its General Recommendation no. 19:

'[...] *Under general international law and specific human rights covenants, States may also be responsible for private acts if they fail to act with due diligence to prevent violations of rights or to investigate and punish acts of violence, and for providing compensation'.*[50]

Following the Second World Conference on Human Rights in Vienna in 1993, the UN General Assembly adopted the Declaration on the Elimination of Violence against Women.[51] After defining violence against women as a violation of the rights and fundamental freedoms of women in its preambular paragraph, the Declaration stipulates that States should not excuse violence against women by referring to custom or tradition, but that they should exercise due diligence to prevent, investigate and punish acts of violence against women no matter whether these acts have been committed by state actors or by private persons.[52]

---

47 Literally the Court found that: 'An illegal act which violates human rights and which is initially not directly imputable to the State (for example, because it is the act of a private person or because the person responsible has not been identified) can lead to international responsibility of the State, not because of the act itself but because of the lack of due diligence to prevent the violation or to respond to it as required by the Convention'. [...] 'The State has a legal duty to take reasonable steps to prevent human rights violations and to use the means at its disposal to carry out a serious investigation of violations committed within its jurisdiction, to identify those responsible, to impose the appropriate punishment and to ensure the victim adequate compensation'.

48 KENNETH ROTH, 'Domestic Violence as an International Human Rights Issue', in: REBECCA J. COOK (ed.), *Human Rights of Women; National and International Perspectives* (Philadelphia: University of Pennsylvania Press, 1994), 330.

49 Although the most important human rights instruments do not address domestic violence directly, they do refer to the right to life, the right to physical and mental integrity, the right to equal protection before the law and the right not to be discriminated against. THOMAS, supra n. 15, 241-244.

50 CEDAW, General Recommendation no. 19, on Violence Against Women, 1992, UN Doc. A/47/38, 1992, para. 9.

51 General Assembly Resolution 48/104, UN Doc. A/48/49, 1993.

52 Art. 4(c) of the Declaration on the Elimination of Violence against Women, which reads: 'States should condemn violence against women and should not invoke any custom, tradition or religious consideration to avoid their obligations with respect to its elimination. States should pursue by all appropriate means and without delay a policy of eliminating violence against women and, to this end, should: [...] c) Exercise due diligence to prevent, investigate and, in accordance with national legislation, punish

In 1994 the UN appointed a Special Rapporteur on the subject of violence against women who paid ample attention to State responsibility in her reports.[53]

Recently, the Human Rights Committee (HRC) reaffirmed that in order to fulfil its positive obligations under the Covenant a State not only has a duty to protect its citizens from violations by its agents,

'[…] but also against acts committed by private persons or entities that would impair the enjoyment of the Covenant rights in so far as they are amenable to application between private persons or entities. There may be circumstances in which a failure to ensure Covenant rights as required by article 2 would give rise to violations by States Parties of those rights, as a result of States Parties' permitting or failing to take appropriate measures or to exercise due diligence to prevent, punish, investigate or redress the harm caused by such acts by private persons or entities'.[54]

From the above it has become clear that States can no longer dismiss domestic violence as a private matter and that they may not give in to traditional ideologies that propagate that women are subordinate to men and thus condone violent behaviour by men. Their first obligation is to prevent violence by eliminating laws and practices that maintain the unequal power relations between men and women. If violence occurs, States must investigate, prosecute and punish the perpetrators, just as they would with any other violent crime. Furthermore, protection measures should be taken and compensatory regulations should be available for the victims. The way in which States may or should react is the subject of the next sub-section.

4.1. The duty to prevent domestic violence

The first task States have is to prevent domestic violence. Since the primary cause of domestic violence is the culturally-determined, subordinate socio-economic position of women, prevention will entail bringing about a change of mentality. This is of course, no easy task. Stereotypical ideas about men and women's characteristics and roles in society are so ingrained that it is very difficult to abolish them. However,

---

acts of violence against women, whether those acts are perpetrated by the State or by private persons'.

[53] Radhika Coomarswamy was appointed as Special Rapporteur on Violence Against Women by the UN Commission on Human Rights in its resolution 1994/45 of 4 March 1994. Already in her Preliminary report she addresses the issue of State responsibility and States' obligations. UN Doc. E/CN.4/1995/42, paras 99-112. Ms Coomaraswamy was succeeded as Special Rapporteur by Dr Yakin Ertürk in August 2003.

[54] General Comment no. 31, nature of the general legal obligations imposed on States Parties to the Covenant, 2004, UN Doc CCPR/C/21/Rev.1/Add.13, para. 8.

culture is not a static phenomenon, but is a social construction and thus a living and flexible concept. There is no society today that still adheres to exactly the same rules as it did a century ago. It is especially this ability to change that gives hope for women's future.[55] Information and education are the best options. Besides bringing about the general literacy of women, human rights education should be provided. Both women and men should be made aware of the rights women have and the respect for these rights that is due both from the State and other citizens. The adoption and implementation of legislative measures may be regarded as clear evidence of a change in policy and attitude of the public authorities. In the criminal law sphere a strong signal of disapproval should be given by pursuing a zero tolerance policy, while in the civil law code, domestic violence should be listed as a reason for divorce and entitlement to alimony, should a woman be in need of financial support.

4.2. The duty to protect in cases of domestic violence

After ages of non-interference, some States have taken up their responsibility to deal effectively with cases of domestic violence. Especially during the last three decades, State interference has increased. States may respond in several ways. In some States, domestic violence is criminalized;[56] perpetrators are prosecuted and punished, while in others, the State's activity concentrates on a system of mediation and conciliation. Protection of the victim may be done by way of issuing court orders, providing counselling service, maintenance and shelter, or by evicting the batterer.

In many States that criminalize domestic violence, it is not treated as a separate offence, but its various forms can be brought under the heading of general crimes, like assault.[57] In cases of criminalization *per se*, it is often not treated as a common crime but as an excusable offence.[58] If the victim 'forgives' the perpetrator or withdraws her complaint, no further action is taken. If the case is tried in court, many judges will pass a much

---

55 CHRISTINE CERNA & JENNIFER WALLACE, 'Women and Culture', in: KELLY D. ASKIN, DOREAN M. KOENIG (eds.), *Women and International Human Rights Law*, Vol. 1 (Ardsley, New York: Transnational Publishers, Inc., 1999) 625.

56 As regards the dilemmas of criminalization see the chapter by Renée Kool in this book.

57 This is the case in the Netherlands where the Criminal Code does not include a specific provision on domestic violence. See RÖMKENS, supra n. 18, 135, and Ministerie van Justitie, *Project voorkomen en bestrijden 'huiselijk geweld'; plan van aanpak*, Den Haag, 14 februari 2001, 7-8.

58 For instance in Romania, reconciliation with the husband (which often occurs under pressure) exonerates him from criminal responsibility. IHF, supra n. 23, 361.

more lenient judgment in cases of domestic violence than they would do in similar cases of assault by a stranger. Sometimes the 'honour defence' is accepted as a mitigating circumstance.[59] In some countries it is felt that arrest of the perpetrator is the best action. It provides the woman with immediate safety and conveys the message that society will not tolerate this kind of behaviour.[60] In Brazil special women's police stations have been created that deal exclusively with domestic violence.[61]

An important drawback of criminalization in general is that the whole family may suffer financially if a man is arrested or fined for his crime. Usually, the man will be the main breadwinner and if he is incarcerated, the family income is dramatically reduced. If he is fined, the money that has to be paid will come out of the housekeeping allowance.

In the USA criminalization also has another, unintended but serious, side effect on the situation of the woman if the couple lives in a subsidized rented house. If a man has a history of domestic violence, the whole family may be evicted. Thus the woman (and children) is two times victimized; not only has she been battered, but she will also be rendered homeless.[62]

---

[59] This is particularly true for countries in Eastern Europe, South East Asia and Latin America. THOMAS, supra n. 15, 228-230.

[60] This policy is predominant in Australia, Canada and the United Kingdom. UN Doc. E/CN.4/1995/42, para. 128.

[61] The first woman's police station was established in Sao Paolo in 1985. In 1996 there were already 152 of such stations all over the country, with a heavy concentration in Sao Paolo (124). Nevertheless ,the bulk of domestic violence cases is still dealt with by regular police stations. Report on the mission of the Special Rapporteur on Violence Against Women to Brazil, UN Doc. E/CN.4/1997/47/Add. 2 of 21 January 1997, paras. 47-50.

[62] In several states of the USA, a.o. Oregon, California, Colorado, Louisiana, Massachusetts and Michigan, subsidized-housing policies have been developed that provide for affordable housing to low-income groups. To be eligible for such a housing subsidy, people have to meet with certain criteria. These include that no member of the family must have a history of criminal activity, disturbing the neighbours or destroying property. The aim is to make housing in subsidized buildings for all tenants as safe as possible. The result is, however, that if one of the family members behaves violently, the whole family may be evicted. Eviction is possible even if the tenant was not actually arrested or convicted. In this way not only the perpetrator, but the victims of domestic violence are rendered homeless as well. Moreover, once one has been evicted it is very difficult to qualify for future housing programmes. See ROBIN HAMMEAL-URBAN AND JILL DAVIES, *Building Comprehensive Solutions to Domestic Violence*, Publication #6, A Policy and Practice Paper, Federal Housing and Domestic Violence: Introduction to Programs, Policy and Advocacy Opportunities, available at: <www.vaw.umn.edu/FinalDocuments/fedhouse.asp>, consulted on 28 August 2001. Also TAMAR LEWIN, *Zero-Tolerance Policy Is Challenged*, The New York Times, 11 July 2001.

Some Governments are hesitant to treat domestic violence as a common crime. It is primarily looked upon as a private matter the couple has to cope with. In some States more specifically the woman, must try to find a solution.[63] If this is not possible, the police and/or (local) authorities may provide mediation and conciliation services.[64] In many cases where alcohol or drugs abuse are considered to be the cause of the violent behaviour, the abuser may be offered counselling and treatment. Less often, counselling services for the survivors of abuse are available.[65]

As far as the housing situation of the victim is concerned, two different approaches may be discerned. The oldest and best known is the establishment and upkeep of shelters where the battered women may find refuge. A more recent method that is not yet widely spread is the eviction of the perpetrator from the family home. The latter method will be discussed first.

4.2.1. Eviction of the perpetrator

An interesting new policy that up till now has only been adopted by a few States, is to provide for eviction of the perpetrator from the family home.[66] Argentina, Austria, and Germany are examples of States where such legislation is already working.[67] Evicting the perpetrator seems the most logical solution in cases of domestic violence, but it is not always possible or advisable. If, however, the victim is mentally up to it, it seems appropriate that the victim should stay in the family home while the

---

[63] That domestic violence might be viewed as a private family problem that must be solved by the woman herself becomes clear from a thorough investigation that was carried out by the International Helsinki Federation for Human Rights (IHF) in 29 central and south-eastern European countries. See IHF, supra n. 23.

[64] In countries like Egypt, Greece, Malaysia, Nigeria and Thailand police officers try to conciliate and dissuade the victims to take legal action. THOMAS, supra n. 15, 222.
In Uzbekistan cases of domestic violence are first and foremost dealt with by the *mahalla*, a form of local government. The chairperson of the *mahalla* will form a reconciliation commission with the objective to eliminate the need for legal action in what is considered a family affair. Victims may be subjected to conciliation attempts for months, or even years, before they are 'allowed' to go to the police or to divorce. See HRW , supra n. 41, 19-23.

[65] THOMAS, supra n. 15, 239.

[66] UN Doc. E/CN.4/1995/42, para. 135.

[67] Report by the Special Rapporteur, 1999, UN Doc. E/CN.4/1999/68, para. 74. The German law is called the *Gewaltschutsgesetz (Gesetz zur Verbesserung des zivilgerichtlichen Schutzes bei Gewalttaten und Nachstellungen sowie zur Erleichterung der Überlassung der Ehewohnung bei Trennung)* that entered into force on 1st January 2002. In the Netherlands the labour party (*Partij van de Arbeid*) has requested the Government to introduce a similar law. See Manifest *Stop Huiselijk Geweld!*, supra n. 18, 1, also RÖMKENS, supra n. 18, 136. Also see Katinka Lünnemann's chapter in this book.

perpetrator should seek lodgings elsewhere. Besides the moral justice aspect it is also a pragmatic solution; the socio-economic situation of men is still such that they will be sooner in a position to be able to afford housing than their female partner, while in the case of couples with children, it is easier to find adequate housing for just one person than for several persons.

A problem of this method is, however, that many women are afraid to remain at an address that is known to their (former) partner. They may feel like sitting ducks, especially if they have already experienced ongoing harassment. A solution may be that these women obtain injunctions against their (former) partner forbidding him to come near her home or even neighbourhood.[68] This solution is rather inadequate, however, since the perpetrator will not be under 24 hour surveillance and thus the violation of the victim's housing rights and privacy may continue.

4.2.2. Shelters

In many States, battered women have the option to go to shelters. The number of shelters is, however, invariably too small.[69] Those shelters that are available are constantly filled to capacity.[70] In countries where there are several shelters, the usual policy is to send the woman to another city for safety reasons. The shelters may be State-supported or financed by churches and other NGOs. Normally, women can stay a limited period in these homes while they are advised and helped to get their life back on the rails.[71] States should see to it that housing in a temporary shelter meets the normal requirements as to adequacy; housing conditions should be spacious enough to allow for some privacy, and families

---

68 In the Netherlands for example, there are many cases dealing with such situations. If a woman obtains an injunction, the court order is mostly based on the right to security of the person and hardly ever refers to her right to housing or her right to privacy. VERHEY, supra n. 8, 243.

69 It should be borne in mind that many of the shelters that exist are not financed by Governments, but by private initiative, sometimes international NGOs. The shelters in the Netherlands, for instance, were initially established by the churches and by the '*Blijf van mijn lijf*' foundation, a national women's NGO. Meanwhile, however, the (local) government is now financing most of the shelters. RÖMKENS, supra n. 18, 139. The only shelter that is available in Bulgaria is run by NOVIB, a Dutch NGO. IHF, supra n. 23, 116. Also see supra n. 39.

70 In the Netherlands, almost half of the women who seek refuge have to be turned away because the shelters are full. Women who are (still) illegally in the country are not even included in the figures, because they may not be taken in. 'Mishandelde vrouwen staan vaak in de kou', *NRC Handelsblad* (Dutch newspaper), 28 November 2001.

71 Usually the maximum period that women can stay in these safe houses is six months.

should be able to stay together.[72] Ideally, there should be specific shelters for battered women and general shelters for other homeless people. If these women and their children have to live in general shelters, together with drug addicts, alcoholics and mentally disturbed people, this may be a traumatic experience.

It goes without saying that safety is the first precondition. Addresses of safe-houses are to be kept on a need to know basis only in order to prevent harassment by vengeful partners. Violation of the right to housing and privacy continues if women are harassed by their (former) partners. The authorities have failed in their duty to protect the rights of battered women if the addresses of such shelters are publicly known or can be easily obtained.[73]

4.3. The duty to repair in cases of domestic violence

Reparation may take various forms.[74] In cases where domestic violence is the cause of the infringement of the right to adequate housing, rehabilitation, restitution and compensation might be the most relevant. Rehabilitation will entail medical and psychological care of the victim as well as legal and social services. Restitution is reparation in kind that may take two forms. When the perpetrator can be evicted and the victim feels safe, she (and her children) may be (re-) installed in the family

---

[72] In several States, including the Netherlands, some shelters do not allow sons over 12 years of age.

[73] In the Netherlands, *e.g.* addresses of safe-houses are not so difficult to obtain. Many women living in such shelters are harassed by their (former) partners who make it very unsafe for them to leave the house. In March 2004 for example, a man succeeded in tracing his wife time and again by way of accessing internet data of their common health insurance company. When he caught her in front of the fourth shelter she had taken refuge in, he killed her in front of their three children. *NRC Handelsblad*, 26 March 2004.

[74] Reparation is the general term for all forms of indemnifying a victim for violations that have been suffered. Reparation may be both material and non-material. Restitution is used to indicate that the situation is restored as much as possible to the situation prior to the violation while compensation indicates monetary indemnification. Other forms of reparation include rehabilitation (the provision of legal, medical and psychological care as well as the restoration of dignity and reputation) and satisfaction and guarantees of non-repetition. See for instance SIM Special No. 12 on the Seminar on the Right to Restitution, Compensation and Rehabilitation for Victims of Gross Violations of Human Rights and Fundamental Freedoms (Utrecht: SIM, 1992) 11-12; and UN Doc. E/CN.4/Sub.2/1993/8, 2 July 1993, Final report submitted by Mr Theo van Boven, Special Rapporteur, Chapter IX on Proposed Basic Principles and Guidelines, particularly sections 8-11 on Forms of Reparation. See further the latest version of the Basic Principles and Guidelines on the Right to a Remedy and Reparation for Victims of Gross Violations of International Human Rights Law and Serious Violations of International Humanitarian Law, in UN Doc. E/CN.4/2005/59, Annex I.

home. If, however, the victim has fled the family home and she is not inclined to return to it, permanent relocation to alternative adequate housing may be the best option. Compensation is a solution if restitution is for some reason not possible or advisable. Monetary indemnification may be in order if a victim is so afraid of her former partner that she wishes to settle someplace secret, unknown even to the (local) authorities or so far away that it may fall outside of the administrative area of such authorities. In addition to restitution and compensation interdicts or injunctions banning the perpetrator from the house or neighbourhood might be warranted. Moreover, the (former) partner as the actual perpetrator should be compelled to contribute financially to his victim's housing condition should she be unable to provide for adequate housing herself. Since the State is also responsible, financial contributions in the form of housing subsidies in cases where the perpetrator is unable to pay, or his contribution falls short, may be called for.

5. CONCLUSION

From the above it has become clear that housing and privacy rights of women are not respected and protected adequately if there is a policy of non-interference in what is considered the family sphere. An unequal power balance resulting in domestic violence can make these rights illusory for many women. Instead of a sanctuary, home may be a dangerous place, even with more hazards than living in the streets. International law recognizes domestic violence as a human rights abuse and States have an obligation to prevent it and to protect and indemnify the victim should prevention have failed. The primary cause for domestic violence is the subordinate socio-economic position of women in society. Therefore, the most effective way of preventing domestic violence is to relinquish traditional laws and views that regard women as subordinate and to bring about a change in mentality and policy. States should start by showing respect for the equal and individual right of women to live in adequate, safe and private housing conditions.

In what form protection may be offered should depend on the circumstances and the victim's needs and wishes. Either eviction of the perpetrator from the home or housing the victim in a safe house may commend themselves. Reparation may consist of permanent relocation of the victim or (re-)installing her in the former family home. Both measures may be accompanied by other forms of reparation, notably rehabilitation, compensation, housing subsidies, interdicts, or restraining orders.

Only if women are regarded as autonomous individuals, entitled to their housing and privacy rights on an equal basis with men, could they too, come to regard their home as their castle.

THE LEGAL ARRANGEMENT OF EVICTION

Katinka Lünnemann

1. INTRODUCTION

paradigm shift is taking place with regard to domestic violence, at least in the Western world. Violence within the family is no longer regarded as a private problem without relevance for the government. Nowadays it is regarded as a social problem involving public interest. Domestic violence is seen as a violation of human rights, such as the right to physical integrity and privacy. States have a duty to protect victims of domestic violence and to take preventive measures. Different legislative measures are needed to protect the victims.[1]

In this article I will focus on eviction of the perpetrator as a legal arrangement of crisis intervention in cases of domestic violence. Westendorp already wrote about adequate housing in cases of domestic violence and mentioned the possibility of eviction of the perpetrator from the family home. I will give more detailed information about eviction as a measure of crisis intervention. But eviction is just one instrument of protecting victims of domestic violence. To protect victims of domestic violence, several legislative measures supported by protective and preventive measures are needed.

I will first sketch the Act of eviction of perpetrators of domestic violence in Austria and Germany. Thereafter, I will comment on the responsibility of the State to enhance legislative and other protective measures, which are needed to protect and prevent violence against women. I will conclude with some topics of discussion.

2. EVICTION AS A MEASURE OF CRISIS INTERVENTION

In Austria[2] and Germany[3] the police have the possibility to evict the perpetrator of domestic violence for a short period. The victim is able to request eviction for a longer period under civil law.

---

1   See the articles of Ineke Boerefijn and Ingrid Westendorp in this book.

2   The *Bundesgesetz zum Schutz vor Gewalt in der Familie [federal law to protect the family against violence]*, for short *Gewaltschutzgesetz*, got effect in 1997 and was reformed in 2000 and 2004. The term was extended from seven days till ten days.

3   The *Gesetz zum zivilrechtlichen Schutz vor Gewalttaten und Nachstellungen [private law act to protect against acts of violence and threats thereof]*, also for short *Gewaltschutzgesetz*, in Germany got effect in 2002. The police have the power to intervene with an order of eviction to prevent danger.

The perpetrator may be ordered by the police to leave the residence (*Wegweisung [eviction order]*) and be prohibited from entering a certain area (*Betredungsverbot [restraining order]*) when there is sufficient ground for fearing 'harm to life, health, or freedom' or a danger to 'body, life and freedom'. Its purpose is to protect everyone who faces a situation in his or her house that endangers his or her life, health, or freedom. The maximum term of this order is ten days. The order is communicated orally and should thereafter be put in writing. A report should describe the circumstances that led to the order. The police should demand an address from the evictee so that official documents can be served. The police should also check within three days whether the perpetrator is complying with the order. Thus far, the measure of eviction is the same in Austria and Germany. However, in Austria a senior police officer (*Sicherheitsbehörde*) can test the legality of such an order within 48 hours and if necessary, withdraw it, while in Germany the written report may be contested in an administrative court procedure. When the evictee is not complying with the order in Austria, this is considered to be an offence - a *Verwaltungsübertretung [administrative offence]* (Article 84 *Sicherheits-polizeigesetz [police safety act]*, for short SPG) - for which he or she can be fined under administrative law. Upon failure to pay this fine, the perpetrator's freedom may be restrained for a maximum of two weeks, or he may be detained (Article 35 *Verwaltungsstrafgezets [administrative penal law]*).[4] If the perpetrator does not comply with the order in Germany, he may be detained (Article 35 section 1 NW *Polizeigesetz [police act]*, for short PolG) or forced to comply through administrative coercion.[5]

If the victim wishes the perpetrator to leave the residence for a longer period of time and/or desires a longer-term restraining order, she should appeal to the civil court judge. In Austria and Germany the rules are not quite the same, yet in both countries this arrangement of eviction only applies if there is a family relationship between victim and perpetrator (as opposed to eviction through police order, which is applicable to everyone), and one condition is that there must be concrete danger for another instance or threat of violence against the victim. What is important is that the measure of eviction is connected to the civil restraining order.

---

[4] For practical purposes, and in conformity with the situation in the majority of the cases, the male pronoun is used to indicate the perpetrator, while female form is used for the victims.

[5] K.D. LÜNNEMANN, J.P.J. TAK & D.J.G. PIECHOCKI, *Interventie door uithuisplaatsing* (Utrecht: Verwey-Jonker Instituut, 2002).

The police in Austria and Germany are given leeway to intervene in crisis situations, besides the usual competencies under criminal law, while Austrian and German civil law allows for protection of the victim (upon her request) and calls on the police to ensure compliance with protective measures. Failure to comply is regarded as a criminal offence in Germany. This construction is similar to Anglo-Saxon legislation: the *Order of Protection* resembles the temporary measure in Austria and Germany and, as in Germany, failure to comply with the *Order of Protection* is also considered to be a criminal offence.

3. ARRESTING OR EVICTION OR BOTH?

The Anglo-Saxon system calls for mandatory arrest, which obliges the police to arrest a suspect of domestic violence immediately and bring him to the police station. The positive aspect of mandatory arrest is that the police arrest the suspect instantly and restore peace in the short term. In the long-term, however, the effects of such a measure are less uniform.[6] A significant disadvantage is that criminal procedures may ignore the needs of victims of domestic violence. Particularly for socially and economically-underprivileged groups, mandatory arrest usually produces more harm than security.[7] Arrests prevent immediate recurrence of violence, but also have a stigmatising effect.

In Austria, the negative aspects of a criminal law approach led to a search for another foundation for crisis intervention by the police. A positive effect of eviction based on the police law is that the perpetrator is removed from the residence and confronted with a restraining order immediately, allowing the victim to calm down and take time to make her own arrangements. The infringement on the perpetrator's freedom is minimal and he can for example, continue to go to work or visit friends. He is not stigmatised by arrest under criminal law. In that sense an eviction is less of an infringement of human rights than an arrest.

However, an eviction order represents a violation of the right to housing, personal freedom and family life (Article 8 European Convention on Human Right and Fundamental Freedoms [ECHR]). Therefore, a law authorising the police to evict needs to account for such a violation. In the Netherlands the Government has decided to legalize a measure of crisis intervention by making an Act of eviction (home prohibition).[8] The proposed Act of eviction will differ from the Acts of Austria and

---

6   L.W. SHERMAN, *Policing Domestic Violence*, The Free Press 1992.

7   D.L. MARTIN & J.E. MOSHER, Unkept Promise: Experiences of immigrant women with the neo-criminalization of wife abuse, in: *Canadian Journal of Women and Law*, 1995, 3-44.

8   A bill will be proposed in 2005.

Germany in the sense that a judge will have to decide on the legitimacy of the eviction. The police can, with the consent of the mayor, order the perpetrator to leave the residence and prohibit entering the area around the family home, but a judge has to consider the conflicting human rights of victim and perpetrator; the right to housing, personal freedom and family life of the perpetrator and the human rights of physical integrity and personal freedom of the victim. In the Netherlands the discussion concentrates on the question 'at which point an eviction can be ordered'. Is it only possible when there is ground for fearing harm to life, health, or freedom, or also when there is a suspicion of an offence? In Austria ground for fearing harm to life, health or freedom can be based on a suspicion of an offence,[9] but in the Netherlands it seems only possible when there is a danger to body, life or freedom. When there is a suspicion of an offence, the suspect has to be arrested and eviction is not an option.[10] In practice, though, domestic violence usually does not result in detention of the perpetrator and if it does, the length of deprivation of liberty is as a rule not more than three days. Currently, the period of detention is often too short to develop a plan to protect the victim's safety by making arrangements for alternative housing and assistance to the victim and perpetrator.[11] The victim needs a longer period of rest to recover from the violence, resume her normal life, and take measures under civil law to remain in her residence. Also current measures under civil law do not offer solutions in times of crisis. Therefore, the immediate safety of the victim cannot be guaranteed. Starting from human rights and the obligation of States to enhance the legislative possibilities to protect victims of domestic violence, eviction should be possible in all situations where the police can consider a danger to body, life or freedom, based on a suspicion of an offence or on non-criminal aspects.

Besides legal arrangements, the State is obliged to take protective and preventive measures. The creation of advisory agencies is an important prerequisite for effective implementation of the law (*i.c.* stopping the violence), as we can learn from Austria. These advisory agencies (*Interventionsstellen*) in Austria help guarantee the safety of the victim. When the police order an eviction, they immediately send their official report to an advisory agency, enabling it to contact the victim. In addition to formulating a protection plan, the advisory agency offers

---

[9]   *Ibid.*, 3.

[10] Letter from the Minister of Justice to the Dutch Lower House of Parliament, 12 July 2004.

[11] Project *Voorkomen en bestrijden 'huiselijk geweld'* (Preventing and combating domestic violence), plan van aanpak, Ministerie van Justitie, Den Haag 2001, 8.

practical as well as social and legal support. Both the support of the individual victim and cooperation between the various organizations is crucial to make eviction effective in stopping the violence. The advisory agencies bring the various parties together and develop a framework for intervention and cooperation. Eviction actually creates room to develop a protection plan, offer help, and it creates time for the victim to decide whether she will request a formal eviction under civil law.

4. EVICTION AS A TOPIC OF DISCUSSION

The manner in which eviction of domestic violence offenders is organized in Austria and Germany could serve as an example for legislation in this area. Moreover, the legislative trajectory followed by these two countries indicates which aspects need to be discussed before drafting legislative proposals. Three themes are particularly important as subjects of discussion; protection of victims, child-related aspects and technical issues.

4.1. Protection of victims

The following questions arise in relation to the protection of victims: Should the victim be involved in the decision to evict in a crisis situation? How should the notion 'danger to body, life or freedom' be defined? What role should advisory agencies and support agencies for perpetrators play in the eviction trajectory? Victims of domestic violence are often in shock after a violent incident and, therefore, not in a position to decide whether eviction is necessary. An order to evict indicates that the government disapproves of violence, also when it occurs behind closed doors, and assigns more value to the victim's right to bodily integrity than the perpetrator's right to his residence. That is why in Austria and Germany the police now have the right to give an order to evict without the victim's consent, but only the police in Austria send an official report of the eviction to the advisory agency without prior approval of the victim. In Austria the assumption is that the victim is isolated and that the advisory agency may contact her to find out whether she requires assistance. In Germany, this is considered an overly invasive breach of privacy.

An order to evict is only possible in case of a danger to body, life and freedom. In Austria, eviction usually only occurs in cases of physical violence, rarely in cases of sexual and psychological violence, as the former is easier to prove. It is easier to get approval for eviction under civil law with an official police report of eviction during a crisis, as this is an important piece of evidence and reduces the relevance of the perpetrator's testimony. The question is; how should we define 'a danger to body, life and freedom'? Eviction is only effective, that is the protection of victims of domestic violence can only be achieved, if advisory agencies offer the victim social and legal support and if the perpetrators are supported in changing their violent habits and behaviours.

4.2. Child-related aspects

Child-related aspects include the child as a victim and the problems concerning interaction between the child and the evicted parent. The most important questions in this area are: To what extent should eviction of the perpetrator of child molestation be possible? Should eviction only be possible in crisis situations or also under civil law? Should the arrangements for contact with the evicted person be cancelled during eviction in crisis situations as well as under civil law? Both in Austria and Germany, the parent who abuses his or her child may be evicted on the basis of a police order as a form of crisis intervention. By the way, eviction in crisis situations is rare in Austria, especially if the offending parent is also the caring parent. But in Austria, children may request the eviction of the offending parent in case of eviction under civil law, while a Council for Child Protection (*Jugendwohlfahrtstrager*) may request a temporary solution if the child appears to be growing up in a violent environment. In Germany, eviction of the perpetrator of child abuse under civil law is impossible. In addition, the arrangements for contact with the children are often cause for conflict in cases of violence between partners. In Germany, much of the discussion during the legislative process concerned the preservation or suspension of the right to contact, as contact between children and the evicted parent frequently leads to tension and violent incidents. In Germany, the judge informs the Council for Child Protection of the eviction, enabling intervention where necessary. The question is whether the Council for Child Protection in a country should take on this preventative role, or whether the right to contact should be suspended in cases of eviction.

4.3. Technical issues

The most important technical aspects concern the time frame for police eviction orders and evictions under civil law; which legal guarantees are required for crisis eviction and eviction under civil law, which role should the police play if eviction occurs under civil law and whether disobeying an eviction order and a restraining order under civil law should be made punishable under criminal law. The time frame of eviction in crisis situations needs to be short, yet not too short; the victim needs time to take the necessary steps required for longer-term eviction. Further, there should be enough time to develop a safety plan and arrange support. Experiences in Austria show that the time frame should be at least ten days, with an option of extension if a civil order to evict is initiated. The time frame for eviction under civil law is more complicated. In Austria, it is three months with a possible extension of another three months, whereas in Germany, depending on the ownership situation, there is either no maximum term or the maximum term is six months. In Austria, the duration of eviction is usually only six weeks. A longer term of six months however, primarily applies to older women who are financially dependent and who do not want a divorce, or to female immigrants who do not have their own residence permit.

These topics of discussion will need to be dealt with during a legislative process. Eviction seems to be an important instrument to protect the victim in situations of imminent danger.

5. ADAPTING LEGISLATION

An eviction order represents a violation of the right to housing, personal freedom and family life (Article 8 ECHR). A law needs to account for such a violation.

There are three complementary paths toward protecting victims of domestic violence:

First, providing the police with power to evict or restrain the perpetrator as a form of crisis intervention. This means that crisis intervention by the police must gain legal footing, as it is an effective instrument to protect the victim of domestic violence.

Secondly, increasing the possibilities for issuance of eviction and restraining orders under civil law. The possibilities for eviction under civil law need to be elaborated for domestic violence; the possibilities under civil law should be adapted in such a way that they allow the victims of domestic violence to get an eviction or restraining order quickly and easily (and in connection with the eviction in time of crisis). Special attention should be paid to under-aged children as victims of domestic violence or as witnesses of violence between parents.

Thirdly, combating domestic violence through criminal law provisions. The parameters for eviction under criminal law must be clarified. It is essential to carefully deliberate on the criminal law route in dealing with (extremely) serious cases of violence against the partner or children, and to evaluate whether the present set of instruments is sufficient or requires fine-tuning. A discussion should be started on the best system of law enforcement to deal with disobedience in case of a conviction. A clear sanction against failing to comply with a police order to evict, or with eviction as a temporary measure, is an essential prerequisite for effective protection of domestic violence victims.

Achieving better implementation of the law may necessitate a separate police department dealing exclusively with domestic violence and a family court for handling all procedures related to domestic violence (involving procedures under family, civil, criminal and, if necessary, administrative law). Improving the protection of victims of domestic violence and embedding clear legislation within a strong infrastructure should be the primary goals. This requires support for the victims, assistance for the perpetrators to prevent recurrence of violence, effective regional cooperation structures and appropriate education for the professional groups involved, especially within the police and the judiciary.

CHILDREN'S RIGHTS AND THE PREVENTION OF CHILD ABUSE AND NEGLECT: THE QUEST FOR A TRIAS PEDAGOGICA OF CHILDREN, PARENTS AND SOCIETY[1]

Jan C. M. Willems

'[All kinds of] studies point to the need for children (…) to have both stable emotional attachments with and touch from primary adult caregivers, and spontaneous interactions with peers. If these connections are lacking, brain development both of caring behavior and cognitive capacities is damaged in a lasting fashion'. (Bruce Perry[2])

'[F]amily violence research demonstrates that abusive experiences change the body. (…) Survivors of childhood abuse often suffer from health problems long after the abuse has ended. (…) [A]dmonitions to abstain from smoking or substance abuse are likely to be unsuccessful until the traumatic past events that are driving these harmful activities are addressed and resolved'. (Kathleen Kendall-Tackett[3])

1. INTRODUCTION

Domestic, that is inter-parental violence, witnessed or sensed by the child is a form of (psychological) child abuse, and child abuse (any form) is a form of domestic violence that is any violence in the domestic sphere. The World Health Organization's definition of child abuse (child abuse and neglect, child maltreatment) reads as follows:[4]

Child abuse or maltreatment constitutes all forms of physical and/or emotional ill-treatment, sexual abuse, neglect or negligent treatment or commercial or other

---

[1]   This chapter is an adaptation and elaboration of my presentation at the International Conference on Child Abuse & Neglect: The Facts; Meeting the Experts, organized by Prof. Dr. Peter Adriaenssens, Leuven, December 1-3, 2004 (available at: <www.kinder-mishandelingleuven.be/congres>).

[2]   BRUCE D. PERRY, 'Childhood experience and the expression of genetic potential: what childhood neglect tells us about nature and nurture', in: *Brain and Mind*, 2002, 79 (adapted from BRUCE D. PERRY, 'The neuroarcheology of childhood maltreatment: the neurodevelopmental costs of adverse childhood events', in: KRIS FRANEY, ROBERT GEFFNER, ROBERT FALCONER (eds.), *The Cost of Child Maltreatment: Who pays? We all do* (Family Violence & Sexual Assault Institute: San Diego, California, 2001)).

[3]   KATHLEEN KENDALL-TACKETT, 'Exciting discoveries on the health effects of family violence: where we are, where we need to go', in: *Journal of Interpersonal Violence*, 2005, 251-257 (i.f.); KATHLEEN KENDALL-TACKETT, 'The health effects of childhood abuse: four pathways by which abuse can influence health', in: *Child Abuse & Neglect*, 2002, 715 and 725, respectively.

[4]   See <www.who.int>, definition child abuse (child abuse and neglect).

exploitation resulting in actual or potential harm to the child's health, survival, development or dignity in the context of a relationship of responsibility, trust or power.

Through interpersonal and trans-generational transmission mechanisms, child abuse (*i.e.* all forms of child abuse and neglect, including sexual abuse) may be seen as one of the root causes, if not *the* root cause of domestic and other forms of violence in the broadest sense.[5] A psycho(patho)logical 'right' to destructiveness (towards self and others) acquired in (early) childhood, appears to be at work here. Child abuse in a broad sense is any form of neurobiological, neuropsychological, psychosocial and overall developmental damage (actual or probable harm) inflicted on children by caregivers and/or society through action or negligence. This chapter will focus on child abuse in the domestic sphere,[6] without being insensitive, however, towards the fact that many risk factors in society especially poverty, ignorance, xenophobia and sexism[7] may contribute to child abuse and neglect. As a matter of fact, the core risk factor in (Western) society: *transism* (basically, the patriarchal or parentiarchal ideology of 'privacy' or 'parental autonomy', that is of not preparing adolescents for parenthood and not preventatively supporting parents), will be a central theme in this chapter.

Child abuse within the family has led in the past to the erection of structures of support and supervision of parenthood, functioning mainly, however, after serious (neurobiological, neuropsychological, psychosocial and other developmental) damage has been inflicted on (young) children. Since (and even before) the adoption of the UN Convention on the Rights of the Child in 1989 existing *ex post*

---

5   ROBIN KARR-MORSE & MEREDITH S. WILEY, *Ghosts from the Nursery: Tracing the Roots of Violence* (The Atlantic Monthly Press: New York, 1997).

6   For a classification with subtype definitions and severity ratings, translated into Dutch from an American study (DOUGLAS BARNETT, JODY TODD MANLY, DANTE CICCHETTI, 'Defining child maltreatment: the interface between policy and research', in: DANTE CICCHETTI, SHEREE L. TOTH (eds.), *Child abuse, child development, and social policy* (Ablex: Norwood, New Jersey, 1993), see JAN C.M. WILLEMS, *Wie zal de Opvoeders Opvoeden? Kindermishandeling en het Recht van het Kind op Persoonswording (Who will Educate the Educators? Child Abuse and the Right of the Child to Become a Person (with a summary in English))* T.M.C. Asser Press: The Hague 1999, 1038-1062 (Appendix 3).

7   See J.C.M. WILLEMS, 'Als de rechten van het kind de dienst zouden uitmaken …; De pedagogische opdracht van ouders, school, beroepsgroepen, burgers en overheid in het perspectief van internationale mensenrechten', in: H. BAARTMAN, D. GRAAS, R. DE GROOT, TJ. ZANDBERG (eds.), *Wie maakt de dienst uit? Macht en onmacht in opvoeding en hulpverlening* (Agiel: Utrecht, 2004) 259-267 (also, with footnotes, and entitled: 'Kindermishandeling en de rechten van het kind: van transisme naar Trias pedagogica', available at: <http://arno.unimaas.nl/show.cgi?did=3323>).

interventionist and repressive (stigmatizing) structures of support and supervision of parenthood have been adapted, to begin with in law, in a more pro-active and preventative direction, in several states.[8] The *Trias pedagogica* (pedagogical *c.q.* child developmental state responsibilities towards the child-parent-society triad)[9] structures in these states are still relatively weak, however. Other states have proven to be less child rights-minded and more conservative. Notwithstanding many prevention programs, the dominant culture and (hence) structures in, for instance, The Netherlands are still interventionist and (hence) stigmatizing rather than preventative and inclusive. At best, new policies focus on selective early (post-childbirth) intervention rather than on 'universal' early (pre-childbirth) prevention, starting in the schools. The costs of this unfortunate myopia, both in economic[10] and in human terms, are enormous. In most states, however, investments needed to improve psycho-education, mental health, healthy (early) child (brain) development and (thus) prevention of child abuse and neglect are seriously lacking. Recovery and social reintegration of victims and perpetrators, which could also break the trans-generational cycle of (domestic) violence are often highly inadequate too. Children's rights and women's rights do not seem to form a combined framework for the development of a central vision and corresponding pro-active national and local policies tailored to the empowerment of children, caregivers and communities. Nowhere is preparation for parenthood seen as a fundamental human right. In this chapter I would like to address these human rights aspects of the responsibility of states to substantially adapt and strengthen their structures of support and supervision of parenthood, in the benefit of children, parents and society itself. First of all, however, I will highlight the fundamental role of international law in this regard.

---

8   See A.W.M. VELDKAMP, *Over grenzen! Internationaal vergelijkende verkenning van de rol van de overheid bij de opvoeding en bescherming van kinderen,* Ministerie van Justitie: Den Haag, 2001.

9   See JAN C.M. WILLEMS, 'The children's law of nations: the international rights of the child in the Trias pedagogica,' in: JAN C.M. WILLEMS (ed.), *Developmental and Autonomy Rights of Children; Empowering Children, Caregivers and Communities* (Intersentia: Antwerpen (etc.) 2002) 69-102 (also available at: <http://arno.unimaas.nl/ show.cgi?did=3150>).

10 For an example, see SUZETTE FROMM, *Total Estimated Cost of Child Abuse and Neglect in the United States: Statistical Evidence* (2001), available at: <www.preventchildabuse.org/learn_ more/research_docs/cost_analysis.pdf> ($ 94 billion per year in the US alone, which would, *grosso modo*, amount to some $ 5 billion annually for The Netherlands). See also H. WATERS ET AL., *The Economic Dimensions of Interpersonal Violence*, World Health Organization: Geneva 2004, 15-17 (available at: <www.who.int/violence_injury_prevention/publications/violence/economic_dimens ions/en>).

2. INTERNATIONAL LAW AND THE EMANCIPATION OF THE CHILD

In 2002 children for the first time addressed a formal session of the United Nations in New York. Gabriela Azurduy Arrieta, 13 years old from Bolivia, and Audrey Cheynut, 17 years old from Monaco, spoke to the General Assembly of the UN. On May 8th, 2002 they delivered to the UN General Assembly Special Session on Children the following message from the Children's Forum:[11]

We are the world's children. We are the victims of exploitation and abuse. (…) We are children whose voices are not being heard: it is time we are taken into account. We want a world fit for children, because a world fit for us is a world fit for everyone. (…) We are not the sources of problems; we are the resources that are needed to solve them. We are not expenses; we are investments. We are not just young people; we are people and citizens of this world. Until others accept their responsibility to us, we will fight for our rights. We have the will, the knowledge, the sensitivity and the dedication. (…) You call us the future, but we are also the present.

As an international lawyer with a primarily normative (and hence multidisciplinary) interest in the law (as opposed to the law's more monodisciplinary technical aspects), and above all in the emancipatory functioning of law, I will present in this chapter my normative vision on children's rights, human rights of parents and duties of states and societies – including professionals and professional societies – regarding the upbringing and protection of children. At the same time, however, I hope to make clear that international law, and especially human rights law and the international law on the rights of the child, seen in the proper context and dimension, and on the solid basis of the state of the art of research on early child and early brain development[12] on the one hand, and on the physical and mental health consequences of child

---

11 Message from the Children's Forum, delivered to the UN General Assembly Special Session on Children by child delegates, Gabriela Azurduy Arrieta, 13, from Bolivia and Audrey Cheynut, 17, from Monaco on 8 May 2002 (<www.unicef.org/special-session/documentation/childrens-statement.htm>).

12 See especially BRUCE PERRY's work on or via <www.childtrauma.org>. Also 'ZERO TO THREE: Response to *The Myth of the First Three Years* by (JOHN) BRUER,' available at: <www.zerotothree.org/no-myth.html>, or via <http://homepages.luc.edu/~hwei-man/page4psyc.html>, Brain-Based Education and Contemporary Controversies. And see BRAD J. KAMMER, *Trauma & Civilization: The Relationship Between Personal Trauma, Social Oppression, and the Transformative Nature of Trauma Healing (A Biopsychosocial Approach)*, Vermont College (of The Union Institute & University), 1 April 2004, available at: <www.avoiceforfreedom.com/Trauma&Civilization.doc>.

abuse[13] on the other is crucial for the process of emancipation which is needed to implement children's rights – needed, badly needed, to create a world fit for children. And as the child delegates Gabriela Azurduy Arrieta and Audrey Cheynut put it at the UN, and thus to the world: a world fit for children is a world fit for everyone.

Children's rights should be viewed in the context of the duties and – shared – responsibilities of parents and other carers, states and societies, and in the dimension of healthy holistic child development,[14] especially ECD: Early Child Development (which includes, and largely amounts to early brain development).[15] They present the framework through which new research data may not only be put in a normative – legal, moral, political, and also pedagogical – perspective, but through this perspective in an atmosphere of urgency of change which is part and parcel of any process of emancipation. This includes the process of emancipation of children, of which child delegates Gabriela Azurduy Arrieta and Audrey Cheynut testified in the clear language I quoted above, and will quote once again: 'We are not just young people; we are people and citizens of this world. Until others accept their responsibility to us, we will fight for our rights'.

3. HUMAN DIGNITY: RESPECT AND SELF-RESPECT

The first chapter of international law is human rights (in the same manner as, for instance, the Dutch Constitution begins, in Chapter One,

---

[13] See especially the work of KATHLEEN KENDALL-TACKETT (and other researchers of the Crimes against Children Research Center) on or via <www.unh.edu/ccrc> and <www.granitescientific.com>.

[14] Holistic child development means interrelated physical-emotional-social-moral-intellectual child development. For the 'holistic development' stand of the Convention on the Rights of the Child (CRC), see Article 17, Article 19, para 1, Article 23, para 3, Article 27, para 1, Article 29, para 1 sub a, Article 32, para 1, and Article 39 CRC. The CRC also refers to 'spiritual' (well-being and) development (Article 17, Article 23, para 3, Article 27, para 1, Article 32, para 1), which may be understood to refer to forms or elements of theistic, atheistic or posttheistic education, depending upon parental values within the boundaries of Article 14, para 2, and Article 18, para 1 CRC (the evolving capacities and the best interests of the child), and with the exclusion of (psychologically) violent, racist, sexist, militaristic, nationalistic and anti-environmental 'values' (Article 19, para 1, and Article 29, para 1 sub b-e CRC, and Article 5 of the Declaration on the Elimination of All Forms of Intolerance and of Discrimination Based on Religion or Belief, General Assembly resolution 36/55 of 25 November 1981).

[15] See CAROL BELLAMY, *The State of the World's Children 2001: Early Childhood*, Unicef: New York, Geneva 2001; MARY EMING YOUNG (ed.), *From Early Child Development to Human Development; [Proceedings of a World Bank Conference on] Investing in our Children's Future*, The World Bank: Washington, D.C. 2002 (also available at <www.worldbank.org>, Documents & Reports).

with constitutional rights).[16] The fundament – the universal philosophical (moral) and legal fundament – of human rights is human dignity. Human dignity can, in my view, best be described as the inherent right of every individual to be respected as a person,[17] and to be treated as such, and the inherent duty of every individual to both respect others (treat others as human beings and not as objects or means) and not to 'deny oneself',[18] that is to develop his or her own self-respect. In brief: human dignity is, or is about, the combination of respect for others and self-respect. This combination refers to both personal (physical and mental) health and personal (physical and mental) integrity as basic human rights, and implies, among other things, that one should never discriminate between groups (in-and-out groups, 'we' and 'they': we the superior, they the inferior, we the good, they the bad), but only between individuals, and not between individuals on the basis of group characteristics, but only on the basis of their moral (basically, their pro-social versus anti-social) qualities and potential. Pro-social refers to an altruistic (caring rather than claiming), dignitarian (rights go with responsibilities),[19] and humanitarian (empathetic and universalistic or cosmopolitan, inclusionistic, non-discriminatory) attitude to life; anti-

---

[16] MENNO T. KAMMINGA, *De humanisering van het volkenrecht* (Universitaire Pers: Maastricht 2001) 8/9.

[17] On the basis, of course, of the fundamental right of being recognized as a person before the law: *see* Article 6 of the Universal Declaration of Human Rights and Article 16 of the International Covenant on Civil and Political Rights (ICCPR), as well as Article 24, para 2 ICCPR, and Article 7 (birth registration) of the CRC; on the importance of which see THEO VAN BOVEN, 'Children's rights are human rights; Current issues and developments', in: JAN C.M. WILLEMS (ed.), *Developmental and Autonomy Rights of Children; Empowering Children, Caregivers and Communities* (Intersentia: Antwerpen (etc.) 2002) 12-14.

[18] The definition of law of FRANK VAN DUN, 'Recht en rechtswetenschap,' in: FRANK VAN DUN (ed.), *Over leven en recht; Opstellen aangeboden aan Prof. mr. N.H.M. Roos ter gelegenheid van zijn afscheid als hoogleraar Metajuridica* (Shaker Publishing: Maastricht 2004) 115, 122, italics added as 'the order of living together': Law is (the order of) people living together; unlawful is whatever threatens the living together of people, whatever puts human relations in disarray. *Ius est ad alios*. For instance, if human beings do not treat one another as human beings but as objects, reward or punish the wrong person, do not acknowledge the work ('plagiarism') or respect the property of others, do not keep promises, *deny themselves*, do not accept the consequences of their actions (say that others are responsible), etcetera. In other words, law is about making a distinction between humans and objects, and between (right, lawful, pro-social behaviour and wrong, unlawful, anti-social behaviour of) humans. In human rights terms: law is about human dignity in human relations, and human dignity is about respect (for persons, property, promises, etc.) and self-respect.

[19] See Article 29, para 1, of the Universal Declaration of Human Rights, and Article 18 of the Declaration on the Right and Responsibility of Individuals, Groups and Organs of Society to Promote and Protect Universally Recognized Human Rights and Fundamental Freedoms (General Assembly resolution 53/144 of 9 December 1998).

social refers to an egocentric (claiming rather than caring), libertarian (individualistic rights without social responsibilities),[20] or fundamentalist (frustration-based *c.q.* 'God's chosen people' or 'God's most favoured nation' oriented, exclusionist, discriminatory) attitude to life. It is submitted by the author that the latter attitude, generally speaking, is more a matter of (infant and child) nurture than of (human) nature. Human nature may be vulnerable to egocentrism, scapegoating and xenophobia, but this vulnerability should be seen as a risk factor, a very serious one indeed, which can and must be countered by the protective factors of psycho-education of children and adults and nurture of infants and children. Psycho-education and nurture in which we need to invest to a far greater extent than we have done so far. As Perry puts it:[21]

In an age where more people must share increasingly limited resources (...) it is imperative that our children develop the capacity to share, be empathic and understanding of others. We must provide an investment in socio-emotional development comparable to our investment in cognitive development. The world, natural and manmade, now more than ever, needs the best of humankind.

Respect seems to be a key word in the debate at this moment in several European countries on integration, citizenship, religious minorities, 'norms and values'. But who is talking about self-respect? Self-respect is crucial for respecting others. Human dignity is, in my opinion, some way or other the combination of both.

The fundament of self-respect is to be found, in the first place in the first years of life,[22] in ECD – Early Child Development –, in secure attachment[23] of infants and toddlers to their mothers and other carers, and in between them; and therefore in the preparation – the socio-emotional (mental health, psycho-hygiene, parental awareness), cognitive (psycho-education, knowledge on child development and child

---

[20] On the dignitarian (UN) *versus* the libertarian (Anglo-American) tradition of human rights, see MARY ANN GLENDON, *Rights from Wrongs*, quoted in: HENRY J. STEINER, PHILIP ALSTON (eds.), *International Human Rights in Context; Law, Politics, Morals* (Oxford University Press: Oxford 2000, 2nd edition) 152-153.

[21] BRUCE D. PERRY, 'Childhood experience and the expression of genetic potential: what childhood neglect tells us about nature and nurture', in: *Brain and Mind,* 2002, 97.

[22] In Perry's words: 'It is during [infancy and childhood] when social, emotional, cognitive and physical experiences will shape neural systems in ways that influence functioning for a lifetime. This is a time of great opportunity – and great vulnerability – for expressing the genetic potentials in a child'. (BRUCE D. PERRY, 'Childhood experience and the expression of genetic potential: what childhood neglect tells us about nature and nurture,' in: *Brain and Mind,* 2002, 82.)

[23] See on attachment (and disorganized attachment and child abuse) especially RIEN VAN IJZENDOORN's work on or via <www.childandfamilystudies.leidenuniv.nl>.

rearing) and material (work, income, standard of living) preparation – for parenthood. In the second place, it is linked to aims of education, to school curricula, and therefore to psycho- and parenting education (as well as democratic citizenship education[24]) starting at school age. Let me first quote Unicef on ECD (Early Childhood Development), and then Dutch psychiatrist Andries van Dantzig on psycho-education. Unicef stresses (in *The State of the World's Children 2002*):[25]

If States are to fulfill their obligations under the Convention on the Rights of the Child they will have to stop seeing early childhood care as an issue of concern to families alone, as an optional extra, a soft alternative. Investing in ECD [Early Childhood Development] should now be second nature for the human family, as natural and inevitable to our lives as the sun and the rain on a field of rice.

Dutch psychiatrist Andries van Dantzig notes:[26]

Empathy should be taught in primary schools. (…) [However], the results of mental health research have little influence on the knowledge of average men and women. Compare this to the discovery of a new medical cure. It would be in the newspapers the next day, and it would be available the next week, regardless the costs. Society looks after the physical health of every citizen, from before birth until death. Every citizen has the right to intellectual education to become a full member of society. But the care for our mental health, for the proper development of our emotional life and our relationships, lacks far behind the care for our physical and intellectual wellbeing.

Psycho- and parenting education in schools and preparation for parenthood before childbirth should, in my view, be considered as the most important new challenge of human rights law, and ultimately of all law, international and national. After all, the ultimate unit of all law is the human being, the human person, the human child. However, international law and human rights law are still far from the recognition of psycho- and parenting education in schools and preparation for parenthood before childbirth as new – or even emerging – human rights.[27] Their crucial importance for peace, security, democracy,

---

24 Which could – and should – be the subject of a separate article (or even a book), although I turn back to it briefly in this contribution.
25 *The State of the World's Children 2002: Leadership*, 57 (quoted in JAN C.M. WILLEMS, 'The children's law of nations: the international rights of the child in the Trias pedagogica', in: JAN C.M. WILLEMS (ed.), *Developmental and Autonomy Rights of Children; Empowering Children, Caregivers and Communities* (Intersentia: Antwerpen (etc.) 2002) 69.
26 ANDRIES VAN DANTZIG, 'Horizontaal en verticaal verlies', in: *Nexus* no. 39, 2004, 150, 151 (my translation).
27 See, however, Article 24, para 2 sub e and f CRC: States shall pursue full implementation of [the right of the child to the enjoyment of the highest attainable standard of health] and, in particular, shall take appropriate measures (…) to ensure

integration of migrants, the struggle against poverty, ignorance and superstition, racial and gender discrimination, let alone trans-generational discrimination,[28] is far from generally understood, far from common knowledge. Trans-generational discrimination, what is meant by that? Before I come to that, a few observations on racial and gender discrimination and on parental autonomy, should be made first.

4. MULTICULTURALISM OR SOCIAL EXCLUSION?

The first international (UN) human rights treaty that came about after the adoption of the Universal Declaration of Human Rights in 1948 (December 10, 1948)[29] was the International Convention on the Elimination of all forms of Racial Discrimination (ICERD), adopted by the General Assembly of the UN in 1965 (December 21, 1965).[30] The ICERD has since become binding treaty law for 170 out of this world's 194 states (including, since 1994, the United States of America). In its sixth preambular paragraph, ICERD stipulates that doctrines of superiority based on 'racial'[31] group characteristics (ethnicity or natural skin colour), are socially unjust *and* dangerous. States have to limit freedom of speech, assembly and association by banning racist (xenophobic) hate speech, meetings and organizations through legislation and court action.[32] This is similar to the court ban of the racist

---

that (…) parents (…) are informed, have access to education and are supported in the use of basic knowledge of child [physical and (develop)mental? -JW] health (…); [and] to develop preventive [physical and mental? -JW] health care [and] guidance for parents (…). *See* also the 7th preambular paragraph and Article 29, para 1 sub d CRC: the preparation of the child for responsible life (as a citizen *and* as a parent?) in a free (democratic) society. And *see* Article 10 sub h of the UN Convention on the Elimination of all forms of Discrimination Against Women: Access to specific educational information to help to ensure the health and well-being of families (…).

28 Poverty, ignorance (superstition), racial and gender discrimination, and trans-generational discrimination are the Big Five human evils which human rights and the human rights movement endeavour to overcome. The Big Five human rights instruments used in this struggle are ICCPR and ICESCR (the International Covenants on Civil and Political Rights, and on Economic, Social and Cultural Rights, respectively), ICERD (anti-racism/xenophobia), Women's Convention (anti-sexism) and CRC (anti-transism): see main text directly hereafter.

29 Adopted and proclaimed by General Assembly resolution 217 A (III) of 10 December 1948.

30 Adopted and opened for signature and ratification by General Assembly resolution 2106 A (XX) of 21 December 1965.

31 'Racial' is, strictly speaking, an incorrect term. As Article 1, para 1, of the UNESCO Declaration on Race and Racial Prejudice (of 27 November 1978) states and stipulates: All human beings belong to a single species and are descended from a common stock. They are born equal in dignity and rights and all form an integral part of humanity.

32 Article 4 sub a and b ICERD.

or xenophobic Vlaams Blok in Belgium in November 2004. Good news from Belgium. But, unfortunately, there was bad news that month from The Netherlands.

November 2004 was also the month of the murder of filmmaker and free speech libertarian Theo van Gogh by a Dutch-Moroccan Muslim fundamentalist, a very angry young man – obviously in desperate need of attention for individual and collective frustrations. Which religiously motivated murder was followed by putting fire to mosques and Muslim schools by Dutch minors and right-wing extremists, other very angry young people, minors even – obviously as desperately in need of attention for individual and collective frustrations. A lack of work or idleness (as the saying goes, the devil finds work for idle hands), social exclusion, a problematic identity development[33] during puberty and adolescence.[34] Probably in retaliation, also a few churches in The Netherlands were met with (attempted) arson.[35]

Dutch sociologist and professor of migration and integration studies Han Entzinger said in a newspaper interview[36] that 25 years ago, we (Dutch society, the Dutch government and legislator) should have told migrants what we expect from them, and what they can expect from us. In stead, for a quarter of a century we had a *laissez-faire* policy called multiculturalism,[37] which was in effect a policy of social exclusion.[38] But we labelled it: respect for other cultures. Now, in The Netherlands, migrants are made responsible for their own democratic citizenship exam (in Dutch: *verplichte inburgering*), they have to take an exam (*inburgeringsexamen*), but the Dutch government does not want to be

---

33 Which may be a re-enactment of insecure attachment during infancy and childhood, and is at any rate likely to be related to low self-esteem and low self-respect caused by adverse childhood experiences.

34 *NRC Handelsblad*, 27/28 November 2004, 3 (JUTTA CHORUS, AHMET OLGUN, '"Jongeren niet gestuurd door partijen"; Onderzoekster Annette Linden over de aard en drijfveren van rechts-extremisten'; '"Aandacht in de krant gaf een enorme kick"').

35 For a list of attacks on Muslim and Christian targets in The Netherlands in November 2004, see *NRC Handelsblad*, 24 November 2004, 3 ('Incidenten sinds 2 november').

36 In *NRC Handelsblad* of 10 November 2004 ('"Dwang is Nederlands stokpaardje"; Hoogleraar Entzinger over integratie, godsdienstvrijheid en de islam').

37 For multiculturalism – that is positive and pro-active, not relativistic and indifferent multiculturalism – as an international obligation, *see* Article 2, para 1 sub e CERD: Each State Party undertakes to encourage (…) integrationist multiracial organizations and movements and other means of eliminating barriers between races, and to discourage anything which tends to strengthen racial division.

38 Social exclusion, that is, through a lack of combined 'responsabilisation' and empowerment (*see* main text hereafter on 'responsabilisation' and empowerment of parents).

responsible for the 'curriculum,' that is: supervision and control of the provision of good quality *inburgering* courses. Respect in The Netherlands appears to be negative respect: intervention and sanctions after too long a period of false (silent) expectations and 'benign neglect' (to use a Nixonian term). I predict that 25 years from now, probably sooner, something similar will be said about youth policy[39] in The Netherlands, and maybe in many other states as well.

5. PARENTAL AUTONOMY OR TRANSISM?

Apart from lofty sounding phrases in the Dutch Civil Code (Book 1, Article 247) – making parents responsible for the mental and physical wellbeing and the development of the personality of their child – nothing more explicit is required of parents in The Netherlands. Parents-to-be are not told well in advance, what is expected from them in terms of their preparation for parenthood and the parental duties and responsibilities that are awaiting them, nor what they can expect from society and from the state regarding preparation for parenthood and the exercise of child-rearing responsibilities – the huge responsibility of parents to care for the mental and physical wellbeing of their child and to promote the development of the personality of their child. Nor are parents-to-be and young parents told and explained to in advance, what is allowed in child rearing and what is not. Hitting and humiliating your child, for instance.[40] Although The Netherlands is expected to ban corporal punishment and humiliation of children in the family in its Civil Code in the near future,[41] a ban (which now exists in thirteen

---

[39] There is no official child and family policy in The Netherlands.

[40] See BEN PHILLIPS & PRISCILLA ALDERSON, 'Beyond "anti-smacking": challenging parental violence and coercion, in: *Child Abuse Review,* 2003, 282-291. See also J.C.M. WILLEMS, 'Het recht van het kind op leiding zonder opvoedingsgeweld; Ouderlijke tikken strafbaar?', in: K. BLANKMAN, M. BRUNING (eds.), *Meesterlijk groot voor de kleintjes; Opstellen aangeboden aan prof. mr. J.E. Doek ter gelegenheid van zijn emeritaat* (Kluwer: *s.l.* 2004) 59-79; and J.C.M. WILLEMS, 'Een verbod op slaan en de emancipatie van het kind,' in: *FJR – Tijdschrift voor Familie- en Jeugdrecht,* 2005, no. 4 (33), 94-98.

[41] The Dutch government decided on such a ban on 11 February 2005. As the Dutch Prime Minister, mr Balkenende, said (shortly after the Cabinet meeting in which the ban decision was taken): 'One does not hit a child. Period'. ('Kind slaan wordt straks strafbaar; Ook geen "pedagogische tik" (Hitting a child will be a criminal offence; including a "pedagogical slap"),' *NRC Handelsblad,* 12/13 February 2005, 3.) A draft code, containing the ban, is expected to be sent to Parliament by the summer of 2005. It has to be approved by both the Second and the First Chamber (the Second Chamber having the right of amendment) before it can obtain force of law. How long that will take is difficult to predict.

states[42]) is not enough.[43] Parents should be informed about alternatives for hitting, shouting and humiliating; they should be taught non-violent, non-aggressive, non-humiliating ways of 'disciplining' their child.[44]

Instead of such an advance social and legal 'responsabilisation' of parents,[45] linked with collective and where needed, individual empowerment of parents[46] and, not to forget, participation of parents[47] – in brief, instead of combined responsabilisation, empowerment and participation policies – we have a *laissez-faire* policy, called parental autonomy. This is in effect a policy of social – first of all socio-emotional – exclusion. A policy – or non-policy, if you like – of exclusion through inaction, *laissez faire, vis-à-vis* (in the face of) trans-generational transmission of trauma, of insecure attachment, of psychosocial problems, of personality problems, of negative parenting styles,[48] of harmful child-rearing practices[49] – traditional, religious or otherwise. A policy, in other words of trans-generational discrimination, of transism.

---

[42] According to <www.endcorporalpunishment.org>: Sweden (1979), Finland (1983), Norway (1987), Austria (1989), Cyprus (1994), Denmark (1997), Latvia (1998), Croatia (1999), Germany (2000), Israel (2000), Iceland (2003), Romania (2004) and Ukraine (2004).

[43] For recent developments in international law, see Recommendation 1666 (2004), *Europe-wide ban on corporal punishment of children*, of the Parliamentary Assembly of the Council of Europe (<http://assembly.coe.int/Documents/AdoptedText/ta04/EREC1666.htm>).

[44] On the issue of corporal punishment of children, see J.E. DURRANT, R. ENSOM AND COALITION ON PHYSICAL PUNISHMENT OF CHILDREN AND YOUTH, *Joint Statement on Physical Punishment of Children and Youth* (Coalition on Physical Punishment of Children and Youth: Ottawa 2004) available at: <www.cheo.on.ca>. This document 'is based on extensive research evidence and clearly states that not only is physical punishment ineffective but that it can be harmful in the short and long term. It reviews the evidence and gives resources for alternative disciplinary approaches'.

[45] Which must be considered to be a state obligation under, *inter alia*, Articles 5, 18 and 19 CRC.

[46] See, *inter alia*, Article 18, para 2, and Article 24, para 2 sub e and f, and Article 27, para 3 CRC.

[47] Responsabilisation without participation may be seen as equally unconstitutional or undemocratic (certainly in Trias pedagogica terms) as taxation without representation.

[48] A parenting style of affection-based guidance and direction, is called 'authoritative' (or, as the child grows older, 'democratic'). This style is seen as positive and healthy. Negative (and damaging) styles are the authoritarian parenting style (little affection, too much direction: over-control or overprotection), the permissive parenting style (affection with too little direction and guidance), and the indifferent parenting style (lack of affection, guidance and direction): see JAN C.M. WILLEMS, *Wie zal de Opvoeders Opvoeden? Kindermishandeling en het Recht van het Kind op Persoonswording (Who will Educate the Educators? Child Abuse and the Right of the Child to Become a Person (with a summary in English))*, T.M.C. Asser Press: The Hague, 1999, 530-533.

[49] Article 24, para 3 CRC.

A passive policy, a non-policy *vis-à-vis* flagrant human rights violations: child abuse and neglect, that is preventable child abuse and neglect and thereby (from an international legal perspective) a policy of flagrant human rights violations, especially children's rights violations. As I said, a policy of trans-generational discrimination, of transism. A policy as unjustified as negative respect – not intervening but waiting until things go awfully wrong, until problems explode – in the face of racial and gender discrimination, of racism and sexism. But we label our transism: respect for families. Our main family value appears to be: parents do not have to accept any form of intervention as long as their child is not suffering very seriously. What kind of value is that, one may ask. What does it have to do with human rights of parents? What does it have to do with the human right to preparation for parenthood? What does it have to do with the rights of the child?

6. WOMEN'S RIGHTS IN THE BEST INTERESTS OF THE CHILD

Let us now turn briefly to gender discrimination. In 1979 (December 18, 1979), the General Assembly of the UN adopted the Convention on the Elimination of all forms of Discrimination Against Women (the Women's Convention).[50] Article 5 of this Convention refers to, and utterly rejects the idea of the inferiority or the superiority of either of the sexes. Article 5 of the Women's Convention reads as follows:

States Parties shall take all appropriate measures: (a) To modify the social and cultural patterns of conduct of men and women, with a view to achieving the elimination of prejudices and customary and all other practices which are based on the idea of the inferiority or the superiority of either of the sexes or on stereotyped roles for men and women; (b) To ensure that family education includes a proper understanding of maternity as a social function and the recognition of the common responsibility of men and women in the upbringing and development of their children, it being understood that the interest of the children is the primordial consideration in all cases.

For the first time in history (to my knowledge at least), international (UN) law became involved, on a large scale, with the private sphere, to a certain extent even with what is in between the ears of men and women. States have to eliminate practices which are based on the idea of the inferiority or the superiority of either of the sexes, or on stereotyped roles for men and women. States have to ensure parent education based, being based, not only on a proper understanding of maternity as a social

---

[50] Adopted and opened for signature, ratification and accession by General Assembly resolution 34/180 of 18 December 1979.

– and not solely a private – function, but also on the recognition (a) of the common responsibility of both parents, fathers and mothers, in the upbringing and development of their children, and (b) of the precedence of the best interests of the child over all other considerations.[51] This is the normative state of the world since 1979.[52] It involves legal obligations for the states parties to the Women's Convention, which now numbers 180 out of 194 states. (The 14 non state parties are Brunei Darussalam, Iran, Oman, Qatar, Somalia, Sudan, six Pacific island states, the Holy See, and the United States of America – which is however a signatory as of 1980.) Of utmost importance are to be considered, in my view, the state's obligations and responsibilities to enable men and women to (equally) combine work and child-rearing responsibilities,[53] including generous parental leave possibilities and other facilities, as well as easy access, individually and on a (father and mother) group basis, to child health and healthy child development, *c.q.* child rearing, information and counselling,[54] especially in the months before and the first years after childbirth in order to give the new family a healthy start.

7. FROM DEVELOPMENTAL DAMAGE TO TORTURE: ONE OUT OF THREE CHILDREN

Let us, finally, turn back to trans-generational discrimination, or transism.[55] In 1989 (November 20, 1989), the General Assembly of the UN

---

51 See also Article 16, para 1 sub d Women's Convention: The same rights and responsibilities as parents (…); in all cases the interests of the children shall be paramount.

52 Strictly speaking, since 1981, in which year the Convention entered into force, in accordance with its Article 27, para 1. The Netherlands became a party a decade later, in 1991.

53 Article 11, para 2 sub c Women's Convention: In order to (…) ensure [women's] effective right to work, State Parties shall take appropriate measures (…) to enable parents to combine family obligations with work responsibilities (…).

54 Article 10 sub h Women's Convention: Access to specific educational information to help to ensure the health and well-being of families (…).

55 I proposed the term 'transism' in a Belgian publication in 2000: J.C.M. WILLEMS, 'Het belang van het kind, de rechten van het kind, hechting en verwerking: vier katalysatoren in de humanitaire ontwikkeling naar preventieve opvoedingsfacilitering en uitbanning van transisme', in: M. BOUVERNE-DE BIE, R. ROOSE (eds.), *Opvoedingsondersteuning en Jeugdzorg* (Academia Press: Gent, 2000) 5-41. (See also from the same year: J.C.M. WILLEMS, 'Kindervolkenrecht en Trias pedagogica', in: J.R.M. GERRIS (ed.), *Preventie van binnenuit* (Van Gorcum: Assen, 2000) 17; and J.C.M. WILLEMS, 'Kindermishandeling en mensenrechten', in: *Nederlands Juristenblad* 2000, 1240.) In JAN C.M. WILLEMS, 'The children's law of nations: the international rights of the child in the Trias pedagogica', in: JAN C.M. WILLEMS (ed.), *Developmental and Autonomy Rights of Children; Empowering Children, Caregivers and Communities* (Intersentia: Antwerpen (etc.), 2002) 87, I proposed the following definition of transism:

adopted the Convention on the Rights of the Child (CRC).[56] Being the most successful human rights treaty in terms of the total number of states parties, it is legally binding today for 192 out of 194 states (195 if we were to include Taiwan) in this world.[57] Non-state parties are only Somalia and the United States of America (both states, however, are signatories as of 2002 and 1995, respectively). The CRC really is universal law (assuming of course we humans are the only intelligence in the universe, which is too big to ever know anyway) – as universal as the Universal Declaration of Human Rights of 1948. Maybe we should be talking – not of the International (as some lawyers do[58]) but – of the Universal Convention on the Rights of the Child.

Trans-generational discrimination, or transism, does not have so much to do, at least on the outside, with ideas, or doctrines, of inferiority or superiority. But it certainly has a lot to do with subtle, or not so subtle, forms of social exclusion.[59] Let us, therefore, look at some (and face some) Western realities before having a closer look at how the CRC tries to fight transism (as ICERD tries to fight racism and the Women's Convention tries to fight sexism). In order to give an impression of these realities, I propose the following semi- or quasi-hypothetical estimate.[60]

'Transism or trans-generational discrimination stands for trans-generational psycho-traumatisation – or rather the trans-generational transmission of insecure attachment, unresolved trauma and/or psychosocial problems – *in the absence of* structural pro-active policies to break this [familial and societal] cycle of abuse, neglect, violence, indifference, lack of empathy, pain and exclusion. *In the absence of* policies of empowerment and community building'.

[56] Adopted and opened for signature, ratification and accession by General Assembly resolution 44/25 of 20 November 1989.

[57] The 191 UN Member States (available at: <www.un.org/Overview/growth.htm>), minus Somalia and the US (signatories only), and plus the Holy See (Vatican City), the Cook Islands and Niue (both formally part of New Zealand): available at: <www.ohchr.org/english/countries/ratification/11.htm>.

[58] Maybe by way of a hypercorrection caused by other UN human rights treaties that do carry the epitheton 'international'.

[59] The less subtle forms of this social (socio-emotional and socio-economic) exclusion are aggravated and perpetuated, according to Dalrymple, by the present culture and mentality of moral/cultural (value) relativism: see THEODORE DALRYMPLE, *Life at the Bottom: The Worldview that Makes the Underclass* (Ivan R. Dee: Chicago, 2001) (Dutch edition: *Leven aan de onderkant; Het systeem dat de onderklasse instandhoudt* (Spectrum: Utrecht, 2004)).

[60] I presented this (on the basis of US, UK, Belgian and Dutch research data) as an *educated guess* in J.C.M. WILLEMS, 'Als de rechten van het kind de dienst zouden uitmaken ...,' in: H. BAARTMAN *ET AL.* (eds.), *Wie maakt de dienst uit? Macht en onmacht in opvoeding en hulpverlening* (Agiel: Utrecht, 2004) 41-60 (literature on 259-267), 57.

Two out of three children (approximately 67%) in industrialized countries[61] benefit more or less from family life: their parents are 'good enough' (that is not too poorly, too ill-equipped) in terms of their being prepared for parenthood *c.q.* their parental awareness: their emotional maturity, mental health, intelligence, marriage stability, alcohol use, income and employment, neighbourhood situation, etcetera.[62]

One out of five children (approximately 20%) in industrialized countries both benefit and suffer from family life, and are at risk of some form or degree of developmental damage, *c.q.* of developing psychosocial problems; parental behaviour may at times fall in some child abuse and neglect scale or chronically in the lower scales of child abuse and neglect classifications.[63]

One out of ten children (approximately 10%) in industrialized countries see their fundamental rights to physical and psychological security, integrity, dignity and healthy holistic development seriously threatened and violated, they may suffer chronic degrading treatment (for instance chronic negativism and non-communication within the family[64]), and fall within classifications of child abuse and neglect into the upper scales.

One to three out of one hundred children (1 to 3%) in industrialized countries suffer forms of child abuse and neglect to degrees, well in the upper scales, amounting to torture, that is treatment which would be labelled torture if it were not parents or other carers but official or semi-

---

[61] It is very difficult to give a global picture, although a World Health Organization study (ETIENNE G. KRUG ET AL. (eds.), *World Report on Violence and Health*, WHO: Geneva 2002) states (available at: <www.who.int/violence_injury_prevention/violence/world_ report/factsheets/en/childabusefacts.pdf>): 'Child abuse is a global problem that is deeply rooted in cultural, economic and social practices. (…) In some studies, between one-quarter and one-half of children report severe and frequent physical abuse, including being beaten, kicked or tied up by parents. Available data also suggests that about 20% of women and 5-10% of men suffered sexual abuse as children. (…) Many children are subjected to psychological or emotional abuse as well as neglect, though the true extent of these problems are not known'. The UN prepares a global study on (state, family, school and other) violence against children, available at: <www.ohchr.org/english/bodies/crc/study.htm>.

[62] Co-incidentally (?), the number of securely attached children (interview, by STERRE VAN LEER, with RIEN VAN IJZENDOORN, 'Veilig gehechte ouders hebben een grote kans op veilig gehechte kinderen,' in: *Psychologie Magazine*, November 2004, 52): About two out of three children are securely attached. The others are insecurely attached or have a disorganized attachment.

[63] For a detailed classification with five severity scales, see supra n. 6.

[64] *Psychologie Magazine*, February 2004, 17 (MICHAEL RUTTER, quoted by HELEEN PEVERELLI).

official figures who would be responsible for the cruelty, abuse or neglect in question.

So, in a hypothetical group of 30 children, 20 are by and large fine and safe, six have been or will be at risk at some time or are all the time, three are or have been or will be victims of child abuse and neglect, one is or has been or will be victim of one or more very serious forms of child abuse and neglect. In human rights terms: in any group of 30 children, there is one torture victim,[65] three victims of degrading treatment, and six potential or semi-victims. Imagine that in any industrialized country the same were true for any group of 30 more or less vulnerable adults, let us say prison inmates, physically or mentally handicapped or elderly persons or psychiatric patients in understaffed institutions … Imagine the public outrage, and outcry, if such numbers were broadcasted and made public

The parents of the 20 relatively happy children have prepared themselves in one way or other for parenthood or have learned very fast along the way. The 10 other children are likely to have parents with all kinds of problems, from relatively mild to very serious, regardless whether they have prepared or tried to prepare themselves for parenthood.

8. PREPARATION FOR PARENTHOOD AS A HUMAN RIGHT

To really improve public health, the best thing to do is to install sewers and a water supply system.[66] To really improve mental health, you could introduce psycho-education and psycho-hygiene in school curricula. Likewise, a system of preparation for parenthood, based on adequate responsabilisation and empowerment of parents and parents-to-be, is likely to be the best candidate for the psychological and socio-educational equivalent of the installation of sewers and water supply. Considering, on the one hand the two third/one third estimate presented in the preceding paragraph, and on the other hand all the knowledge we have today on the consequences and the prevention of child abuse and neglect, and on early child and early brain development, one feels tempted to present the following thesis as one's very first conclusion: the greatest foe of children's wellbeing, health and

---

[65] On the question of domestic violence (against women) as torture under international law, see the chapter by THEO VAN BOVEN & SABINA PUIG in this book ('Domestic violence against women and torture').

[66] DICK SWAAB, quoted in *NRC Handelsblad*, 5/6 February 2005, Zaterdags Bijvoegsel, 37 i.f. (JANNETJE KOELEWIJN, 'Nee, de baarmoeder is niet veilig').

development is adults' selfishness and short-sightedness, adults' egocentrism and myopia. And by adults I do not mean parents alone, but all of us. Both an American neurobiologist and a European Union lawyer can testify to this. Neurobiologist Allan Schore commented in 2001 on the situation in the US (and The Netherlands appears to be moving very fast in the same direction[67]) where working mothers have no other choice but to send very young babies to sub-optimal day care:[68]

In the US we send mothers back into the work force at 6 weeks, at the exact point of a massive organization of the visual areas of the brain and the period in which face-to-face play interactions just begin. Parents now struggle with the terrible dilemma of how to cope with this problem, without any social-political support at all. In addition the level of day care here is, on average, clearly sub-optimal. (...) As I say this, the first word that comes to describe this attitude towards the youngest members of our societies is 'scandalous'. We, the adults, should definitely feel shame about how we're avoiding this problem, and about how little attention we're paying to our futures.

European Union lawyer, former member of the European Parliament and rapporteur and author of the European Charter of Rights of the Child (adopted on 8 July 1992)[69], Bandrés Molet commented in 1996 (and not very much seems to have changed in this regard since then) on child abuse as a social taboo:[70]

But referring to our so-called advanced societies, we have to recognize that child abuse is under a social taboo which is very difficult to change. (...) All over the world, but also in Europe and even in our surroundings, sometimes due to our silence, children suffer from the consequences of the incomprehension, the selfishness, the indifference, the lasciviousness or the cruelty and brutality of adults.

In the (recent) past, the greatest foe of adults' selfishness and short-sightedness (or egocentrism and myopia) has proven to be, at times at least, the balance of rights and duties as postulated since the Second World War by and in the universal language of human rights.

---

67 See MARIANNE RIKSEN-WALRAVEN, *Wie het kleine niet eert ...; Over de grote invloed van vroege sociale ervaringen*, Inaugural lecture, [Radboud] University Nijmegen, 2002, 19/20.

68 Quoted by MARIANNE RIKSEN-WALRAVEN, *Wie het kleine niet eert ...*, [Radboud] University Nijmegen, 2002,. 20 (reference at p. 23 *i.f.*).

69 European Parliament resolution on a European Charter of Rights of the Child (OJ C 241, 21.9.1992, p. 67). The text of the Charter is included in EUGEEN VERHELLEN (ed.), *Monitoring Children's Rights* (Martinus Nijhoff Publishers: The Hague (etc.), 1996) Appendix 3, 923-930.

70 JUAN MARIA BANDRÉS MOLET, 'Towards a European law on children: the European Charter of Rights of the Child', in: EUGEEN VERHELLEN (ed.), *Monitoring Children's Rights* (Martinus Nijhoff Publishers: The Hague (etc.), 1996) 160.

Fortunately, apart from egocentrism and myopia, human beings have also been endowed by Evolution, or Evolution's Creator, with, however feeble, social, that is pro-social tendencies and potentialities. This is probably why human rights being based on a well-balanced mix of universal rights and responsibilities in relation to liberty, equality and social justice,[71] have been, in industrialized countries to begin with, relatively successful considering their very short legal existence. Thanks of course to the work of many individuals and many IGOs and NGOs (inter- and non-governmental organizations).

This positive turn to a negative thesis immediately brings me to a second – a normative – thesis: preparation for parenthood, starting in schools (that is starting with psycho-education and psycho-hygiene in school curricula), must be proclaimed – on the basis of children's rights and other human rights, such as the important right, proclaimed in 1948 and put in treaty form in 1966, to benefit from scientific progress[72] – as a human right for all parents-to-be.[73] On the same grounds and as an integral part of preparation for parenthood as a human right, parental (assistance and) support must be proclaimed as a basic right for all parents and parents-to-be who have any problems whatsoever which may negatively influence their experience of parenthood – which should be an enriching experience for them and be beneficial for their children. All of these should at the same time be seen as fundamental rights of the child. Supervision of parenthood – that is, monitoring of the healthy holistic development of each child – should be a corollary of these rights of the child. In other words preparation for parenthood and support and supervision of parents are to be seen as fundamental rights of the child. Does the Convention on the Rights of the Child, say so too? Does the CRC make any mention, or give any indication, of the rights of the child to prepared parents, to supported parents and to supervised parents?

---

71 J.C.M. WILLEMS, 'Als de rechten van het kind de dienst zouden uitmaken ...', in: H. BAARTMAN ET AL. (eds.), Wie maakt de dienst uit? Macht en onmacht in opvoeding en hulpverlening (Agiel: Utrecht, 2004) 46-49 (literature on 259-267).

72 Article 27, para 1 of the Universal Declaration of Human Rights, recodified in Article 15, para 1 sub b and para 2 of ICESCR: the International Covenant on Economic, Social and Cultural Rights, adopted by the General Assembly in 1966.

73 Based, apart from the Articles mentioned above, on at least the following Articles: Article 18, para 2, Article 19, para 2, Article 24, para 2 sub e and f, and Article 27, para 3 CRC, Article 16, para 3, and Article 25, para 2, of the Universal Declaration of Human Rights, Article 23 (International Covenant on Civil and Political Rights), Articles 10, 11, and 12 (International Covenant on Economic, Social and Cultural Rights), and Articles 5, 10 sub h, 11, and 16 (Convention on the Elimination of all forms of Discrimination Against Women).

In other words, to what degree does the CRC account for the fact that children may only have a more or less equal start in life in so far as the mental health of parents including their emotional and cognitive intelligence and parental awareness, the standard of living of parents, and their knowledge of emotions, relationships, human communication and interaction, and more specifically on child development, child care and child rearing are adequate for healthy holistic child development, especially ECD (Early Child Development)? Let us look at some CRC state obligations in this regard. Let us look first, however, at what I call the CRC's paradigm of the Trias pedagogica.

9. TRIAS PEDAGOGICA: FROM CONSTITUTIONALISATION TO OPERATIONALISATION

Walk upstairs, open the door gently, and look in the crib. What do you see? Most of us see a picture of innocence and helplessness, a clean slate. But, in fact, what we see in the crib is the greatest mind that has ever existed, the most powerful learning machine in the universe.[74]

Not only the learning machine in the crib, but also the less powerful minds around the crib have (and have had) a lot of learning to do with respect to the tasks, rights, duties and responsibilities – developmental, parental and all the other ones that come with life and parenthood – that are awaiting them. This message is conveyed by the term Trias pedagogica. The term Trias pedagogica basically signifies three things:
(1.) three actors are at work: the child, the parent, and the state, in a constitutional framework of rights of children, preparation, support and supervision of parents, child and parent participation and related state obligations; (2.) in the context of duties state obligations towards parents and children and parental duties and responsibilities towards the child as legislated by the state on the basis of its international legal obligations; (3.) in the dimension of healthy holistic child development: the child is a subject of rights (of interrelated, and overlapping, provision, prevention, protection, participation and reparation rights, of interdependent developmental and autonomy rights) which guarantee (promote and protect) his or her personal security and integrity, affection-based guidance and direction by carers and adequate care for the optimal

---

74 GOPNIK ET AL., *The Scientist in the Crib: What Early Learning Tells Us about the Mind* (2001), quoted by MARIANNE RIKSEN-WALRAVEN, *Wie het kleine niet eert ...; Over de grote invloed van vroege sociale ervaringen*, Inaugural lecture, [Radboud] University Nijmegen, 2002, 4.

development of his or her personality and his or her development
towards 'responsible democratic citizenship'.[75]

A true Trias pedagogica starts with constitutionalisation: the translation
– and implementation in law and policy on the basis thereof – of human
rights in constitutional rights, of treaty law in constitutional law.[76] I have
drawn up a draft article to give an impression of what this could mean,
to indicate what could be an example of a constitutional provision in any
country one likes to fill in:

- Every child in (Belgium, Brazil, Canada, China, Egypt, Ethiopia,
  India, Japan, Mexico, The Netherlands, New Zealand, Nigeria,
  Somalia, South Africa, the United States of America …) has the
  right to have his or her physical and psychological integrity
  respected and protected, and to receive the affection, direction
  and guidance of adults, preferably his or her own parents, as
  well as adequate care for the optimal development of his or her
  personality, in order to become, to the fullest potential of his or
  her talents and abilities, a responsible democratic citizen.
- To ensure and promote the rights mentioned in the first
  paragraph, the government will provide for and maintain an
  integrated system of socio-educational institutions, services and
  facilities, youth care (including family counselling,
  psychotherapeutic services and family guidance), foster care,
  and child protection.
- Socio-educational services and facilities will include information
  and advice concerning child health and child development,
  especially early and pre-school child development, educational
  allowances and leave, and educational assistance and support
  for all parents.
- The government will provide, or see to the provision of, school
  education and training on child development, child care and
  child rearing, as well as all other education and training which
  should help school age children and adolescents to fully develop
  their personality and prepare themselves for responsible

---

[75] In relation to 'responsible democratic citizenship', Article 29 CRC and the General
Comment of the UN Committee on the Rights of the Child on this Article: General
Comment No. 1, 2001, CRC/GC/2001/1 (<www.ohchr.org>, <www.unhchr.ch>), *The
aims of education*.

[76] JAN C.M. WILLEMS, 'The children's law of nations: the international rights of the child
in the Trias pedagogica', in: JAN C.M. WILLEMS (ed.), *Developmental and Autonomy Rights
of Children; Empowering Children, Caregivers and Communities* (Intersentia: Antwerpen
(etc.), 2002) 88-89.

democratic citizenship and for responsible and fulfilling parenthood.
- The government will see to the proper participation of both children and parents in or in relation to, all policies, institutions, services and facilities affecting the wellbeing of families and the healthy holistic development of children.

Such a constitutional article is today's Utopia, but hopefully tomorrow's reality. This hope is based on the involvement not only of several IGOs (Unicef and others) and many NGOs (Defence for Children International and many others) but also of growing numbers of professionals and professional organizations (such as ISPCAN[77] and many national and international ones) in the process of emancipation of children, especially the very young. Unfortunately, but this may change in the near future as awareness grows, professionals and professional organizations do not yet take a united stand and make a common front together with IGOs, NGOs and other stakeholders – thus making the Trias pedagogica a Trias of children, parents and society, not of children, parents and the state alone.

Albeit, as a lawyer, rather than an activist, let alone a prophet, I will limit myself now to the building blocks for a constitutional Trias pedagogica – children's rights, parental support rights, state obligations – as they are clearly to be found in the Convention on the Rights of the Child. I will not bother the reader with a full list of articles and extensive legal analysis. However, I will pick out, and comment upon, a few.[78]

10. THE CRC: BUILDING BLOCKS FOR A CONSTITUTIONAL TRIAS PEDAGOGICA

Article 5 CRC states that States Parties shall respect the responsibilities, rights and duties of parents (the parental child-rearing duty-right[79]).[80]

---

[77] ISPCAN, the International Society for Prevention of Child Abuse and Neglect, stoutly entitled a history book for its 25th birthday: *An International Movement to End Child Abuse* (Carol Stream, Illinois 2002).

[78] See also (in general and in relation to the Articles mentioned) RACHEL HODGKIN, PETER NEWELL, *Implementation Handbook for the Convention on the Rights of the Child*, Unicef: New York, Geneva 2002, 2nd edition.

[79] Formulated as a duty and a right in Article 1:247, para 1, of the Dutch Civil Code.

[80] See also Article 3, para 2 CRC: States Parties undertake to ensure the child such protection and care as is necessary for his or her well-being, taking into account the rights and duties of his or her parents (…). And Article 18, para 1, second sentence CRC: Parents (…) have the primary responsibility for the upbringing and development of the child. (Article 14, para 2 CRC seems superfluous in light of Article 5 – although it

The state duty to respect this family life duty-right involves both negative and positive respect obligations. Negative respect: no arbitrary – but only justified and adequate – interventions in family life. Already here, much has to be improved. Some 75% of state interventions through the courts in Dutch families could be avoided, according to Dutch psychologist and professor of educational sciences Jo Hermanns, if institutions were to work more professionally, were more evidence-based, and also were to co-operate in a much more professional manner. With adequate budgets, of course, to do their job.[81] Unfortunately, welfare and child protection institutions seem to function on the basis of low budgets rather than on the basis of high professional standards.[82]

Jo Hermanns leads, together with Myra ter Meulen, the so-called RAAK regions in The Netherlands (RAAK is a Dutch foundation called Reflection and Action Group on Child Abuse and Neglect).[83] In these (four) state-subsidized regions attempts are being made to work and co-operate more professionally, on the basis of the concept of an evidence-based so-called 'continuum of care'[84] (that is combined universal, selective and indicated prevention – to which I will return in the next paragraph).[85]

---

speaks of 'direction' only, and not of 'direction and guidance' of the child as a parental right and duty.)

[81] Interview in *Vrij Nederland*, 11 January 2003, and emails to the author 21 January 2005.

[82] See also: <www.johermanns.info>, Actueel, Discussiëren over de jeugdzorg (21 January 2005). One of the main causes of the poor performance of Dutch welfare and child protection institutions seems to be the misuse of power and power play by high-ranking civil servants: see letters KLAAS GROEN and J.C.M. WILLEMS in *NRC Handelsblad*, 4 and 7 December 2004, respectively.

[83] See <www.raak.org>, or go directly to <www.samenopvoeden.nl>.

[84] See JO HERMANNS, *Het bestrijden van kindermishandeling: welke aanpak werkt?* (COACT Consult: Woerden, 2003); for an (earlier) English version, see JO HERMANNS, *Towards Advice and Reporting Centres against Child Abuse in the Netherlands Antilles* (COACT Consult: Willemstad/Woerden, 2001) (for information on these reports, see <www.coact.nl> or <www.johermanns.info>).

[85] See also JOHN W. KYDD, 'Preventing child maltreatment: an integrated multisectoral approach', in: *Health and Human Rights*, 2003, 34-63 (also at <www.ispcan.org/documents/vid/prevention.kydd.pdf>); MATTHEW R. SANDERS, WARREN CANN & CAROL MARKIE-DADDS, 'Why a universal population-level approach to the prevention of child abuse is essential', in: *Child Abuse Review*, 2003, 145-154; MATTHEW R. SANDERS, WARREN CANN & CAROL MARKIE-DADDS, 'The Triple P-Positive Parenting Programme: a universal population-level approach to the prevention of child abuse', in: *Child Abuse Review*, 2003, 155-171; JANE BARLOW & SARAH STEWART-BROWN, 'Why a universal population-level approach to the prevention of child abuse is essential; Letter to the editors', in: *Child Abuse Review*, 2003, 279-281.

Arbitrariness and lack of professional standards do not stop there, however. As recent research (by Wim Slot and others) indicated:[86] only in one third of (state *c.q.* court) interventions in the family, the situation improved for the damaged children. In one third of interventions, the situation became even worse for the children concerned in spite of their right under Article 39 CRC, the important article on trauma reparation, a unique provision in international law. Article 39 states:

States Parties shall take all appropriate measures to promote physical and psychological recovery and social reintegration of a child victim of: any form of neglect, exploitation, or abuse (...). Such recovery and reintegration shall take place in an environment which fosters the health, self-respect and dignity of the child.

Then of course, there is a child's right to intervention (well-known Article 19 CRC). But only few people report[87] to the Dutch AMK's (Child Abuse and Neglect Advise and Reporting Centres).[88] Or there are

---

[86] N.W. SLOT, A. THEUNISSEN, F.J. ESMEIJER, Y. DUIVENVOORDEN, *909 Zorgen; Een onderzoek naar de doelmatigheid van de ondertoezichtstelling*, Vrije Universiteit (Faculteit der Psychologie en Pedagogiek, Afdeling Orthopedagogiek): Amsterdam 2002. See also J.M.A. (JO) HERMANNS, 'Effectieve hulp in het kader van een dwangmaatregel', in: H. BAARTMAN, D. GRAAS, R. DE GROOT, TJ. ZANDBERG (eds.), *Wie maakt de dienst uit? Macht en onmacht in opvoeding en hulpverlening* (Agiel: Utrecht, 2004) (literature on 259-267), 107.

[87] There is no mandated reporting in The Netherlands. For the Dutch situation, see H.E.M. BAARTMAN, L. DE MEY, 'Protecting, reporting and supporting: child abuse and the assessment of risks in The Netherlands', in: MICHAEL FREEMAN (ed.), *Overcoming Child Abuse: A Window on a World Problem* (Ashgate/Dartmouth: Aldershot (etc.) 2000) 281-304. For the very negative effects ('a bankrupt policy') of mandated reporting in the US, see GARY B. MELTON, 'Mandated reporting: a policy without reason', in: *Child Abuse & Neglect*, 2005, 9-18. Whereas the US system appears to be one of investigation ('What happened?'), the Dutch system, which is as much or as little preventative as the American child protection system, at least is more welfare oriented ('What can we do to help?'; *cf.* MELTON, at p. 14). That is, if there are no waiting lists for abused children and their families. Also highly negative on mandated reporting is an Australian study by MARIA HARRIES & MIKE CLARE ET AL., *Mandatory Reporting of Child Abuse: Evidence and Options; Report (...) for the Western Australian Child Protection Council*, July 2002, available at: <http://fcs.wa.gov.au/_content/miscellaneous/mandatory_reporting.pdf>.

[88] See a recent survey by NOVA (a Dutch TV news program) on <www.novatv.nl> and <www.geheimgeweld.nl>. See also CEES HOEFNAGELS & MACHTELD ZWIKKER, 'The bystander dilemma and child abuse: extending the Latané & Darley model to domestic violence', and [CEES HOEFNAGELS], 'Signaleren en melden van vermoede kindermishandeling door omstanders: de rol van demografische en attitudinale factoren en eerdere ervaring met kindermishandeling', in: C.J. HOEFNAGELS, *Met recht van spreken; Enkele theoretische en empirische bijdragen ten behoeve van de secundaire preventie van kindermishandeling* (SWP: Amsterdam, 2001) 171-195 and 196-246, respectively.

waiting lists for maltreated children and their families: Article 19 states (italics added):

1. States Parties shall take all appropriate legislative, administrative, social and educational measures to protect the child from all forms of physical or mental violence, injury or abuse, neglect or negligent treatment, maltreatment or exploitation, including sexual abuse, while in the care of parent(s), legal guardian(s) or any other person who has the care of the child.
2. Such protective measures should, as appropriate, include effective procedures for the establishment of *social programmes to provide necessary support for the child and for those who have the care of the child, as well as for other forms of prevention* and for identification, reporting, referral, investigation, treatment and follow-up of instances of child maltreatment described heretofore, and, as appropriate, for judicial involvement.

Much, therefore, still needs to be done in relation to the negative respect (that is the *ex post*) obligations (after damage has occurred): improving professional standards and co-operation, raising budgets, promoting, reporting *('What can we do to help?)*, improving intervention and reparation. But what about the positive respect obligations, state obligations to positively respect parental responsibilities? Here, we encounter the child's right to (universal) prevention. Two CRC articles deal with fighting 'parental poverty' for child development. Article 27, para 1 and 3, deals with material parental poverty:

1. States Parties recognize the right of every child to a standard of living adequate for the child's physical, mental, spiritual, moral and social development.
3. States Parties, in accordance with national conditions and within their means, shall take appropriate measures to assist parents and others responsible for the child to implement this right and shall in case of need provide material assistance and support programmes (…).

Further, Article 18, para 2, deals with mental and emotional parental poverty (lack of intelligence, mental health and/or basic knowledge on healthy holistic child development):

For the purpose of guaranteeing and promoting the rights set forth in the present Convention, States Parties shall render appropriate assistance to parents and legal guardians in the performance of their child-rearing responsibilities and shall ensure the development of institutions, facilities and services for the care of children.

So, the state must positively respect parental responsibilities by assisting parents both financially and pedagogically for healthy holistic child development (as formulated in Article 27, para 1). This is linked to Article 4, which makes these state duties a national priority; all the knowledge, financial and organizational means in the country have to be directed towards healthy holistic child development. Article 4 states (italics added):

States Parties shall undertake all appropriate legislative, administrative, and other measures for the implementation of the rights recognized in the present Convention. With regard to economic, social and cultural rights, States Parties shall undertake such measures *to the maximum extent* of their available resources and, where needed, within the framework of international co-operation.

Like the human right to work (that is, a just combination of work and care responsibilities for men and women[89]) and the human right to found a family[90] (sometimes called reproductive rights, especially in relation to certain aspects of the right *not* to found a family) and to raise one's children,[91] the (proposed and, *inter alia*, CRC based) human right to preparation for parenthood and to parental support (facilitation, empowerment and participation of parents) are duty-rights, which means that they entail all kinds of responsibilities for adults, not for states alone. States, however, have three implied duties in this regard: (1.) legal and social responsabilisation: saying in the law and in public campaigns, and through any other means, what is expected of parents (not hitting and humiliating children, offering children affection-based guidance and direction); (2.) school and pre-childbirth education, information and preparation of parents-to-be; and (3.) pre-, peri- and post-natal empowerment of parents, *c.q.* parents-to-be. These threefold duties follow from the (CRC based) rights of the child to preparation for parenthood and support and supervision of parents as well as from the (proposed and, *inter alia*, CRC based) general human rights of

---

89 Article 11, para 1 sub a Women's Convention refers to the right to work as 'an inalienable right of all human beings.' Article 11, para 2 sub c Women's Convention goes on to state: In order to (…) ensure [women's] effective right to work, State Parties shall take appropriate measures (…) to enable parents to combine family obligations with work responsibilities (…). Article 18, para 1 CRC reinforces 'the principle that both parents have common responsibilities for the upbringing and development of the child'.

90 Article 16, para 1 Universal Declaration of Human Rights: Men and women of full age (…) have the right (…) to found a family. ('Of full age' should be read, and may be read some time in the future, as 'of full age and maturity' – parallel to Article 12, para 1 CRC.) Article 23, para 2 ICCPR refers to the right of men and women 'of marriageable age' to found a family. (Of course, marriageable may, some time in the future, be understood in both a biological and a psychological sense.)

91 Article 18, para 1 CRC: both parents having the best interests of the child as their basic concern. Article 9, para 1 CRC: a child shall not be separated from his or her parents unless such separation is necessary for the best interests of the child. Article 7, para 1 CRC: the right of the child to know and be cared for by his or her parents.

preparation for parenthood and parental support of parents and parents-to-be.

The question then arises: what structures of parenthood preparation, support and supervision exist in industrialized countries? And how can they be improved in light of the, *grosso modo*, 30 percent of children in industrialized countries who would greatly benefit therefrom or whose lives or minds could be saved by the establishment and/or improvement of comprehensive systems of combined universal, selective and indicated prevention.

11. CONTINUUM OF CARE: COMBINED UNIVERSAL, SELECTIVE AND INDICATED PREVENTION

To my knowledge, a comprehensive and integrated system of combined universal, selective and indicated prevention exists nowhere (in spite of the outstanding efforts made in the Dutch RAAK regions I mentioned above). Many changes in law and policy have been made, however, in some countries in this direction.[92] The main aspects that are missing in my view are: preparation through psycho-education in school and at pregnancy; the watertight combination of the three successive forms of prevention (universal, selective and indicated - Hermanns's continuum of care) and adequate supervision.

Universal prevention refers, for the purposes of this chapter, to all sorts of facilitation and information, courses and training, programs and services that are open to all parents and parents-to-be; *selective* prevention refers to all sorts of (evidence-based) programs and services that try to address certain risk factors or at risk populations and at risk neighbourhoods (in so far these risks, and especially the cumulation thereof, are not sufficiently compensated or buffered by protective factors in the individual, family or community concerned); *indicated* prevention refers to all sorts of (evidence-based) programs and services that try to address situations where pregnant women, children or families are having serious problems of whatever kind (from personal to personality problems, from practical to psychosocial problems, etcetera). Let us

---

[92]   See A.W.M. VELDKAMP, *Over grenzen! Internationaal vergelijkende verkenning van de rol van de overheid bij de opvoeding en bescherming van kinderen*, Ministerie van Justitie: Den Haag, 2001. See also VELDKAMP's English abstract in: MARIANNE BERGER, *Parenting Matters; Verslag [van] een Europese expertmeeting over de mogelijkheden van drang in de opvoedingsondersteuning* (NIZW Jeugd: [Utrecht 2005]) 4-5 (for information on this report, available at: <www.nizw.nl>, and contact NIZW Youth or NIZW International Centre).

rephrase this, on the basis of the estimate of (arguably preventable) developmental damage of children presented above, in terms of parental autonomy, both legal and emotional or personal autonomy, that is. The following hypothesis (and connected legal reform suggestion[93]) may then be put forward:

- 67% of parents are sufficiently autonomous – that is mentally healthy *c.q.* emotionally mature, in terms of the level of development of the rational, moral and authentic aspects of their personality – in order to leave their legal parental autonomy fully intact; they may welcome, and benefit from, or may not be overly interested in universal prevention facilities;
- 20% of parents may see their personal autonomy lifted through universal and selective prevention to a full legal parental autonomy level;
- 10% of parents may see their personal autonomy lifted through selective and indicated prevention to a higher, or even full, legal parental autonomy level;
- 3% of parents may see their personal autonomy lifted through indicated prevention (including 'reparation' of youth trauma and 'rehabilitation'[94]), although some of them may never reach a full legal parental autonomy level; several of these parents will see their (young) children being raised by other adults able to give these children affection, guidance and direction. As long as their children are minors and in the care of others, these parents should be entitled to counselling and guidance.

12. CONCLUSION

Let me come to my conclusion. Children's rights is a concept that basically has to do with two things: (1.) children are not the property of their parents or other caregivers, nor of anybody else, they are subjects and persons in their own right; and (2.) children are entitled to the best that society has to offer regarding their healthy holistic development, especially their pre-school emotional development, their physical and emotional wellbeing during the first years of life, the years of brain,

---

[93] Legal parental autonomy levels may be associated with existing or new measures of child protection. These measures could be part of agreements with parents, but ultimately may be court imposed.

[94] Article 39 CRC applies, so to speak, to the traumatized child within the parent(-to-be). If he or she is not a minor, the legally (more) correct Article to invoke would, of course, be Article 18, para 2 CRC.

attachment and personality formation and organization. Unicef
executive director Carol Bellamy once said:[95]

*States are obliged to protect children against violence wherever it occurs and it is vital
that they do so. What happens to children determines society's attitudes to violence.
Protecting them from violence today is crucial to the prevention of violence throughout
society in the future.*

Human rights scholars, students and activists, committed, each in his or
her own way and within his or her means, to the causes and principles of
peace, human dignity, sustainable human development and democratic
governance, cannot or can no longer, ignore – and allow themselves not
to study – violence against children as a root cause of many other forms
of violence, including material and mental poverty, despotism,
criminality, hatred, intolerance and indifference – all of which constitute
a direct threat to everything they have committed themselves to.
Therefore, I would like to propose a thought experiment.

Imagine all of us working in the field of human rights today could have
a second life. After our death we wait for the last one of us to die, behind
a veil of ignorance.[96] And then, resurrected, we have to decide, all
together, democratically, where we would like to be born. We have two
options. We can choose a country, any country we like. Or we can choose
parents, that is, parents with an average income and mental health in
any country where governments, communities, professionals and others
are fighting transism on the basis of a constitutional Trias pedagogica.
Would we, with everything we know about child abuse and neglect, the
ensuing abnormal brain development, and other preventable
developmental damage to infants and children, choose a rich country to
be born in? A country with many opportunities, liberties, good schools
etcetera, like Belgium, or maybe, still, The Netherlands? Or would we
choose parents, with an average income and mental health, in any
country providing families with information and adequate support and
supervision? Maybe we can ask Carol Bellamy to take the vote.

---

95 CAROL BELLAMY, addressing the 2nd Intergovernmental Conference on Making Europe
   and Central Asia Part of a World Fit for Children, Sarajevo 13 May 2004 (*see*
   <www.unicef.org/media/media_21164.html>, retrieved 3 February 2005).
96 See RAWLS's 'veil of ignorance', on which see SUSAN NEIMAN, *Het kwaad denken; Een
   andere geschiedenis van de filosofie* (*Evil in Modern Thought; An Alternative History of
   Philosophy*, 2002) (Boom: Amsterdam, 2004) 328; and JAN C.M. WILLEMS, *Wie zal de
   Opvoeders Opvoeden? Kindermishandeling en het Recht van het Kind op Persoonswording (Who
   will Educate the Educators? Child Abuse and the Right of the Child to Become a Person (with a
   summary in English)]*, T.M.C. Asser Press: The Hague 1999, 181.

All countries in the world are parties to the Convention on the Rights of the Child, all the countries of the world, which is absolutely unique, except Somalia and the USA, which states have, as we know, divergent problems with their membership of the world community. As an international lawyer with some knowledge of psychology and a keen interest in the normative (moral, political and pedagogical) aspects of the law, especially of human rights law, I have done and continue to do research into the meaning and the potential of the CRC for the prevention of developmental damage to children (especially child abuse and neglect) and the promotion of the healthy holistic development of children (especially ECD, Early Child Development). After more than 15 years of work in this field, I have come to the conclusion that the most important implication of the CRC for Western states, to begin with, is the fundamental legal and social change from repressive and stigmatizing systems (early 20th century systems) of child protection towards (21st century) pro-active and inclusive (integrationist) systems of parenthood preparation, support and supervision. With all the investments it takes, which will pay back[97] in many ways that will promote peace and security, democracy and sustainability, wellbeing and freedom in the world.[98]

This change should start in the schools: psycho-education and psycho-hygiene should be part of all school curricula, and psycho-education and psycho-hygiene should include information on child development and on child care and child rearing. This school education should continue in the form of (more specific) information for parents-to-be, pre-, peri- and postnatal ECD programs, including home visiting[99] starting early in pregnancy, video-feedback, counselling and therapy, in combination with generous (paid) parental leave for both parents during at least the first two to three years of life of children, community new mother groups and new father groups, financial and practical support, high quality child care, relationship therapy, social work, mediation, and so on and so forth, for young parents. There should be a continuum of care for (young) parents. Combined with a system of foster care and counselling for parents who do not raise their own children – in those cases, of course, where it would be irresponsible if society did not see to it that

---

[97] See H. WATERS et al., The Economic Dimensions of Interpersonal Violence, World Health Organization: Geneva 2004 (available at: <www.who.int/violence_injury_prevention/ publications/violence/economic_dimensions/en>).

[98] See on these and other fundamental values and key objectives, the United Nations Millennium Declaration (General Assembly resolution 55/2 of 8 September 2000).

[99] JANE BARLOW ET AL., 'Working in partnership: the development of a home visiting service for vulnerable families', in: Child Abuse Review, 2003, 172-189.

children's rights to affection-based guidance and direction are being met
by other adults than the biological parents, who, for whatever reason or
through whatever cause, are not in a position to meet these rights
themselves even with the support of others.

There must also be legal change. The law should not only define the best
interests of the child. In The Netherlands this is broadly defined as 'the
mental-and-physical wellbeing of the child and the development of his
or her personality.'[100] But the law should also define parental
care/authority, not only indicate that parental care/authority is both a
right and a duty,[101] a (vague) parental responsibility, but also be much
more specific on the kind of responsibilities, and the exact duties, this
involves: not hitting and humiliating children, offering children
affection-based guidance and direction, sending children to school and
to sporting clubs, giving them tasks and responsibilities in the household
and in the community, and so on and so forth. At the same time, the law
should define not only what is expected from parents, but also be very
clear and specific on what parents can expect from society and the state,
in terms of the above mentioned continuum of care, that is of universal,
selective and indicated prevention in one integrated and comprehensive
system of parent-and-child care.

In many countries this fundamental legal and social change amounts to
no less than a minor or even major cultural revolution. Family values are
no longer a matter of negative respect – state abstention and '*ex post*
interventionism' (*laissez-faire* and 'after damage' intervention) – only.
Positive respect is required from society and the state. Positive respect
obligations, stemming from children's rights and CRC principles and
provisions, are to be fulfilled. *Laissez-faire* systems are to be replaced by
pro-active systems of shared responsibility, within communities, of
parents, volunteers and professionals. Repression and stigmatization
have to be replaced by prevention and inclusion. This cultural revolution
should be triggered, apart from the CRC and positive state obligations,
by raising awareness of the enormous numbers of abused and neglected
children, and the impact of child abuse and neglect on individuals,
families and society – an impact (psychological, economic, trans-
generational; health, mental health, crime, domestic violence, violent
crime, and so on and so forth related) which is hard to over-estimate.
Child abuse and neglect figures and impact are multiplied by the huge
scope of and suffering caused by, preventable developmental damage to

---

[100] In Article 1:247, para 2, of the Dutch Civil Code.
[101] As in Article 1:247, para 1, of the Dutch Civil Code.

children, damage which may or may not fall within definitions and classifications of child abuse and neglect.

I just said 'apart from the CRC (and positive state obligations)'. What the CRC adds however, is the rights-based approach which has already triggered so many a process of emancipation (of workers, of homosexuals, of women). What the CRC also adds, is the basis and the direction of this emancipation process. This basis is the rights of the child as a human being and citizen dependent on affection-based guidance and direction; including tasks and responsibilities, inclusion and participation, social reintegration and rehabilitation, which are all part of healthy holistic child development, and which are all included in CRC positive state obligations. This is the basis the CRC offers, but the CRC (in combination with other human rights instruments) also shows the direction of this emancipation process: the rights of parents to be prepared and to parental support, and thus to the acknowledgement of their fundamental role in creating and maintaining families, societies and ultimately a world 'fit for children'.

In spite of the brave words of Gabriela Azurduy Arrieta, from Bolivia, and Audrey Cheynut, from Monaco, who spoke to the General Assembly of the United Nations – the brave words I quoted at the beginning (directly after the introduction) of this chapter – in spite of these brave words, children cannot and should not fight for their rights all by themselves. They need adults: parents, professionals and others, to stand by their side. So, I would like to conclude by expressing my hope that adults, all over the world, can and will say after, and to, Gabriela Azurduy Arrieta and Audrey Cheynut: We adults will join you in your fight for children's rights. We have the accumulated knowledge of many disciplines, we have the will (and in the West the wealth), the sensitivity and the dedication.

DOMESTIC HOMICIDE - AN OFFENCE AT THE EXTREME END OF A VIOLENT CONTINUUM

Frans Koenraadt and Marieke Liem

1. INTRODUCTION

The closed nature of the family acts as a protective cover, behind which abuse and ill-treatment may continue undisturbed. This greatly complicates any investigation of the motives and actual course of events. Domestic violence covers a wide range of delinquent behaviour, where homicide is a lethal one at the extreme end of a continuum of violence. On the basis of research and literature in the domestic area, we explore in this contribution, the patterns and motives of killing ones relatives. In the family, special attention is paid to the relationship between (structural) domestic violence and fatal killings.

After a short introduction on the prevalence of domestic homicide, especially at a national (Dutch) level (sections 1-3) we will focus on a description of different types and patterns of domestic homicide; the killing of spouses (section 4), children (section 5), parents (section 6), and siblings (section 7). Some case vignettes are presented. Finally, some concluding remarks will be made (section 8).

2. FATAL VIOLENCE WITHIN FAMILIES

The family is a social organization that is very vulnerable to the application of violence, a phenomenon which can be understood by the following factors, that by themselves cannot offer an adequate explanation,[1] but in connection with each other make the family sensitive to conflicts and the use of aggression. The long period of time that family members are in contact with each other or dependent on each other increases the risk of conflict. A broad range of activities and interests might cause tension among the relatives. In every family, stressful events such as accidents, illnesses or deaths occur which require coping with. This kind of interaction is characterised by intensity. The membership of the family is not a voluntary one, if the members did not have a choice to become a member or not. The family is a private organization where social control by outsiders is limited and outside intervention is a last resort. The family members have broad insights into each other's

---

[1] M. STRAUS AND G. HOTALING, *The Social Causes of Husband-Wife Violence* (Minneapolis: University of Minneapolis, 1980).

personal history which may be used as an extra instrument in family conflict situations.

The bond between relatives gives violence a special meaning, but in fatal cases the bond defines the aggressive act. In the domestic area several types of fatal violence can take place:

aviolicide, killing of grandparent(s) by the grandchild, parricide, killing of parents by their son or daughter, matricide, killing of mother by her son or daughter, patricide, killing of father by his son or daughter, sororicide, killing a woman by her brother or sister, fratricide, killing a man by his brother or sister, uxoricide, killing a man or woman by his or her spouse, filicide, killing of a child by the parent, infanticide, killing a child in the first year of life by the parent, neonaticide, killing of a child within 24 hours after birth by the parent, extended suicide, a parent committing suicide and killing the child who is fully dependent on her or his care, familicide, killing more than two family-members.

Most of these lethal acts will be discussed in this chapter.

3. THE DUTCH SITUATION

From 1992-2001, 2549 cases of murder and manslaughter took place in the Netherlands. In 474 cases (19 %) uxoricide was involved, in 85 cases a filicide and in 48 cases (2 %) a parricide.[2] This distribution results in the conclusion that a quarter of the homicide cases are the immediate result of domestic violence.[3]

Whereas in the past, filicide was considered to be a predominantly female offence, nowadays the gender of the perpetrator is evenly distributed, as illustrated by table 1. With regard to the killing of spouses and parents, males are the main perpetrators and females the main victims.[4]

Table 1   Gender distribution among perpetrators and victims in 607 domestic homicide cases in the Netherlands

	Perpetrator		Victim	
	Male	Female	Male	Female
Uxoricide	86 %	14 %	30 %	70 %
Filicide	49 %	51 %	56 %	44 %
Parricide	94 %	6 %	44 %	54 %

---

2 G. LEISTRA AND P. NIEUWBEERTA, *Moord en doodslag in Nederland, 1992-2001* (Amsterdam: Prometeus, 2003).

3 This equals 29 % of the solved cases, as not all of the 2549 cases have been solved.

4 LEISTRA AND NIEUWBEERTA, supra n. 2, 47.

The place where the offence was committed was at home in 73 % of the uxoricides, in 80 % of the filicides and in 81 % of the parricides. Although the majority of the domestic homicides takes place at home in spite of the name, a considerable part of the cases were committed outside the house.[5]

Now that we have considered some baseline characteristics of the perpetrators involved, let us take a closer look at the sanctions imposed on these crimes.

The measure *terbeschikkingstellen (tbs)* [to place an offender under a hospital order] is a special sanction in the Dutch Penal Code exclusively for delinquents who are suffering from a mental disorder at the time of the offence and who are considered to be at risk for recidivism. Apparently, almost half of the filicides and more than half of the parricides were committed by delinquents who suffered from mental disorders. Therefore, the judge imposed a *tbs*-sanction in order to detain and treat the offender in a special forensic mental hospital (see table 2).[6] This sanction appears to be used frequently, especially if compared to offences with another criminal background, where only 7 % of the offenders receive a *tbs*-sanction.[7]

Table 2   Distribution of sanctions

	Prison sentence	Prison + Tbs	Tbs	Youth sentence
Uxoricide	73 %	23 %	4 %	0 %
Filicide	54 %	36 %	10 %	0 %
Parricide	41 %	31 %	26 %	2 %
Total	77 %	17 %	4 %	2 %

In 2004 the total number of homicides decreased to 204 with 47 domestic victims.[8]

---

5   Domestic does not refer to the location of the violence, but to the persons involved. See T. VAN DIJK, S. FLIGHT, E. OPPENHUIS AND B. DUESMANN, 'Domestic Violence: A National Study of Nature, Size and Effects of Domestic Violence in The Netherlands', in: *European Journal on Criminal Policy and Research*, 6, 1998, 8.

6   In cases of male perpetrators who killed their partner the *ter beschikking stellen* is more frequently imposed (23 %) in comparison with female perpetrators (9 %).

7   LEISTRA AND NIEUWBEERTA, supra n. 2, 59.

8   LEISTRA, 2005; these relatives were 30 (ex-) spouses, 7 children, 7 parents, and 3 brothers.

4. KILLING OF SPOUSES

Case 1: The 36 year old administrative assistant James, and his 34 years old wife Mary had two children, a boy of 5 and girl of 2. They met 10 years ago and shortly afterwards Mary moved into James' house.

Gradually Mary developed a drinking problem and several months after she gave birth to her son she lost her job, continued drinking heavily and became more and more depressive. She received psychotherapy and medication from a clinic for out-patient treatment. Mary once threatened James with a knife.

James is an introvert and compulsive kind of person who feels extremely responsible for his children, especially since his wife has withdrawn more and more from the taking care of and educating the children. Mary called James several times a day at his work telling him that he had to come home, etc. More and more, he fulfilled the roles of both father and mother. To friends and family they tried to uphold a normal life, but in fact they had a relationship with many quarrels and fights.

One day after she threatened to kill both the children, James killed his wife by stabbing her to death. He tried to hide her dead body and finally he was accused of murder.

He was sent to a hospital for residential forensic multidisciplinary mental health assessment. He appeared to have an above average IQ, and suffered from a personality disorder with schizoid and compulsory traits. He was considered to have diminished responsibility. The risk of recidivism was estimated to be very low. Assistance and support by the probation service was recommended in order to deal with the traumatic experiences and to support his contact with his children.

The court found him guilty and imposed a prison sanction of nine years. Two other experts were hired and came to the same conclusion. The court of appeal imposed a prison sanction of eight years.

The mutual obligations between people are affected by institutions and frameworks for social action, and these vary according to the social context. The tendency to harm spouses, kin or in-laws is affected by daily frictions stemming from the composition of the household, disputes over the division of roles, domestic stress, the principles and practices of ascription and inheritance, the residence of married couples, etc.[9]

Preliminary results of a research project in 83 cases of spouse-killing derived from the Dutch residential observation hospital for forensic mental health assessment reveal that:

---

[9]   G.M. KRESSEL, 'Sororicide/Filiacide. Homicide for Family Honour', in: *Current Anthropology*, 22, 2, 1981, 141-158.

- male perpetrators of uxoricide tend to be slightly older than female perpetrators.
- for female perpetrators (attempted) uxoricide was the first offence, whereas male offenders had already committed previous offences. Among male perpetrators we see more recidivists than among female.
- male perpetrators mostly commit the offence alone, whereas female perpetrators sometimes have assistance in committing the offence.
- female perpetrators are often maltreated by the later victim, whereas male perpetrators often maltreat their spouses.[10]
- male perpetrators tend to be more dependent and more often fear being left alone compared to female perpetrators.[11] As a result, wives are much more likely to be slain by their husbands when separated from them, than when co-residing.[12]
- when we compare the recidivists and the first offenders, the relationship between perpetrator and victim is considered to be more intense in the group of first offenders.
- it is not surprising that history is expected to repeat itself; the forensic mental health experts fear a bigger chance of recidivism for the recidivists rather than for first offenders.
- the percentage of female perpetrators seems to increase gradually over the recent decades.[13]

5. KILLING OF CHILDREN

Historically, child homicide is not a new phenomenon, as in previous centuries it was used to control family size and weed out weak, abnormal, deformed and illegitimate children, and to limit the number of females.[14] Although the killing of unwanted female children is still a common event in certain developing countries, filicide in general is still a significant cause of infant mortality in wealthy parts of the world. The most vulnerable person in the family is the small child. The younger the child, the greater the risk he or she has of becoming a victim of fatal violence. In 2003, UNICEF published a report in which it was concluded that almost 3,500 children under the age of 15 die from maltreatment

---

[10] A.P. DE BOER, *Partnerdoding. Een empirisch forensisch-psychiatrisch onderzoek* (Arnhem : Gouda Quint, 1990).

[11] J.K. ZWEMSTRA, *Partnerdoding*. Bijdrage aan het Voorjaarscongres van de Nederlandse Vereniging voor Psychiatrie, 1999.

[12] M. WILSON AND M. DALY, 'Spousal Homicide Risk and Estrangement', in: *Violence & Victims*, 8, 1993, 1.

[13] ZWEMSTRA, supra n. 11.

[14] L. DEMAUSE, *History of Childhood* (New York: Psychohistory Press, 1974).

every year in the developing world. Every week two children die from abuse and neglect in Germany and the United Kingdom, three in France, four in Japan, and 27 in the United States. In the great majority of the cases, children are maltreated by their parents or other relatives.[15]

Although child deaths from maltreatment appear to be in decline in the majority of the countries in the developing world, there still remain inconsistencies of classification and a lack of common definitions and research methodologies. This means that few internationally-comparable data exist and that the extent of child maltreatment is almost certainly underrepresented by the statistics.[16]

A small group of countries have an exceptionally low incidence of child maltreatment (between 0.1 and 0.3 per 100.000 children under the age of 15 year).[17] Three countries have rates that are between 10 and 15 times higher than the average for the leading countries.[18]

5.1. Filicide

In many countries, children under the age of one year face a greater risk of homicide than any other age group.[19] Some research projects reveal that homicide is the only cause of death of those under the age of 15 and this has increased over the last 30 years. Parents or the *de facto* parents commit the majority of child homicides. Pre-school age children are almost never the victims of homicides by strangers. The latter cases are almost always about an adult male who had sexual contact with a young child. Fear of public exposure and the subsequent wish to silence the child, will induce the perpetrator to kill it. Children rarely represent a direct threat, which may trigger personal violence by their killers. The threat may be indirect as in cases where the perpetrator is concerned that the child is about to reveal a criminal activity on his part. Non-family child homicide perpetrators mostly deny having committed the offence, whereas in cases of filicide the family members mostly confess. The criminal sanction imposed by the judge is in general more severe when

---

15 UNICEF, *A league table of child maltreatment deaths in rich nations* (Florence: UNICEF Innocenti Research Centre, Innocenti Report Card No.5, 2003) 2 and 8.

16 *Ibid.*, 6-7; N. TROCMÉ AND D. LINDSEY, 'What Can Child Homicide Rates Tell Us About the Effectiveness of Child Welfare Services?', in: *Child Abuse & Neglect*, 20, 3, 1996, 171-184.

17 Spain, Greece, Italy, Ireland and Norway.

18 These countries, United States, Mexico and Portugal also have exceptionally high adult death rates.

19 M. MARKS, 'Parents at Risk of Filicide', in: G.F. PINARD AND L. PAGINI (eds.), *Clinical Assessment of Dangerousness. Empirical Contributions* (Cambridge: Cambridge University Press, 2001) 158-180.

family ties are involved than in cases of a non-family child homicide.[20] The younger the child, the most likely it is that the child will be killed by a parent and this is as likely to be the child's mother as the father. Although historically filicide is known as a crime predominantly committed by women, research indicates a more or less equal distribution of both genders.[21] This finding might be explained by two factors. Firstly, in the case of fatal child abuse, men's force tends to be stronger than women's. In other words, when men batter children, the victim is more likely to be severely hurt than when women batter, thereby causing an overrepresentation of male filicide offenders. Secondly, it might be possible that the legal system gives a different connotation to cases of fatal child abuse in the case of male perpetrators compared to female perpetrators. The latter cases may be treated more leniently – indicating 'severe maltreatment leading to death' - than offences committed by men – indicated by '(attempted) murder or manslaughter'. As the child grows up, the risk of homicide shifts to outside the family and in those cases, the offender is more likely to be male,[22] and so is the victim.[23]

Silverman & Kennedy (1993) point out that homicide rates tend to decline after the age of five and argue that this is a reflection of the children's removal from the parents as a source of conflict or violence. They note that the daily activities of children over five take them out of

---

[20] C.M. ALDER AND K. POLK, *Child Victims of Homicide* (Cambridge: Cambridge University Press, 2001).

[21] *Ibid.*; D. BOURGET AND J.M. BRADFORD, 'Homicidal Parents', in : *Canadian Journal of Psychiatry*, 35, 3, 1990, 233-238; J.F. CAMPION, J.M. CRAVENS AND F. COVAN, 'A Study of Filicidal Men', in: *American Journal of Psychiatry*, 145, 9, 1988, 1141-1144 ; T. HARDER, 'The Psychopathology of Infanticide', in: *Acts Psychiatrica Scandinavia*, 43, 1967, 195-245; C.P. MALMQUIST, 'Psychiatric Aspects of Familicide', in: *Bulletin of the American Academy of Psychiatry and the Law*, 8, 3, 1980, 298-304 ; L.K. SOMANDER AND L.M. RAMMER, 'Intra- and Extrafamilial Child Homicide in Sweden', in: *Child Abuse and Neglect*, 15, 1-2, 1991, 45-55 ; T. VANAMO, A. KAUPPI, K. KARKOLA, J. MERIKANTO AND E. RASANEN, 'Intra – familial Child Homocide in Finland 1970-1994 : Incidence, causes of death and demographic characteristics, in: *Forensic Science International*, 117, 2001, 199-204.

[22] BOURGET AND BRAFORD, *ibid.*; M.J. LOMIS, 'Maternal Filicide. A Preliminary examination of Culture and Victim Sex', in: *International Journal of Law and Psychiatry*, 9, 4, 1996, 503-506; M.N. MARKS AND R. KUMAR, 'Infanticide in Scotland', in: *Medicine, Science and the Law*, 36 , 4, 1996, 299-305; MARKS, supra n. 20; G.B. PALERMO, 'Murderous Parents', in: *International Journal of Offender Therapy and Comparative Criminology*, 46-2, 2002, 123-143.

[23] Based on our own data, victims of filicide inside the family tend to be more often boys than girls. This overrepresentation of male victims may be related to the increased physical vulnerability of male infants compared to female infants. Or it may be a consequence of parental attributions about the infant's behaviour, for example that male infants are perceived as more aggressive and requiring harsher discipline than female children (Marks 2001), thereby causing an overall larger percentage of male victims.

the house for large parts of the day and thus away from those who are most likely to harm them, namely their parents.

Some research indicates that children living in stepfamilies have elevated risks of exposure to violence,[24] an assumption also referred to as the Cinderella hypothesis.[25] Although this hypothesis is related to the folk tale in which the child becomes the victim of the wicked stepmother, it is more often the stepfather committing the crime. In these cases, the cause of the filicide is frequently (fatal) physical abuse.

5.2. Neonaticide

Case 2: A 16-year old girl was still living at her parents' house. She worked in a supermarket, was socially active, had a good relationship with her parents but appeared to be able to keep her pregnancy secret, even from her parents. One friend noticed some change in her clothes.
During one night in winter time she gave birth to a boy in the lavatory bowl, when her parents were asleep upstairs. She cleaned the baby and laid him behind the garden fence.
Forensic mental health assessment revealed that she denied her pregnancy; she did not make any preparations for birth. Her personality structure appeared to be naive and superficial. At the time of the offence there was a narrowing of thinking and a disassociated state.
She was considered to be severely diminished responsible. The risk of recidivism was estimated to be very low. Psychotherapy on an outpatient basis was recommended.

Strictly speaking, the term filicide refers to the killing of one's child between the age of 1 to 12. Those not surviving the first 24 hours of their life are referred to as victims of neonaticide.[26] The latter type of child homicide has appeared to be clearly distinct from the killing of older children in terms of the psychological processes underlying the offence as well as socio-demographic characteristics. Neonaticides are almost exclusively committed by women. These mothers tend to be young and unmarried, often still living with their parents at the time of giving birth. It has been suggested that this overrepresentation of very young women in this type of offence is due to their naïveté (a lack of awareness of what

---

[24] M. DALY AND M.I. WILSON, 'Step-Parenthood and the Evolved Psychology of Discriminative Parental Solicitude', in: S. VOM PARMIGIANI AND F.S. SAAL (eds.), *Infanticide and Parental Care* (Lausanne: Harwood Academic Publishers, 1994) 121-134.

[25] ALDER AND POLK, supra n. 20, 147-149.

[26] P.J. RESNICK, 'Murder of the Newborn: A Psychiatric Review of Neonaticide', in: *American Journal of Psychiatry*, 126, 1970, 1414-1420; PALERMO, supra n. 22.

sexuality and pregnancy entail), a restricted social environment, and a passive personality.[27] These women tend to deny that they are pregnant or assume that the child is stillborn. This denial is not merely directed towards the environment; rather, it becomes part of their own belief. Many of them go as far as to wear wide clothing, continue their daily activities without making preparations for the delivery and some even do not cease to menstruate during their pregnancy. When reality is thrust upon them by the infant's first cry, they respond by permanently silencing the intruder,[28] thereby attempting to continue their denial.

5.3. Suicidal killings

Literature on filicide often mentions previous suicide attempts of the perpetrator. In several studies, it appears that it is not uncommon for the filicide offender to express suicidal impulses or exhibit suicidal behaviour at the time of the killing. Some of these suspects who actually tried to harm themselves said that they had wanted to die, but failed for various reasons, such as insufficient effect of the drugs or poison used. In almost all of these cases the suspect's suicidal feelings were part of the filicide incident, rather than a later reaction of having killed the child. Suicidal impulses or behaviour appear to be markedly more common in filicide than non-fatal abuse. Most of the cases were perceived by the parents as involving some elements of altruism - that is, the parents perceived the killing as being in their children's best interest. In the so-called altruistic cases there was no evidence of hostility towards the victim, and it appeared that the parents wanted to kill themselves but could not face leaving their children behind, defenceless and unprotected to face the world alone.

In these cases, the child was seen as dependent on and an extension of the offender, without a separate personality or independent ability to live. As noted in other research, the perpetrators in these altruistic extended suicide-filicides also tended to have strong religious views, particularly of Catholicism. Suicidal impulses and attempts were more common in the female rather than in the male cases of filicide. In several cases of extended suicide, it appeared that the man killed his child or children after his wife had left him. Here, the Medea-complex is illustrative, for these men are too dependent on the partner and the

---

[27] MARKS, supra n. 20; F. KOENRAADT, 'Doding van een pasgeborene - een verborgen delict', in: T.I. OEI AND M.S. GROENHUIJSEN (eds.), *Actuele ontwikkelingen in de forensische psychiatrie* (Deventer: Kluwer, 2003) 201-226.

[28] M. MENDLOWICZ, M.H. RAPAPORT, K. MECLER, S. GOLSHAN AND T.M. MORAES, 'A Case-Control Study on the Socio-Demographic Characteristics of 53 Neonaticidal Mothers', in: *International Journal of Law and Psychiatry*, 21, 2, 1998, 209-219.

relationship with her to live a life of their own; the idea of living alone is unbearable. In complete misery or induced by feelings of revenge towards the partner they kill what is most beloved by both him and his ex-partner, namely the child or children, thereby destructing 'the jewels of the partner.'

Research has shown that perpetrators of homicide-suicide in the family share more characteristics with those who commit suicide than with those who commit homicide without suicide.

It has been found that homicides followed by suicide were most often attributable to male proprietary behaviour or mental illness.[29] By contrast, none of the murders that occurred as a result of violence by the victim, child abuse, family conflict, or financial/criminal motives was followed by suicide. Ongoing violence appears to be characteristic of all non-suicide filicides.

The killing of one's own child is closely connected to the suicidal experience of the mother. This is especially true for the extended suicide, where the mother commits or attempts suicide at the same time as killing the child. In forensic psychological assessment the course of the mother-child relationship and the specific disturbing influences has to be examined. From a psychodynamic point of view we often see in these cases that the killing mother has not succeeded in experiencing herself as permanently separated from her own mother.[30] Here a detailed analysis of the personal history, especially her relationship with her own mother is necessary. In fact, she is not aware of the child as an independent person, but as an extension of herself, or even as an object that is still united with her in symbiosis.

In these women, aggression has not been allowed to be fully experienced during her childhood, as this seemed to be too dangerous for her own person.

Whereas women predominate in extended suicide statistics, men tend to prevail with regard to so-called familicide offences, not only killing their child(ren), but also their spouse. In these cases, it appears that the primary object of the man's action is the wife instead of the children. The motives for these crimes include fear of abandonment, anger because of actual abandonment or rejection; motives unrelated to the children as such, but instead, related to their spouses. Secondly, these drives can be regarded as stemming from a man's feeling of losing control over his

---

[29] M. WILSON AND M. DALY, 'Sexual Rivalry and Sexual Conflict. Recurring Themes in Fatal Conflicts', in: *Theoretical Criminology*, 2, 3, 1997, 291-310.

[30] A. WIESE, *Mütter, die töten. Psychoanalytische Erkenntnis und forensische Wahrheit* (München: Fink, 1996).

wife and his family. The man, according to this theory, is the focus of the nucleus family and thus assumes he is the one in control.[31] When his position of control is challenged, he feels personally threatened and undermined in his power. His position can be challenged by (a threat of) abandonment or by factors outside the family sphere, such as finances or occupational problems. This perceived lack of power leads to an extreme feeling of inadequacy, combined with the conviction that his children and spouse are not able to live a life on their own. Often shaped in the form of extended suicide, they victimize not only themselves, but the whole family.[32]

6. KILLING OF PARENTS

Not only the killing of the mother (matricide) and the killing of the father (patricide) are considered to be parricide, but also those who kill their grandparents (aviolicide) are referred to as having committed the offence of parricide.

6.1. Parricide

Case 3: Mr. A was a 23 year old man who grew up in an unsafe family environment. His father appeared to be a very threatening, sadistic, aggressive person who abused a great deal of alcohol and often maltreated his wife and children. The parents had many quarrels. Mr. A felt very responsible for his mother and was a supporting person for her. He grew up protecting his mother against his father's impulsive behaviour. He had a dependent and protective bond with his mother and it was impossible for him to live his own life. His mother put him in a father-replacing position against the threatening father. The father's aggression fulfilled a bonding role in his contact with his mother, but caused him to use reactive violence; by killing the father he also loosened the bond with his mother.

Within the family setting, the killing of a parent occupies a special position because perpetrator and victim belong to different generations, share blood ties and a long common history. The relationship with the victim was neither chosen by the perpetrator nor was it symmetrical.

---

[31] C.P. EWING, *Fatal Families: the Dynamics of Intra-Familial Homicide* (Thousand Oaks, California: Sage, 1997).

[32] Based on our own data, 3 of the 13 offenders of familicide attempted to commit suicide directly after the offence. The majority of the 13 cases were almost exclusively motivated by a fear of abandonment, actual abandonment or a fear of rejection.

Research into the prevalence of parricide in several, predominantly Western European countries shows – in so far as data are available – that on average, parricide accounts for 2-3% of all killings each year.[33] Perpetrators of patricide are usually younger than perpetrators of matricide. Fathers are more often victims than mothers.

From a developmental-psychological perspective, an occasional child's death wish or fantasy with regard to his or her parents is a general phenomenon and it is surprising how rarely this develops into an attempt at, or threat of parricide. As harbingers of actual parricide, such attempts or threats are alarming, but insufficient. Many parricides are committed without any previous threat or attempt.[34] Neither need there be any increase in violence by the future perpetrator of parricide.

Young parricide offenders have fewer psychological problems than adult offenders. The youthful perpetrators of this offence are usually first offenders who are struggling to escape parental tyranny. In the turbulent period of adolescence, there is a tension between the bond with parents and its loosening. Parricide by young people is often characterised as a reaction to long-standing provocation, torment or ill-treatment, in some cases accompanied by long-term sexual abuse by a parent or parents. This parental behaviour is clearly situated in the nature of permanent provocation. Compared to adult parricides, the adolescent offender's behavioural prognosis is more favourable.[35] The victims of a reactive parricide were dominant, tyrannical and aggressive, not only towards their children but also towards their partner who was often relatively weak, helpless, passive and dependent.

Although matricide is often regarded as a schizophrenic killing,[36] there is insufficient support for this view in research literature. However, matricides do appear to be more psychologically disturbed than patricides, and show more serious forms of psychopathology.[37]

---

[33] S. BORNSTEIN, J.F. MOTTE-MOITROUX AND M. BALETTE, 'A propos d'une forme rare de parricide. Le meurtre de la grand- mère ou aviolicide', in: *Revue de la Gériatrie*, 9, 9, 1984, 483-486.

[34] B.M. CORMIER, C.C.J. ANGLIKER, P.W. GAGNÉ AND B. MARKUS, 'Adolescents Who Kill a Member of the Family', in J.M EEKELAAR AND S.N. KATZ (eds.), *Family Violence. An international and interdisciplinay study* (Toronto : Butterworths, 1978) 466-478.

[35] CORMIER ET AL., *ibid.*, 476; K.M. HEIDE, *Why Kids kill Parents. Child abuse and adolescent Homicide* (Ohio State University Press, 1992).

[36] M. YVONNEAU, Matricide et vampirisme', in: *L'évolution Psychiatrique*, 55, 3, 1990, 576-577; F. KOENRAADT, *Ouderdoding als ultiem delict* (Deventer: Gouda Quint, 1996).

[37] KOENRAADT, *ibid.*, 258-259 and 173-177.

Several serial and mass killers have also killed their parents. A series of murders sometimes begins with the death of the father or mother, or both.[38]

Adoptive children are extra sensitive for existential dilemmas about parentage and origin of their existence. This also explains why more than a proportionate number of adopted children become involved in murder cases and especially in (double) parricide.

In examining the psychic condition of the perpetrator and the motives that underlie parricide we mainly come across psychopathological phenomena of psychosis, schizophrenia, catathymic crisis, personality disorder, post-traumatic stress disorder and neurosis.[39] The motives for parricide that, to a greater or lesser extent, lead to parricide are the following:[40] incest,[41] honour,[42] reactive act,[43] jealousy or envy,[44] altruism, financial gain, the victim's request and psychotic reasons.

6.2. Aviolicide

Case 4: David was a 30 year old man accused of murdering his grandmother. He was born into a family with a low socio-economic status. The parents divorced and since his third year he was raised by his grandparents. His grandmother was very dominant, he could not trust her and she was extremely eager to save money. She was involved in many quarrels. The grandmother forbade him to have contact with his parents.

He was raised in problematic and conflict situations and developed a personality disorder. He had problems in personal contacts and abused alcohol, he had financial problems, and problematic relationships with female partners.

At the time of the offence his financial situation was unbearable. Hoping to get support from his grandmother he paid her a visit and asked for

---

[38] See e.g. M.W. KAHN, 'Psychological Test Study of a Mass Murderer', in: *Journal of Projective Techniques and Personality Assessment*, 24, 1960, 48-60.

[39] KOENRAADT, supra n. 36, 202-213. But also rare cases of vampirism (see e.g. PH D. JAFFÉ, CH. TSCHOPP AND F. DiCATALDO, 'Expertise d'un vampire. Mythologie et psychopathologie', in: *Bulletin de Psychologie*, 47, 1994, 349-356), cannibalism, epilepsy, mental defects.

[40] See also KOENRAADT, *ibid.*, 214-222 and 262-273.

[41] K. VELDENZ, *Die Kriminologie in der Praxis* (Hamburg: Kriminalistik Verlag, 1966).

[42] Y. YEŞILGÖZ, Allah, satan en het recht. Communicatie met Turkse verdachten (Arnhem: Gouda Quint, 1995); R. LEMPP, *Jugendliche Mörder* (Bern/Stuttgart/Wien: Huber, 1977).

[43] CHR. VON MAHLSDORF, *Ik ben mijn eigen vrouw* (Amsterdam/Antwerpen, Manteau, 1992).

[44] H. VON HENTIG, *Der Muttermord und sieben andere Verbrechenstudien* (Neuwied: Luchterhand, 1968).

her help. When she let him know that he could not expect anything from her, he left and walked the dog. As soon as he returned he took an axe and beat his grand-mother to death. He took her money and left her house.

The assessment revealed that he had an average IQ and was suffering a personality disorder and that at the time of the offence he was severely diminished responsible for committing the offence.

The court imposed five years imprisonment and a *terbeschikkingstelling*-order.

Killing of parents (parricide) is relatively rare, killing of grandparents (aviolicide) is even rarer. Professional literature does not (with a few exceptions) pay attention to the killing of grandparents. If killing of grandparents happens, it appears that mainly grandmothers are the victim. Few authors present cases in which the grandfather was the victim.[45] The demographic fact that there are more old women or widows rather than old men or widowers, contributes to the fact that relatively more grandmothers than grandfathers are killed as a result of aviolicide. It appears that mainly grandsons commit these offenses. In our analysis of the literature of 40 cases we came across three cases of aviolicide committed by granddaughters. When we compare parricide (killing of parents) with aviolicide (killing of grandparents) in many countries we see that granddaughters play a much bigger role in committing these offenses against their parents, although grandsons commit most of these offenses. We might conclude that mainly grandmothers – presumably because on average they live longer than grandfathers – are killed as a result of a homicide committed by their grandsons. In cases of parricide, however, fathers constitute the biggest group of victims. Not only do grandmothers on average live slightly longer than the grandfathers, but grandmothers also more often play an active role in taking care of their grandchildren.

Bornstein et al. (1984) concludes that in cases of aviolicide the victims are characterized by their proximity to the perpetrator; for grandchildren, the grandparents are available as a replacing parent. The older age contributes to the physical vulnerability, although these grandparents appear to be very vital; intellectually as well as morally. These homicides should be interpreted as committed by persons who suffer from the development of a disharmonious affect and the killing is a disastrous breakthrough of not discussing and not solving (long lasting) family conflicts. In these cases the anger, the aggression towards (one of) the

---

[45] J.P. DE WAELE, *Daders van dodingen. Vergelijkende analyses* (Antwerpen/Arnhem: Kluwer, 1990); HEIDE, supra n. 35.

parents is transferred to the grandparent, who is seen as the root, the source of the parents.

7. KILLING OF SIBLINGS

To actually kill someone is a big step to take and this also applies to the killing of one's own brother or sister. One cannot choose the relationship with a brother or sister, on the contrary; it is a special one that cannot be made undone. It is an everlasting relationship, emphatically different from that between partners or between parents and children, a blood relationship from the same parentage, a relationship that, in our Western society is very rarely deliberately terminated. In other cultures, the killing of a sister (sororicide) in order to protect the family honour happens more frequently.[46] Kressel (1981) mentions as characteristic for these cases that the perpetrators are always male, that the act is always premeditated and is always a group affair, involving brothers and fathers. The reason for the act is forbidden sexual contact. The act is not revenge; on the contrary, it is an act for which the perpetrators gain honour. Murder can enhance prestige and it may be a planned investment in improving, not maintaining social status. Remarkably, this also accounts for victimizing one's family members.

In cases of fratricide, however, the motives are mainly unsolved conflicts, jealousy, sibling rivalry and severe mental illness.[47] In many of these cases, substance abuse plays a facilitating role.

8. CONCLUSION

Research has shown that at least a quarter of all homicide cases are the immediate result of domestic violence and that a considerable part of the domestic homicides were committed outside the domestic territory. Daily clinical forensic mental health practice reveals that many other crimes are committed as an indirect consequence of domestic violence.

If domestic homicide is considered as the extreme end of a continuum of violence it is often looked upon as an ideographic tendency in both perpetrators' and victims' lives that the violence increases gradually; from neglect, to abuse, to severe maltreatment or attempt of killing and finally to the lethal act. Research indicates that many cases of domestic homicide, however, are not preceded by maltreatment or abuse. From a factual point of view, there is no doubt that homicide lies at the extreme end of a continuum of violence. Whatever the motives for domestic

---

[46] KRESSEL, supra n. 9; KOENRAADT, supra n. 36, 196-198.
[47] KOENRAADT, ibid., 273-278.

homicide might be, another fact is that what is happening behind the closed doors of the family may remain unnoticed by the outside world. Even cases of domestic homicide can take place without outsiders being informed. In the cases where only the perpetrator and victim are witnesses, the dark number of domestic homicide can increase silently.[48] In research in general and in preventive and therapeutic intervention specifically, special attention has to be paid to those cases where there is no manifest kind of increasing aggression towards the (possible) victim.

---

[48] KOENRAADT, supra n. 27, 219.

NOTE ON CONTRIBUTORS

INEKE BOEREFIJN

Ineke Boerefijn is a senior lecturer in international law of human rights at the Netherlands Institute of Human Rights (SIM) of Utrecht University. Her research mainly concerns the United Nations human rights treaty bodies, women's human rights and violence against women.

THEO VAN BOVEN AND SABINA PUIG

Theo van Boven is professor of international law at Maastricht University. Among the functions he held was United Nations Special Rapporteur on Torture.

Sabina Puig has been working with the UN Office of the High Commmissioner for Human Rights as research-assistant for various mandate holders of the Commission on Human Rights, including the Special Rapporteur on Torture. She studied Political Science (Universitat Autònoma de Barcelona, Spain) and completed an LLM in International Human Rights Law (University of Essex, United Kingdom).

FRANS KOENRAADT AND MARIEKE LIEM

Dr. Frans Koenraadt, forensic psychologist and criminologist. He teaches forensic psychology and psychiatry at Utrecht University (since 1980) and Maastricht University (since 1997). His dissertation was on parricide. He is a forensic psychologist at the Pieter Baan Centre for Forensic Psychiatry in Utrecht. He has a private practice in forensic psychology, he serves as a forensic psychological expert in Dutch criminal courts, he published widely on mentally ill offenders and forensic mental health and has (co-)edited several books in the area of law and mental health. His current research is on domestic homicide and on (the history of)law and psychology.

Marieke Liem obtained her Bachelor's degree in Social Science at University College Utrecht and her Master's degree in Clinical Psychology at Utrecht University. She has been conducting research together with Frans Koenraadt in the field of domestic homicide, paying particular attention to filicide. Currently she is employed as a junior researcher at the Willem Pompe Institute, Utrecht and enrolled in an MPhil programme in Criminological Research at Cambridge University.

RENÉE KOOL

Renée Kool works as senior researcher/lecturer at the Willem Pompe Institute, University of Utrecht. In het Ph.D. project she explored the criminalisation of sexual abuse of minors (1999). Her research concentrates on the fields of the vice law, the position of victims of crime within the criminal justice system, punishment and restorative justice.

KATINKA LÜNNEMANN

Katinka Lünnemann used to work as a researcher for almost fifteen years at different Faculties of Law (in Leiden, Utrecht and Nijmegen) in the field of gender and (criminal) law. Her main specialisation is violence in the family and the law. She conducted mostly qualitative research in this field on regulation of domestic violence by criminal law and issues of domestic violence in civil law. Her PhD study was about criminal law and battered women, especially the way prosecuters handle cases of domestic violence and possibilities of adequate legal protection.
Since 2001 she works as senior research officer at the research Institute Verwey-Jonker in Utrecht where she is responsible for the programme Law, protection and prevention.

RENÉE RÖMKENS

Dr. Renée Römkens is currently Senior Researcher at IVA (University of Tilburg) in the field of Criminality and Safety. The research for this article was conducted while working as Visiting Professor at the Institute for Research on Women and Gender at Columbia University in New York (between 2001-2005). The focus in her work are women's rights and violence for the past two decades. She conducted the first national survey on violence against women in the Netherlands and has published extensively in this area. Her current research focuses on socio-legal and cultural aspects of the increasing regulation of violence against women, in particular through criminal law and international human rights law.

INGRID VLEDDER

Ingrid Vledder is coordinator Discrimination and Identity at the Dutch Section of Amnesty International. She is working for Amnesty's Stop Violence against Women Campaign and co-author of the booklet *Hebt u haar gezien? Geweld tegen vrouwen raakt iedereen.*

INGRID WESTENDORP

Ingrid Westendorp is Lecturer in law, especially woman and law, with the International and European Law Department of the Faculty of Law, Maastricht University. She has almost finished her Ph.D. thesis on 'Women's housing rights: The influence of gender on the realization of adequate housing for women'.

JAN WILLEMS

Jan C. M. Willems is at the Department of International and European Law and the Maastricht Centre for Human Rights, Universiteit Maastricht. He is Professor of Children's Rights at Amsterdam Vrije Universiteit. He publishes and teaches on human rights and children's rights and the responsibility of states to improve structures (laws, policies, institutions) of support and supervision of parenthood in order to promote healthy child development and prevent child abuse, neglect and exploitation.

RIA WOLLESWINKEL

Ria Wolleswinkel is Associate Professor of Women and Law at the University of Maastricht, Member of the Board of the Maastricht Centre for Human Rights and National Director of the European Master in Human Rights and Democratisation in Venice. In research her main focus is gender perspectives of family rights of prisoners and their families. In the field of education she teaches a multidisciplinary course on "Victims in (criminal) law".